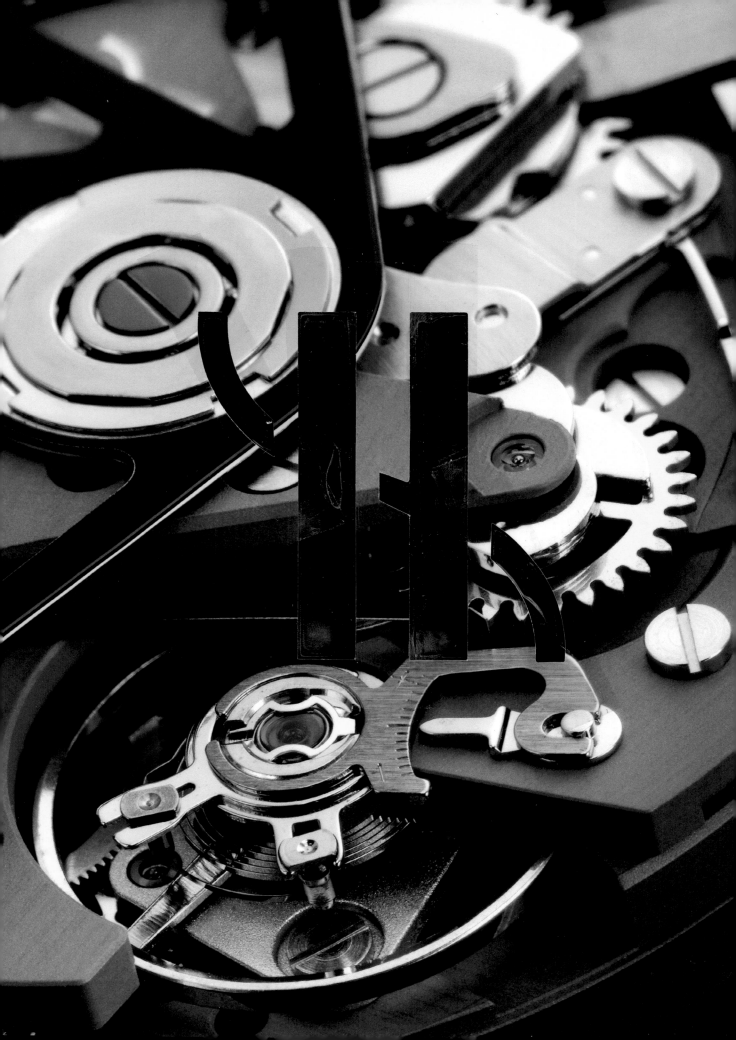

HUBLOT

GENEVE

The fusion between Tantalum and Rubber.

«Grand Prix d'Horlogerie
de Genève»

GRAND COMPLICATIONS®

THE ORIGINAL ANNUAL OF THE WORLD'S WATCH COMPLICATIONS AND MANUFACTURERS®

SPECIAL MULTICOMPLICATIONS

First published in the United States in 2008 by

TOURBILLON INTERNATIONAL, LLC.
A MODERN LUXURY COMPANY
11 West 25th Street, 8th floor
New York, NY 10010
Tel: +1 (212) 627-7732   Fax +1 (212) 627-9093
www.tourbillon-watches.com

CHAIRMAN AND CEO Michael Kong

VICE CHAIRMAN Stephen Kong

COO Michael Lipson

PUBLISHER Caroline Childers

EDITOR IN CHIEF Michel Jeannot

SENIOR VICE PRESIDENT OF FINANCE John Pietrolungo

In association with  **RIZZOLI** INTERNATIONAL PUBLICATIONS INC.

300 Park Avenue South, New York, NY 10010

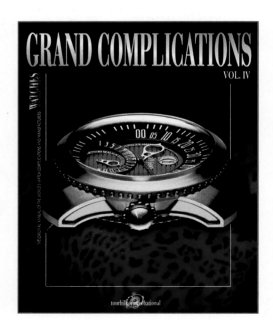

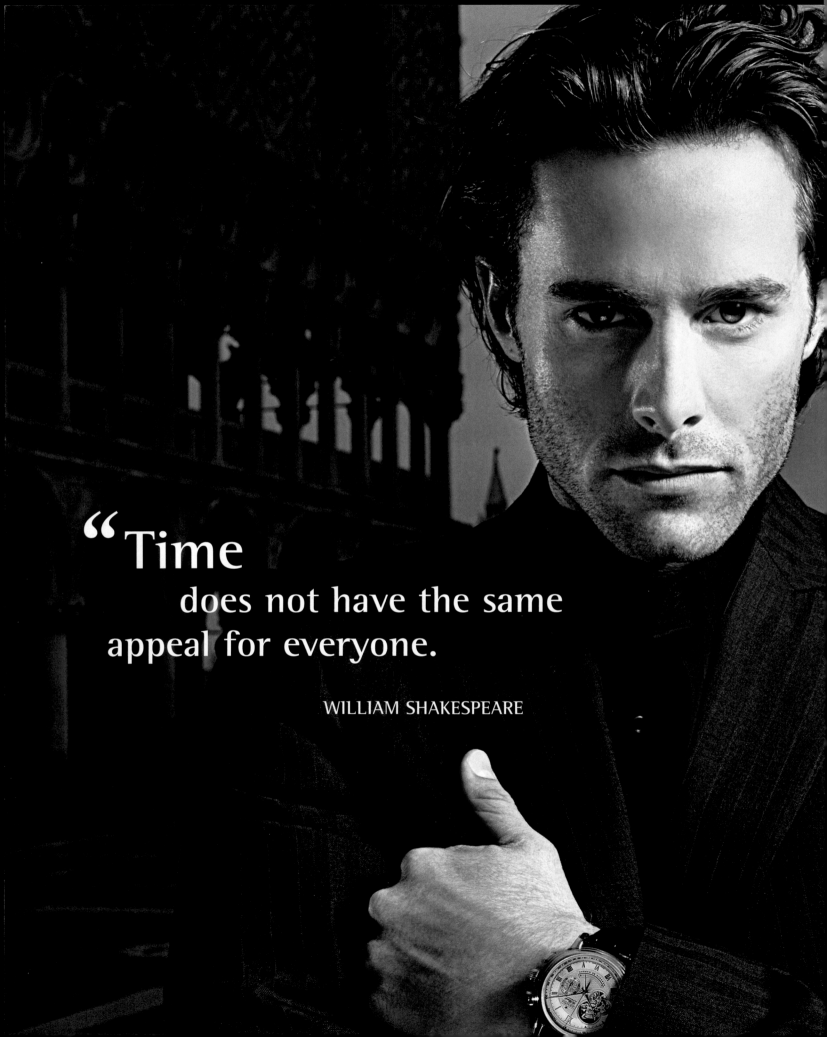

"Time
does not have the same
appeal for everyone.

WILLIAM SHAKESPEARE

ZENITH

SWISS WATCH MANUFACTURE

SINCE 1865

CHRONOMASTER
Open
El Primero

CHRONOMASTER
Open
El Primero
GRANDE DATE

ChronoMaster Open, ChronoMaster Open Grande Date – Venice, Italy : Perfect marriage of Tradition and Modernity.
Icon of the ZENITH Manufacture, ChronoMaster Open reveals the 36,000 vibrations of the legendary El Primero Automatic Chronograph. Traditional yet Modern, the ChronoMaster constantly borrows the conventions of the past and projects them into the future. The collection is now enriched by the addition of a complication. The Open Grande Date has a patented three-disk mechanism housed in a grey or rose gold case that reveals a semi-transparent silver guilloché dial – a world premiere. The 4039 caliber manufactured in-house is driven by 331 components and has a 50-hour power reserve. The hand-made guilloché on the dial and the double fluted case hark back to the watchmaking heritage whilst the asymmetric design, with its play on openness and transparency, gives it a subtle touch of modernity.

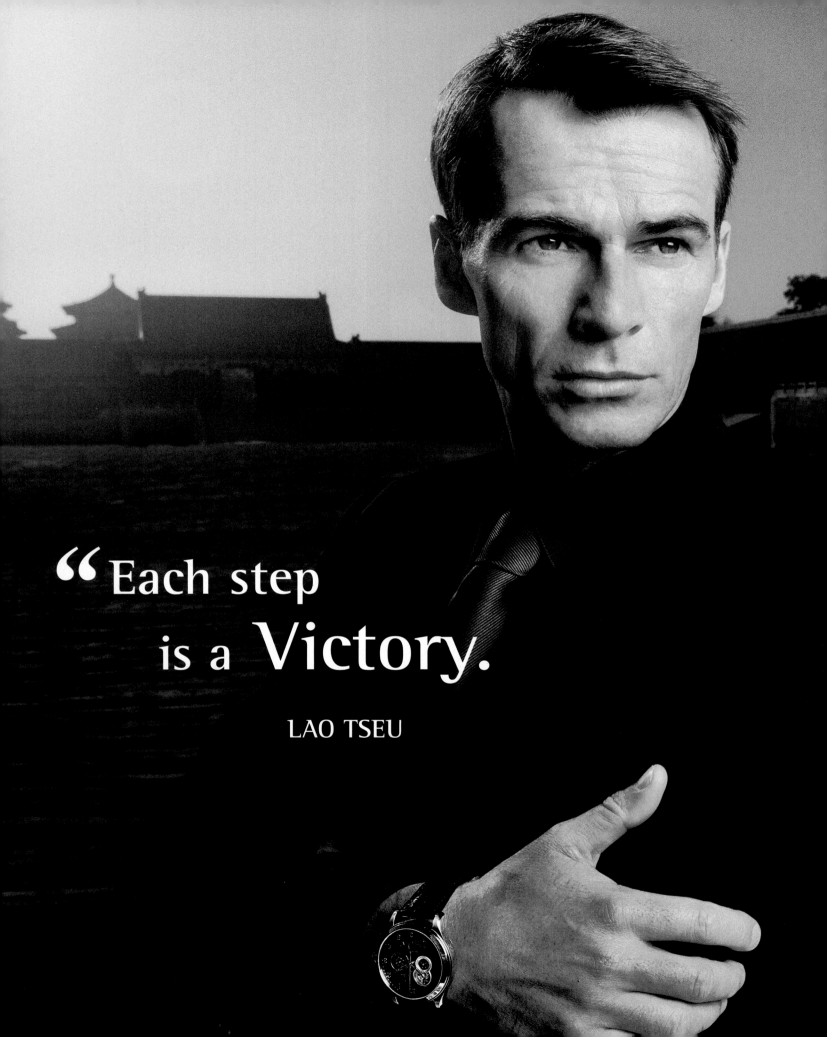

ZENITH

SWISS WATCH MANUFACTURE

SINCE 1865

CLASS
Elite

CLASS
MOONPHASE
El Primero

CLASS
RÉSERVE DE MARCHE
Elite

Class - Beijing, China : New Classical Renaissance
Continuing the traditional watchmaking values of the collection, three new timepieces have been added to this classical yet modern range. The new Automatic Elite Class with a central second hand says what it needs to say with sobriety. The Elite Power Reserve Class has kept its subtle refined look in the new larger case. For the Moonphase Class, the mechanical excellence of the El Primero movement is embellished with the addition of moon phases and a triple date, day and month calendar. The hand-finished guilloché, true to the aesthetic principles that underpin this range, gives the dials a highly exclusive finish. These New Classics are available in two sizes ; 44mm XT and 40mm T cases, in stainless steel or rose gold.

ZENITH INTERNATIONAL   TEL. +41 32 930 62 62   WWW.ZENITH-WATCHES.COM

CELLINI JEWELERS
NEW YORK, NY

ABOVE Cellini's flagship store was established in 1977 at the Hotel Waldorf-Astoria.

LEFT This award-winning, one-of-a-kind masterpiece features petal-shaped diamonds adorned with fancy colored diamonds and is edged with white diamond pavé in 18-karat gold.

The Adams family established a tradition of timeless taste 30 years ago

when it began assembling what would become one of the world's most extensive collections of rare European timepieces and bespoke jewelry designs. Over the years, both of Cellini's New York City boutiques have earned respect and raves for their dedication to rarity and sophistication. "It's nice to look back and see where we've been and what we've accomplished, but I'm more excited about where we're going," says Cellini's president, Leon Adams.

With the original location in the Hotel Waldorf-Astoria and a second on Madison Avenue, Cellini's superlative collection of exclusive watches continues to grow, reflecting Adams's passion for high horology. Savvy collectors from around the world make the pilgrimage to Cellini to experience the unparalleled selection of rarities and world-class personalized service. More than just a gathering place for the handiwork of today's most acclaimed watchmakers, Cellini has become an arbiter of style and an important proving ground for young watch brands.

Before they were highly successful watch companies, Cellini was among the first to offer A. Lange & Söhne, Audemars Piguet and F.P. Journe to name but a few. "One of the things I'm most proud of is that we've never been afraid to take a chance on something new or spend the time nurturing a talented watchmaker. Cultivating those long-standing relationships with the industry's rising stars is what's insured our access to hard-to-find watches today."

These one-of-a-kind pieces highlight Cellini's vast assortment of natural colored diamonds with an extraordinary array of pink, blue, green, orange and yellow stones.

RARE FINDS

In the watch industry, it is a rare honor when a watchmaker creates a special edition for one of its dealers. In the past, IWC, A. Lange & Söhne and others have produced exclusive timepieces for Cellini. This year, a trio of brands will commemorate the company's 30-year anniversary. Parmigiani and Panerai will each offer limited-edition collections exclusively at Cellini that feature unique executions of their popular models. Restricting production to 30 pieces, Parmigiani will offer a special Kalpa Tonda GMT in steel while Panerai will deliver 30 of its own special-edition Radiomirs in rose gold.

For the Kalpa Tonda GMT, Parmigiani's round Tonda case is fitted with dual day-night indicators and the ability to set the second time zone to the minute, rather than to just the hour as with traditional GMT models. The exclusive Radiomir features Panerai's in-house P.2002 movement paired with a rare blue dial, an eight-day power reserve and a GMT function.

Audemars Piguet, featured at Cellini from the start, has created a one-of-a-kind Grande Complication in titanium especially for the occasion. This exceptional timepiece takes every finishing detail to the extreme, combining examples from the three main categories of watchmaking—split-seconds chronograph, perpetual calendar, and minute repeater.

Cellini is also proud to welcome a new trio of Swiss watchmakers to the fold this year—two Swiss and one French. The first is H. Moser & Cie from Schaffhausen. Earning the coveted award for favorite complicated watch at the Grand Prix d'Horlogerie in 2006, H. Moser & Cie is making its U.S. debut exclusively at Cellini.

The second addition is De Bethune. Highly collectible for their rarity and artistry, the watchmaker's creations deftly straddle the line between modern technology and time-honored tradition.

Guy Ellia is the third brand to join Cellini's collection this year. Driven by his passion for pure design, Ellia's watches include complicated movements created by master watchmakers Michel Parmigiani, Christophe Claret and Frédéric Piguet. "We hold all the brands we carry to higher standards," Adams explains. "Ultimately, it's a matter of trust. We've earned our clients' trust over the years so it's important that we believe in every watchmaker you see in our stores."

After spending three decades on the forefront of high horology, it's easy to see why any conversation about the world's best watch shops would be incomplete without a discussion of Cellini.

SCINTILLATING SPARKLE

But watches tell only half of the story. Cellini is also one of New York City's premier jewelers with a superb selection that ranks among the city's best. "The depth of our collection means our designs are limited only by our imaginations," Adams says. "We can create pure simplicity with flawless diamond stud earrings, or high drama with some of the world's finest colored diamonds or rarest gemstones."

Just this year, Cellini introduced a magnificent necklace that crackles with the high-wattage twinkle that only 42 carats can provide. Although the 11 colored diamonds account for just four of those carats, they are undoubtedly the stars of the show. Suspended tantalizingly from a trio of white marquises, the colored diamonds—including blue pears, green and yellow radiants, pink asschers and an orange heart—are surrounded by white round brilliants.

Cellini has also created a bracelet that evokes the indulgent luxury of the necklace on the wrist with 6.5 carats of colored diamonds. An orange oval conducts this sparkling symphony, which includes two pink ovals and two yellow radiants surrounded by matching rounds. The fiery explosion of color is intensified by the 12 carats of white diamonds that encircle the wrist.

This past fall, Cellini also introduced a one-of-a-kind bracelet, ring and set of earrings from the La Reina Collection. Winner of the diamond category at the 2007 *Town & Country* Couture Design Awards, these floral-themed treasures are immediately captivating thanks to the diamond petals and the unorthodox cut used to create them. The stone's natural inclusions remain intact giving the flower a realistic, organic texture. "It's rare to see a diamond cut like this because it wastes so much of the stone," Adams explains. "It's a daring cut on a large scale."

Scintillating micro-pavé edges the petals as they stand guard around the flower's bejeweled center, rendered elegantly with thin gold prongs and colored diamonds taking the place of the stamen and the pistil. "The natural flow of the design, the unique cut of the diamonds—everything comes together giving each piece a special dimension," says Adams. "This is artistry working on a higher level; truly inspiring."

The same could be said of Cellini. After 30 years, visitors still leave smitten and spellbound by the unparalleled collection of high-style jewelry and rare timepieces.

CHANEL

J 12

CHANEL

J12
AUTOMATIC

SWISS

Michael Kong   Stephen Kong

Note from the Chairmen

What can we say? We love watches. If you know us, you're aware that they're almost an obsession. And it goes far beyond having something to get us to an appointment on time. A well-designed watch is a treasured object of intricate machinery and craftsmanship. The best are timeless (or perhaps I should say, time-honored) works of art.

So it's with great pleasure and pride that we welcome *Watches International* to the Modern Luxury family of publications. As the nation's largest publisher of luxury city magazines, all 25 of our Modern Luxury titles—including *Angeleno*, *CS*, *Riviera*, and soon *Manhattan*—highlight the latest news on the sophisticated worlds of fashion, interior design, dining, travel, jewelry and culture, all presented with distinctively breathtaking photography.

Watches International fits perfectly into the Modern Luxury fold. We look forward to making this already great publication even better in coming months, lending both our expertise in the world of luxury goods and our enthusiasm for putting out great magazines. And we are thrilled that Caroline Childers, founder and publisher of *Watches International* will continue to lead both this publication and *Grand Complications*. She's a legend in the watch business, known by every major watch manufacturer in the world. Her breadth of experience and knowledge in this industry is an invaluable asset. We're excited to grow in this direction and look forward to bringing the best to you. And also we can't wait to check out some of those watches ourselves.

MORE THAN 250 YEARS OF CONTINUOUS HISTORY...

1929. When the world's first twin lens camera, the legendary Rolleiflex, was launched, Vacheron Constantin was 174 years old.

Collection Musée de la Photographie, Vevey

MALTE CHRONOGRAPH

Caliber 1141 handwound mechanical movement. Column-wheel chronograph mechanism. Telemetric scale with 1-kilometer graduations and tachymetric scale; 30-minute totalizer. Manually engine-turned gold dial with applied hour markers and a subdial for the seconds. Diameter 41.5 mm. Sapphire-crystal caseback. Water-resistant to 30 meters (~100 feet). Standard buckle. White gold.

47120/000G-9098

...DEDICATED TO PERFECTION

VACHERON CONSTANTIN
Manufacture Horlogère. Genève, depuis 1755.

RICHARD MILLE

OFFICIAL TIMEKEEPER

OFFICIAL TIMEKEEPER

Grand Prix d'Horlogerie
de Genève

Golden Hand · 2007

THE DIAMOND CRUNCHER

RICHARD MILLE

SEVEN SEAS RACING CLASS

OFFICIAL TIMEKEEPER

OFFICIAL TIMEKEEPER

Grand Prix d'Horlogerie
de Genève

Golden Hand • 2007

MARINE CALIBER RM 015
TOURBILLON PERINI NAVI CUP

Manual winding movement
Carbon nanofiber baseplate
Variable inertia balance
Fast rotating barrel
Power reserve indicator
Torque indicator
Function selector
Second time zone
In line escapement
Ceramic center pivot
Winding barrel teeth and third-wheel pinion
with central involute profile
Modular hand setting and winding mechanism
fitted against the case back

Available in 18-carat red or white gold, and platinum

From 223 650 €

Letter from the Publisher

Winners!

Unprecedented! At no point in watchmaking history has the industry experienced such spectacular development. From whichever angle you look at it—from innovation to the increase in production capacity—there are signs of clear progress, massive growth and revolutionary ideas. We could start by saluting a promising trend: brands are increasingly adopting verticalization policies that are beginning to bear fruit. By grouping the full range of manufacturing activities under a single roof or within an effective network, they have accelerated their reaction times in order to respond faster to exponential demand. Then there is the ever more fervent quest for quality and precision. Witness the initiative to reinforce the Swiss made label, which guarantees standards of quality and origin, promoted by the watch brands themselves. Another eloquent example can be found in the research and development departments, which are acquiring increasing importance within many manufactures. And finally, one can sum it all up with the impressive rise in Swiss watch exports: +16.2% in 2007! This growth clearly shows that fine watchmaking is steadily intensifying its presence worldwide, and that more and more clients are showing their undeniable interest in its products.

Tourbillon International, publisher of this book, has followed a very similar path, achieving acknowledged success and ongoing growth. Modern Luxury Media, LLC, publisher of many prestigious titles in the largest American cities, recognized the quality of work accomplished by our company, and decided it wished to own it in order to extend its activities. By accepting this proposal, Tourbillon International is confirming its position as a benchmark player in this field and is acquiring the means to further intensify its global presence. This union also paves the way for new projects that had been on the back burner until now. So Tourbillon International is making a new start that will enable it to become even more adaptable and resourceful, enhance its editorial strength, and reinforce its position as a key player in its favorite areas. And who stands to gain most from these strategic moves? You!

Caroline Childers

BVLGARI

WESTIME
LOS ANGELES & BEVERLY HILLS, CA

Proudly located in two of the most prestigious locations in Southern California,

Westime places great emphasis on the art of horology, guided by its intense knowledge of watches and watchmaking history. A visit to Westime is not just a shopping trip, but an opportunity for education, as Westime's well-trained staff shares its horological expertise with the customers, helping them understand the hows and whys of each watch's particularities and charms.

Westime began as the idea of a second-generation watchmaker who dreamt of bringing together the world's finest—and rarest—watches for a discerning clientele. The first turning point in Westime's history was the move from an upstairs location in a mall to a much larger location on West Pico Boulevard, complete with valet parking. With the move, Westime became not simply a watch store but a "destination," a shopping experience for watch connoisseurs to see rare and limited pieces in person. Westime understood the value of the physical experience—people want to be able to pick up a watch, hold it in their hands and listen to it tick rather than rely on a picture, however beautiful, in a catalog. Westime's expansion to its second location on Rodeo Drive in Beverly Hills marked another stage in the store's history. The move to this luxury mecca placed Westime in the position, quite literally, to cater to a truly international clientele of world travelers, as well as loyal Beverly Hills customers—anyone with an interest in the most exquisite timepieces in the world.

THIS PAGE   RM 018 tourbillon "Hommage a Boucheron" (Richard Mille)

FACING PAGE   Westime boutique on Rodeo Drive in Beverly Hills.

THIS PAGE Westime boutique on West Pico Blvd., Los Angeles.

FACING PAGE Three Minds (HD3)

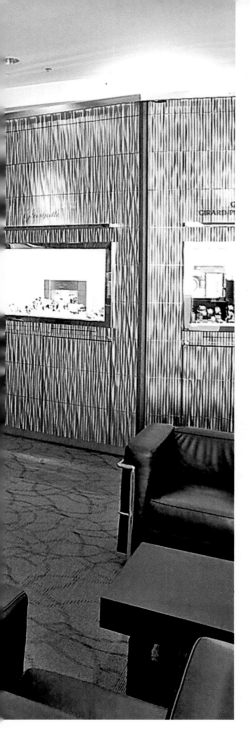

WATCH BRAND LISTING

A. Lange & Söhne	Corum	HAUTLENCE	Richard Mille
Audemars Piguet	Ebel	HD3	Roland Iten Mechanical Luxury
Baume & Mercier	Eberhard	Hermès	Swiss Army
Bell & Ross	Franck Muller	Hublot	TAG Heuer
Blancpain	Gérald Genta	IWC	TB Buti
Bovet	Girard-Perregaux	Longines	Tissot
Breguet	Glashütte	MB&F	URWERK
Breitling	Greubel Forsey	Michel Jordi	Vacheron Constantin
Chanel	Guy Ellia	Milus	Vertu
Chopard	Hamilton	Omega	Wyler Genève
Concord	Harry Winston	Parmigiani Fleurier	Zenith

Westime makes a point of carrying the best and most exclusive timepieces available; though no one can truly predict the future, Westime's staff comes close and always anticipates which timekeepers will pass through its doors so as to satisfy its customers' demands for watches that are difficult, if not almost impossible, to find elsewhere.

Watch aficionados are extremely knowledgeable about their passion, and Westime recognizes the critical importance of having staff members who are just as well informed as the clientele they serve. Every manufacturer represented at Westime provides extensive training throughout the year for every sales representative. Most of Westime's staff members are seasoned professionals with a career's worth of experience behind them, and all are fluent in three languages.

The upcoming years promise to be fruitful ones, as Westime vows to continue in its quest to please its clientele in every way possible and to make the purchasing experience pleasurable and memorable. The watch lovers who frequent Westime know they can count on the store to find them what they are looking for—that special timepiece not to be found anywhere else, along with impeccable service and attention to detail. Whether a customer spends $100 or $100,000, he or she receives the royal treatment at Westime.

STORE LOCATIONS

10800 West Pico Blvd., #197, Los Angeles, CA 90064 • TEL: 310.470.1388 • FAX: 310.475.0628

254 North Rodeo Drive, Beverly Hills, CA 90210 • TEL: 310.271.0000 • FAX: 310.271.3091

www.westimewatches.com

Letter from the Editor

No limits

Faster, slimmer, more resistant, more innovative, more complex: the list of adverbs and adjectives used to describe the various types of technical progress being achieved in the watch industry is virtually endless—and quite rightly so. In 2007, François-Paul Journe pushed back the limits of short-time measurement in spectacular fashion with his Centigraphe Souverain. Thanks to dials displaying both a scale of time and a tachometric scale, along with a patented chronograph mechanism, this watch measures speeds running from 6 to 360,000 km/h. Jaeger-LeCoultre and later Ulysse Nardin also made their marks on history, each presenting its own lubricant-free movement within the space of a few months. By comparison with the space race, that would be the equivalent of man's first step on the moon: a truly major accomplishment. In the featherweight category, while the RM 009 by Richard Mille still tops the list of the world's lightest watch (at just 30 grams), Hublot has decided to take up the challenge. Its Mag Bang model presented in October 2007 also contains Hublonium, an ultra-light proprietary alloy enabling it to weigh in at just 78 grams with the wristband.

But there are certain limits that the watch industry is finding harder to stretch. The oft-discussed lack of manpower is still a very real issue. Various industry authorities have tried to respond by offering fast tailor-made training tracks so as to supply the market with fresh human resources as quickly as possible. The overloaded supplier network, which simply cannot meet orders in time—and has to turn down plenty more!—represents another major obstacle. Badly stung by the sudden market crisis of the 1980s, some suppliers simply refuse to run the risk of having to face a potential new slump and are therefore very reluctant to invest in expanding their production capacities.

Within this strained context, the sale of the Swiss Soprod and Indtec movements to the Chinese watch and distribution group Peace Mark (Holdings) Ltd seems pretty surprising. How is that Swiss watchmakers have allowed such a production tool that was within reach—even if it may require some improvements—to slip through their fingers? Perhaps this is where one of the keys to the watch industry comes into play: the need to aim for long-term targets. By focusing all their attention on sales objectives, it appears that some managers have neglected to consolidate their supply sources. Such shortsighted strategies are already starting to cost the industry dearly…

Octo Chrono Quattro Retro

Self-winding manufactured column-wheel
chronograph movement, entirely decorated by
hand. Jumping hours, retrograde minutes and date,
retrograde chronograph hour and minute counters.
Red gold case, sapphire crystal and transparent
case-back. Water-resistant to 10 atm.

Gérald Genta

HAUTE HORLOGERIE D'AVANT-GARDE

PIAGET

THE ORIGINAL ANNUAL OF THE WORLD'S WATCH COMPLICATIONS AND MANUFACTURERS ®

TOURBILLON INTERNATIONAL
A Modern Luxury Media, LLC company

ADMINISTRATION, ADVERTISING SALES,

EDITORIAL, BOOK SALES

11 West 25th Street, 8th Floor, New York, NY 10010
Tel: +1 (212) 627-7732 Fax: +1 (212) 627-9093
sales@tourbillon-watches.com

CHAIRMAN AND CEO
Michael Kong

VICE CHAIRMAN
Stephen Kong

COO
Michael Lipson

PUBLISHER
Caroline Childers

EDITOR IN CHIEF
Michel Jeannot

EDITORS
Elizabeth Kindt
Elise Nussbaum

TRANSLATIONS
Susan Jacquet

CONTRIBUTING EDITORS
Hervé Genoud
Louis Nardin

COORDINATION
Caroline Pita

INTERNATIONAL ART DIRECTOR
Franca Vitali - Grafica Effe

DIRECTOR OF PRINT PROCUREMENT
Sean Bertram

PRE-PRESS AND COLOR PROOF
Maurizio Zinelli

SENIOR VICE PRESIDENT OF FINANCE
John Pietrolungo

DIRECTOR OF DISTIBUTION
Eric Holden

WEBMASTER
Marcel Choukroun

WEB DISTRIBUTION
www.amazon.com

PHOTOGRAPHERS
Photographic Archives
Property of Tourbillon International,
a Modern Luxury Media, LLC company

DANIEL ROTH

MASTERPIECES IN THE ART OF WATCHMAKING

8-DAY TOURBILLON

Double-face Daniel Roth tourbillon movement, entirely decorated by hand. Off-centered hours and minutes, three-arm small seconds hand on the tourbillon axis, 200-hour power reserve and date displays, upper dial in gold and inside openworked dial in sapphire crystal and gold.

The Americans were the first to set foot on the moon. But it was IWC who brought it under control.

"Aye aye, Sir!"

Portuguese Perpetual Calendar. Ref. 5022: As unlikely as it may sound, the hardy seafarers and conquistadores of Portugal were actually the distant forefathers of the astronauts. Their unequalled gift for navigation on the high seas enabled them to consistently succeed in discovering previously unknown territories. Along with the correct astronomical coordinates, these explorers also had to be sure of the exact time. Centuries later, seafaring was still in the blood of many Portuguese. In the 1930s, two Portuguese businessmen named Rodrigues and Teixeira were on a quest for a wristwatch that had a stainless steel case and all the performance of a deck watch. IWC made this vision a reality by designing a high-precision wristwatch for maritime use, on the basis of a calibre 74 watch movement. And so the foundation was laid for a watch-making family saga that was to remain unmatched in the history of the industry.

F. A. Jones.

The IWC story begins back in 1868, when US watchmaker Florentine Ariosto Jones from Boston set up the International Watch Company in the north-east corner of Switzerland. And ever since then, IWC engineers have been hard at work, creating such diverse watches as the Grande Complication, the Ingenieur series, the Portuguese family, the Pilot's Watches, the Da Vinci and the Aquatimer ranges. Probus Scafusia ("good, solid craftsmanship from Schaffhausen") encapsulates the philosophy of IWC. And this proud claim is substantiated by the striking number of technical achievements and innovations that have originated in the workshops of Schaffhausen, and in the last 139 years have won international renown.

IWC manufactory movement.

Today, IWC is proud to present the Portuguese Perpetual Calendar, featuring the world's largest automatic movement in a 42.3-mm case. Glance through the sapphire glass back cover to see how in no time at all the Pellaton winding system can build up a seven-day power reserve, easily checked on the power reserve display. The perpetual moon phase display is so accurate that it will only show one day's deviation over 577 years. The affiliation of manufacturer's calibre 5000 with the perpetual calendar make the Portuguese Perpetual Calendar watch a truly worthy addition to the Portuguese range.

An ingenious mechanical apparatus ensures that all 109 single parts function in smooth, fully automatic harmony. Together they control and activate the clearly laid-out perpetual calendar indicators with exceptional precision. Also included are displays for seconds, minutes, hours, day, date, month and four-digit year. Preset for up to 2499, probably about the time when the first family homes are being built on the moon. Right in Neil Armstrong's footprints. **IWC. Engineered for men.**

Mechanical manufactured movement | Automatic Pellaton winding system | Seven days' continuous running | Power reserve display | Perpetual calendar (figure) | Perpetual moon phase display | Water-resistant to 30 m | 18 ct. rose gold

IWC
SCHAFFHAUSEN
SINCE 1868

IWC North America, 645 Fifth Avenue, 5th Floor, New York, NY 10022.
For an authorized retailer, catalog or additional information, please call 1-800-432-9330 or visit our website: www.iwc.com.

Summary

Master piece

L.U.C Steel Wings Tourbillon. The crafting of a tourbillon movement remains the exclusive preserve of a handful of watch "Manufactures". As a member of this extremely select circle, Chopard has innovated by creating the world-first variable-inertia balance that greatly simplifies adjustment. The tourbillon carriage visible through the dial is held by a dynamically shaped bridge. Both the case and dial highlight the technical nature, the modern design and the inherent elegance of the new L.U.C collection signature. This subtle sporting touch combines with exquisitely refined details to form an exceptional timepiece. The power-reserve display indicates the over 8-day autonomy ensured by four barrels (patented L.U.C Quattro® system). Representing a masterful development by Chopard Manufacture, Calibre L.U.C 4T is chronometer-certified by the COSC.

L.U.C

MANUFACTURE DE HAUTE HORLOGERIE
LOUIS-ULYSSE CHOPARD

L.U.C Steel Wings Tourbillon: available in a limited, numbered series of 100 in white gold (ref. 161906-1001).

Web Site Directory

Audemars Piguet	www.audemarspiguet.com	**Jacob & Co.**	www.jacobandco.com
Bell & Ross	www.bellross.com	**Jaeger-LeCoultre**	www.jaeger-lecoultre.com
Bovet Fleurier	www.bovet-fleurier.ch	**Jean Dunand Pièces Uniques**	www.jeandunand.com
Bozeman Watch Co.	www.bozemanwatch.com	**Jean-Mairet & Gillman**	www.jean-mairetgillman.com
Breguet	www.breguet.com	**Leviev**	www.leviev.com
Bvlgari	www.bulgari.com	**Maurice Lacroix**	www.mauricelacroix.com
Chanel	www.chanel.com	**Parmigiani Fleurier**	www.parmigiani.com
Chopard	www.chopard.com	**Patek Philippe**	www.patek-philippe.ch
Concord	www.concord.ch	**Piaget**	www.piaget.com
Daniel Roth	www.danielroth.com	**Richard Mille**	www.richardmille.com
de GRISOGONO	www.degrisogono.com	**Rolex**	www.rolex.com
DeWitt	www.dewitt.ch	**Romain Jerome**	www.romainjerome.com
F.P. Journe	www.fpjourne.com	**TAG Heuer**	www.tagheuer.com
Gérald Genta	www.geraldgenta.com	**Ulysse Nardin**	www.ulysse-nardin.com
Greubel Forsey	www.greubelforsey.com	**Vacheron Constantin**	www.vacheron-constantin.com
Guy Ellia	www.guyellia.com	**Vulcain**	www.vulcain-watches.com
Hublot	www.hublot.ch	**Wyler Genève**	www.wylergeneve.com
IWC	www.iwc.com	**Zenith**	www.zenith-watches.ch

GE | GUY ELLIA

TOURBILLON MAGISTERE
WATCH AND CALIBER IN TITANIUM

INSTRUMENTO
Nº UNO

de GRISOGONO
GENEVE

Index

«Grand Prix d'Horlogerie
de Genève»

✛ BIG BANG ✛

The fusion between 18K Red Gold Mat and Rubber.

HUBLOT OF AMERICA, INC. • 800-536-0636 • 954-568-9400 • Hublot TV on: www.hublot.com

BR01 INSTRUMENT TOURBILLON PHANTOM ⌀ 46 MM · Regulator · Power reserve 120 hours · Trust index · Carbon fiber bridges
Titanium case with special carbon finish · Limited edition · Information: Bell & Ross Inc. +1.888.307.7887 · www.bellross.com

INDEX

INSPIRED BY THE PAST, BUILT FOR THE FUTURE.

LUMINOR 1950 8 DAYS GMT.
Hand-wound mechanical movement
P.2002 calibre, three spring barrels,
second time zone with 12/24 hr
indicator, 8-day power reserve with
linear indicator, seconds reset.
Steel case 44 mm Ø. Steel buckle.

PANERAI
LABORATORIO DI IDEE.

www.panerai.com   Toll Free 1-877-PANERAI

Chronomètre à Résonance

The first resonance wristwatch.

F.P.JOURNE
Invenit et Fecit

Invenit et Fecit = Invented and made : The motto of a contemporary watchmaker building his own history.

www.fpjourne.com

At the heart of the movement

"I will try to explain the historical reasons that led me to build such or such a watch. As far as the resonance phenomenon is concerned, the intuition that energy is dissipated without being lost goes back to the 18th century and the research performed by the great chemist A.L. de Lavoisier (1743-1794), who stated his famous theory that is behind my modest convictions: "Nothing is lost, nothing is created, everything is transformed". With the invention of the pendulum, watchmakers noticed that their beat often interfered with their environment and it was not unusual for a pendulum clock to stop of its own accord when the pendulum entered into resonance with the driving-weight suspended from its cords. A particularly brilliant watchmaker, or "mechanical engineer" as he described himself, was the first to have the feeling that one might turn this disadvantage into an asset: Antide Janvier, born in 1751 in St. Claude, France. His idea was to build two complete movements with two precision escapements and to place them close to each other, ensuring that the two pendulums were hanging from the same construction. Just as he imagined, the pendulums recovered the energy dissipated by each other and began to beat together, thus entering into resonance.

Maintained by this wave and thus protected from outside vibrations, this principle considerably enhanced their precision. About 1780, Antide Janvier built two precision regulators, one of which is preserved at the Paul Dupuy museum in Toulouse and the second in the private collection of Montres Journe SA, Geneva. A third desk-top regulator is kept in the Patek Philippe Museum in Geneva. Thirty years later, Abraham-Louis Breguet built a resonance regulator for Louis XVII, King of France, which is now part of the collection of the Musée des Arts et Métiers in Paris, and a second for the King of England, George IV, which is housed in Buckingham Palace. He also made a pocket-watch based on the same principle for each of these illustrious figures. To my knowledge, no-one else in watchmaking took any further interest in this fascinating physical phenomenon!

The advantages of this phenomenon in terms of precision led me to pursue my own personal research and attempts which, after fifteen years, enabled me to adapt it to a wrist-watch for the second model in the Souveraine collection: the Chronomètre à Resonance. I felt that this resonance system was particularly well suited to the various wrist movements that subject watch mechanisms to the repeated jarring which is so detrimental to their smooth running."

François-Paul Journe

Caliber FPJ 1499-2 in 18k solid gold - Platinum case - Dial in gold and silver

INDEX

LEVIEV

Extraordinary Diamonds

PAINTING BY KEN MARSCHALL © 1992

DNA OF FAMOUS LEGENDS

MADE WITH PARTS OF THE TITANIC

INDEX

LEWIS HAMILTON, VODAFONE McLAREN MERCEDES F1 DRIVER

Grand
CARRERA
CALIBRE RS

TAG HEUER INTRODUCES THE CALIBRE RS, THE 1ST MECHANICAL MOVEMENT ENGINEERED WITH THE ROTATING SYSTEM,
INSPIRED BY THE MOST CONTEMPORARY AND TECHNICALLY ADVANCED GT CARS.

WWW.TAGHEUER.COM

TAGHeuer

SWISS AVANT-GARDE SINCE 1860

INDEX

PASSIONNÉ D'EXCEPTION

Academia
Tourbillon Force Constante

Exclusive DeWitt calibre DW8003 mechanical movement, Tourbillon with a constant force device designed to transmit to the tourbillon impulses with identical energy, to exert optimum force control whatever the degree of winding ; a DeWitt patent: "Academia" rose gold case and hand-turned gold dial.

THE FRENCHWAY TRAVEL: 11 WEST 25TH
TEL: 1.212.243.3500 • FAX: 212.243. 3535 • TOLL-FREE

Multi-Complications

photo Ninghetto

CEO Daniel Roth & Gérald Genta

Gérald Roden

Gérald Genta and Daniel Roth, two brands in the Bulgari group, are among the most active in the field of multi-complications. Gérald Roden, their CEO, recalls the path taken over the last few years by the two companies. But first, he addresses the evolution of the multi-complications market over the last ten years.

"An explosion of creativity"

An explosion of creativity characterizes the market right now, which lets Swiss brands maintain their primary position! I still remember my arrival at Daniel Roth in 1997. We were buying movements from Girard-Perregaux, Lémania and Zenith. In the same way as some of them were using ETA movements as a base for creation, at Gérald Genta we were lucky enough to have an incredible legacy of integrated complications and additional plates to relaunch the two brands.

At the time, we halted production of dials and cases to invest in manufacturing movements within our Manufacture de Haute Horlogerie Daniel Roth & Gérald Genta.

Ten years ago, only a few brands were capable of producing multi-complications. Besides these manufactures, only one company—Christophe Claret—produced them. The landscape has changed since, and now many companies are releasing tourbillons combined with other complications. But to my mind, the market for striking harbous the greatest potential in the coming years.

The average price for Swiss watches has gone from 312 Swiss francs (US$285) to 565 (US$516) in 2007, and this trend will certainly continue... at the expense of quantity, certainly. But it repre-

FACING PAGE
Gérald Roden.

THIS PAGE
Detail of the Gefica.

sents a real re-evaluation of our expertise in all the trades—many of them based on hand craftsmanship—that are required to produce exceptional watches!

How has Gérald Genta responded to this evolution?

Since 1998, Gérald Genta has used modern means of design and production to redevelop the movements that made this brand a pioneer in

multi-complications. In 1989, Gérald Genta introduced a tourbillon, and then the small Manufacture, based in both Vallée de Joux and Geneva, released such marvels as the world's thinnest minute repeater, and the undisputed masterpiece of striking watches, at the time the most expensive watch in the world: La Grande Sonnerie with four hammers, tourbillon, minute repeater and retrograde perpetual calendar.

We still haven't finished rediscovering our treasures! That said, the level of quality made possible by new means of production is light-years ahead of what it was 20 years ago. We have an extraordinary level of quality that lots of other brands envy!

And Daniel Roth?

Daniel Roth's position at the time was not as clear-cut. It produced multi-complications, of course, but mainly focused on the horological art at the level of finishing. There was also this philosophy of labor according to which one watchmaker would realize a watch from A to Z, starting from the parts coming straight out of the machine that washed them! The collection included a tourbillon, a minute repeater, a chronograph and a retrograde watch in the style of a Georges Daniels pocket watch. The brand began to find itself at the end of the 1990s, producing simpler watches

in steel. It has always innovated, introducing the first colored dials as part of a strategic approach to the high-end market.

Since then, while still maintaining an extraordinary level of finishing, we have developed some unique complications. The Grande Sonnerie Moon Phases that we released in December 2007 is one example. We also introduced an exceptional watch in 2008—a one-of-a-kind creation in watchmaking. It is a minute repeater with automata—and not jaquemarts. In fact, the animation of the automata will be disassociated from the striking mechanism. This implies two separate mechanisms, instead of the single one found in a traditional striking watch.

What place does each brand occupy in the world of haute horology and complications?

Gérald Genta has found its place as a pioneer of complicated watches, but also of sophisticated, cutting-edge watches, marrying shapes, materials and colors in the universe of haute horology and

according to its values. And Daniel Roth is the brand of the grand Swiss watchmaking tradition.

What are each brand's signal achievements in this field?

The launch of Gefica in 2007, which has a movement that is impossible to copy—featuring jump hours and retrograde minutes—marked the fruition of Gérald Genta's rebirth; the brand is finding success again after long years of the industrial restructuring that is necessary to offer one-of-a-kind products of high quality and technical standards. The Arena and Octo collections also welcomed the reintroduction of grand strike, tourbillon and perpetual calendar movements. The year 2004 saw Gérald Genta's revival, not only in terms of design with the launch of the Octo collection, but also in terms of movements, with the exclusive use of Manufacture-made movements.

As for Daniel Roth, the end results of the most high-technology research in the great watchmaking tradition will be revealed when we introduce the first minute repeater automaton ever produced.

How would you define the clientele that goes for very complicated pieces?

There are several types of clients. The fan, the con-

noisseur, the collector—they have always existed. We have a lot of them at Gérald Genta. They are very demanding—and rightfully so—and they want to learn about all the technical details. They are also interested by the idea that their purchase could be an investment. Some of these aficionados by their watches secondhand.

The second type of client—the kind whose numbers have been growing the fastest over the last few years—wants very exclusive watches. We find a lot of those at Daniel Roth, which produces 1,500 watches per year. Even for the simpler complications, we intentionally limit the number of watches we produce.

Do you see an evolution in these different types of clienteles?

The differences are tending to give way to a certain degree of homogenization, particularly due to the internationalization of watch magazines, but also thanks to the fantastic work done by sites like The Purists or Horomundi.

The popularity of these sites has undeniably unified the clientele, but has also really put the brake on the market for those brands that claimed to be a part of haute horology, while they were really just sticking ETA movements in extremely expensive gold cases. Outside the framework of haute

horology and the principles that are inseparably entwined with it, even multi-complications aren't worth that much!

How can, or should, "legitimate" brands defend their territory?

By being more creative, higher-quality and in line with their DNA, as well as keeping everything within the framework of the values of haute horology. "No gimmicks" is one of our mottos at Daniel Roth and Gérald Genta. The second, somewhat more intangible principle, is to not insult our clients' intelligence!

What are the risks of the current boom?

The pendulum swinging back! Traditionally, market contractions come according to a three-year cycle; for the last five years, the industry has been surfing on these incredible rates of growth! At Daniel Roth and Gérald Genta, we've been able to grow and develop in a structured way, which protects us from any slowdown in the market.

What does the future look like for haute horology?

Excellent, because haute horology is developing in a world of rock-solid values! History has shown that only the companies that have a sense of these values can survive.

President of Bovet

Pascal Raffy

Fleurier
Notre Dame

Under the leadership of Pascal Raffy, Bovet has chosen to go the manufacturing route to realize its exceptional timekeepers. Exemplified by the Fleurier Notre Dame, a minute repeater with tourbillon, three time zones and automata, all Bovet timepieces are the fruit of the passion and know-how of dozens of artisans working in the heart of the manufacture.

> "It is essential to be able to live with your timepiece every day, to wind it, to feel the passion and work that gave it life"

"These timepieces require the symbiotic contribution of dozens of artisans, but they are also by their very nature a journey through three centuries of watchmaking heritage," notes Pascal Raffy, Bovet's president and fierce defender of the horological craft. In the six years since he started leading Bovet, Raffy has taken the time to construct his body of work, step by step, with a very clear vision. "It is our duty to carry on tradition," he says. "But that absolutely does not mean that we must stand still. Though it facilitates certain production processes, technology will never invent a human act; it simply allows us to perfect and improve upon it. So human beings and their passion must remain at the core of our endeavors."

It is by never losing sight of these principles that Pascal Raffy has made Bovet the company it is today, which has come to attract the attention of all those who love and collect these exceptional objects. "In many fields, true luxury has really suffered over the last three decades," Raffy says. "Under the crushing blows of excessive speculation, easy gains and the supposed democratization of luxury, which in fact served purely economic objectives, many people lost the fundamental guidelines. True luxury must primarily be asso-

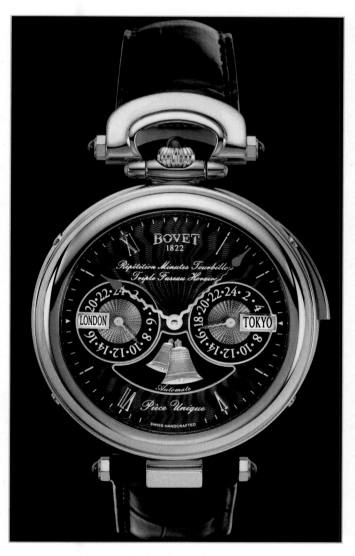

FACING PAGE
Pascal Raffy.

THIS PAGE
Fleurier Notre Dame: a stunning blend of complications and expertise.

ciated with pleasure and emotion—that's what we are trying to convey through our timepieces. In the same way that a collection of paintings should be admired and not hidden in a safe, it is essential to be able to live with your timepiece every day, to wind it, to feel the passion and work that gave it life."

Fresh manufacturing impetus

These are the values governing the crafting of all Bovet timepieces, such as the outstanding Fleurier Notre Dame, which has aroused the enthusiasm of a number of connoisseurs. Merely listing its functions already sets the Fleurier Notre Dame apart as truly exceptional: minute repeater, tourbillon, triple time zone and an automaton with cathedral chimes! This timepiece endowed with such a wealth of complications perfectly reveals Bovet's philosophy of beauty, which it believes should not be visually aggressive. Its 18-karat white-gold Ø 44mm case houses a manual-winding Bovet Haute Horlogerie caliber 12BM09, with tourbillon and minute repeater, beating at 18,000 vibrations per hour, with beveled, flame-blued screws. It displays the hours and minutes by central hands, two independent time zones on counters at 3:00 and 9:00 with city indications in windows (24 cities linked to time zones at 3:00 and 16 cities at 9:00), hour, quarter-hour

and minute repeater activated by a dedicated repeater slide. Showing an impressive display of artistry, the dial is guilloché by hand and graced with fleurisane engraving and time zones in black enamel. This extraordinary timepiece is produced at the rate of eight models per year, each one different.

It is order to master the essential parts of this expertise, representing the true signature of haute horology, that Raffy has forcefully developed the Bovet brand since he acquired it in 2001: "what really counts is not to shine, but to last," recalls Raffy. Almost two centuries after Edouard Bovet founded the company, Raffy has given it a new boost in order to ensure the future of one of the greatest legends of Swiss horology. After purchasing the Môtiers château, in the Val de Travers, original homeland of Bovet, the brand absorbed three manufacturing companies in August 2006 (STT SA, Aigat SA and Spir-It SA), uniting them into a Manufacture of hand-crafted haute horology under a name drawn from Bovet's history: Dimier 1738. Dimier thus incoroporates the savoir-faire that is indispensable for the manufacture of haute horology movements, since it produces mechanical movements with complications, ensures the development of new calibers and creates balance springs. Three months later, Raffy completed Bovet's vertical integration by acquiring the Valor & Lopez workshops, prominent in the production of dials and cases.

Base movement coming soon

From 50 people in 2005, Bovet and Dimier have grown to an over 200-strong workforce today. Since January 2008, a watchmaking unit has been active at Château de Môtiers, which will also serve as the brand museum. The company has also been working for the last three years on a base movement, which will be introduced in 2009. After successfully completing the approval stages, this movement will be deemed worthy to bear—an extraordinary accomplishment in itself —the most demanding seal of approval in the Swiss watch industry, the Fleurier Quality Foundation certification.

The Bovet manufacture produced 1,652 timepieces last year. "And I won't worry if we keep to that same quantity in the years to come," affirms Raffy. "The Bovet brand has never produced in great volume, and we never will We're avoiding giving in to the temptation of going too fast, and we're relearning the lessons of our ancestors; these things take time."

Spotlight on the great complications

The so-called grand complications, describing watches
combining several of the most difficult horological
functions, are a bit like a dazzling violin solo
or when the soprano hits a high C—the ultimate display
of superior talent and virtuosity.

The best watchmakers have always tried to push their
art to the limits, demonstrating their ingenuity by
creating timepieces of extreme mechanical complexity.
These masterpieces of design and manufacture have
found favor not only from connoisseurs but also from
those eager to demonstrate their wealth and power.

Complications returned to the scene following the revival of mechanical watchmaking in the 1980s. Major watch companies resumed the contest to build the world's most complicated watch, and with the help of the hitherto unimaginable power of design software, started turning out timepieces with the maximum possible functions. Many other brands followed suit, often relying on anonymous sub-contractors, and hardly a month goes by without the announcement of a new horological marvel of 400, 600 or even 800 components, or of a fantastic combination of unprecedented functions destined to rewrite history.

This rivalry and determination to excel is most gratifying to enthusiasts of fine watchmaking and to the brands that represent it. Although extremely complicated watches invariably come in a strictly limited edition or as a unique piece, being destined for a small group of collectors or even for the brand's museum, their development serves as a test bed and a means for watch companies to hone their skills. Many of the developments and improvements thus derived find their way into more affordable watches, rather like the application of the technological spin-offs from Formula 1 racing in production automobiles.

However, these attempts at horological record-breaking are not without risks. Quite a few companies seem to focus more on the publicity effects of their announcements, leaving customers to wonder why the watches that made the magazine headlines months or even years ago, are still not in the stores. Have they been conveniently forgotten? Furthermore, under competitive pressure, some brands have the distressing tendency to curtail the necessary development and testing. The word behind the scenes is that the rich buyers of ultra-complicated wristwatches as well as some of the more precocious brands could be in for a surprise when it comes to after-sales service.

Nevertheless there are more positive developments. The last decade has seen the emergence of a trend in user-friendly complications. Stuffing a record number of functions into club sandwich watches is so not in fashion. Further beyond the pale are illegible dials and instruction manuals as fat as bibles. Watchmakers are on a new quest: the maximum functionality and simplicity with the minimum mechanical complexity. Another way of jumping above the crowd is to invent alternative mechanical ways of expressing the classic complications, mostly dating from the 19th century or earlier. The contemporary watchmaking scene is full of novel mechanical constructions, weird materials and tradition-mocking parodies.

Yet the great complications preside eternally over the changing fashions—and this publication has done justice to a worthy subject.

Multi-Complications

With movements assembled from hundreds of parts and multi-function dials, extremely complicated watches bring together all the skills of watchmaking at their highest level. Designing and building a single mechanical superwatch can take a decade of committed effort. But the know-how and the time don't come cheap.

In the old days, such pieces were made for rich enthusiasts; today they are more likely to mark some anniversary in the history of the brand. Alongside commemorative pieces and record-breaking attempts, watchmakers are now also producing a variety of grandes complications where the emphasis is on practicality and ease of use while the complications are kept within limits. These rare pieces are all that meet the growing demand from hobbyists and collectors today.

Time to the sound of bells

Watch- and clock-making didn't progress in a straight line from the simplest to the most complicated devices. The indication of the minute, which we take for granted, couldn't become a practical possibility before the invention of the balance-spring in the late 17th century, yet watchmakers had long been capable of the most complex mechanical devices for watches. It took another century before watches showed the passing seconds. The progress of watchmaking has also been pushed back by the constant miniaturization of mechanisms. Thus the first portable timepieces of the Renaissance were necessarily far simpler mechanically than the great tower clocks of mediaeval times, while today even the most sophisticated wristwatch cannot match the complexity possible in pocket-watches of an earlier generation.

The mechanical measurement of time was first described back in the 14th century. But that doesn't that the first clockmakers started with simple mechanisms. The first clocks we hear about were already very sophisticated, notably the tower clock with astronomical calendar built by Roger Stoke for Norwich cathedral between 1321 and 1325, or Richard de Wallingford's astronomical mechanism constructed in St. Albans between 1330 and 1360. Even these were outclassed by the horological masterpiece of the era, the Astrarium by Giovanni de' Dondi of Padua, completed in 1364.

In the late Middle Ages and in the Renaissance, the church and political leaders promoted, and above all financed, the construction of monumental clocks full of astronomical and astrological indications, and often with elaborate chimes. Among the best known are the astronomical clocks of Lund cathedral in Sweden (1380), the cathedral of Saint-Etienne de Bourges, France (1424), and of St. Mary's church at Rostock in Germany (1472). Also built in the 15th century is the astronomical clock on the north wall of Prague's town hall, which has a 24-hour dial, shows the positions of the sun and the moon, and indicates the saint of the month and the astrological house. Every hour, the clock parades the 12 Apostles; other automated figures include Death, the Turk and Avarice. The builder of the Prague masterpiece is said to have been victim to the legendary expedient of poking out the creator's eyes so he could never construct the like. Strasbourg cathedral's astronomical clock built between 1547 and 1574, features among its complications an orrery showing the movement of the planets, as well as a perpetual calendar indicating the movable feasts over a century. Bern's Zytglogge tower clock, dating from 1530, and the much post-carded pride of the main street in the old town of Switzerland's capital, is celebrated for its astronomical calendar of day, date, month, zodiac and moon phase, as well as

for its hourly carousel of animated figures: a golden rooster that crows thrice, a king turning his hour glass, a parade of bears dressed in the city's colors and accompanied by a jester. A mounted knight above the clock strikes the hours on the bell.

The age of mastery

The first pocket-sized watches at the end of the 15th century could only manage one hours hand. The following century saw the development of astronomical and astrological indications. Watchmakers went on to add other functions, such as alarm, calendar, chimes in passing or repeaters that strike the time on demand. Then they strove to combine as many of these complications as possible in a single watch. This culminated in the mystery-shrouded Breguet watch N° 160, best known as the Marie-Antoinette. In 1783, Abraham-Louis Breguet, the watchmaker in favor with King Louis XVI of France and his queen, Marie-Antoinette, received a strange order from an officer of the queen's guard whose identity remains a mystery. Some,

▶▶ *1* *La « Zytglogge » de Berne*
The "Zytglogge" or clock tower of Berne dates back to 1530. It is famous for its astronomical dial (hour, day, date, month, zodiac, moonphase) as well as for its carousel of figurines that come to life once an hour.

▶▶ *2* *L'astrarium de de' Dondi*
Completed in 1364, the Astrarium of Giovanni de'Dondi, of Padua, demonstrated a remarkable level of complexity.

▶▶ *3* *L'horloge astronomique de Prague*
Built in the 15th century, the Prague Astronomical Clock adorning the wall of the Old Town City Hall features the hour on a 24-hour display, positions of the sun and moon, the day's saint and signs of the zodiac.

TEMPS APPARENT

LEVER DU SOLEIL

COUCHER DU SOLEIL

notably after seeing the Sofia Coppola movie, are romantically inclined to name the handsome count Axel de Fersen, whose attentions to the queen are said to have generously exceeded the requirements of his official functions. The order was for watch that combined all the known and latest mechanical features. The enigmatic agent set no limit as to the price or deadline, but specified that gold was to replace brass or steel wherever possible. It is not known whether the queen was aware of this order, or if she wanted it as a gift to her royal husband. Breguet set to work, but the queen, guillotined in 1793, would never see the mechanical jewel that was completed only in 1827, under the management of Breguet's sons, and after lengthy interruptions. The so-called perpetuelle (selfwinding) watch in a gold case with rock-crystal dial, combined a minute-repeater, a full perpetual calendar, the equation of time, a power-reserve indicator, a bimetallic thermometer and independent sweep seconds in addition to the running seconds. It also featured a number of technical innovations like the double para-chute shock-absorber, a gold balance-spring and several parts in sapphire. The Marie-Antoinette watch had a succession of owners before being stolen in 1983 from a Jerusalem museum in a spectacular break-in that became the subject of a novel. The Breguet company hinted at a reward to anyone who could lead to its recovery, and the firm's constructors and watchmakers were set to devising a replica, when in late 2007, the watch was reported to have reappeared in rather obscure circumstances (see The Marie-Antoinette's amazing comeback).

▶▶ 1 *L'horloge astronomique*
de la Cathédrale de Strasbourg
Close-up on the astronomical
clock of the Strasbourg Cathedral,
built between 1547 and 1574.

▶▶ 2 *Breguet, Marie-Antoinette*
The Breguet N° 160, better known
under the name "Marie-Antoinette,"
integrates all complications and
fine-tuning known at the end
of the 18th century, including,
among others, a minute repeater,
a complete perpetual calendar
and an equation of time.

THE MARIE-ANTOINETTE'S
AMAZING COMEBACK

Did the decision by Nicolas G. Hayek, managing owner of Breguet, to build replicas of the celebrated Breguet N° 160 have any bearing on the intriguing reappearance of the original that had vanished in 1983? Evidence can be found in the remarkable circumstances surrounding the Marie-Antoinette's recovery.

In 2006, Hayek received an astonishing email. "An anonymous person asked me if I wanted to buy the Marie-Antoinette watch which was in his possession. He said he lived near Jerusalem. The individual certainly knew about our advertising around the reconstruction of a brand-new Marie-Antoinette watch," concluded Breguet's boss.

Hayek's anonymous correspondent in Jerusalem does indeed know of the project in hand. He offers to come to Switzerland and hand the treasure over personally to the industrialist in Biel. But this attempt at extortion backfires. "As a good Swiss, I reported this to the federal attorney general," recounts Hayek. "Detectives came to Biel to investigate the matter, but because of this investigation, the anonymous individual who tried to sell me the watch must have known I had contacted the police. I never heard any more from him." Shortly afterwards, in August 2006, the manager of the L. A. Museum of Islamic Art in Jerusalem gets a call from a watchmaker in Tel Aviv. The watchmaker tells her that a young woman lawyer had contacted him and invited him to appraise some 40 watches she had. The watchmaker agrees. He immediately recognizes among them several of the watches stolen in Jerusalem in 1983. The lawyer says that the watches, wrapped in newspaper and stored in three old cardboard boxes, belong to one of her clients, a British woman who had inherited them from her late husband. The widow was prepared to part with them for money and for anonymity. Following the watchmaker's report, experts from the L. A. Mayer museum hurry around to the lawyer's premises where they discover the 40 rare pieces, including the missing Breguet N°160 made for Marie-Antoinette. They spend hours examining the fragile mechanisms. Five of them are irreparable; the thieves had gouged out the jewels and the gold. Four other watches are damaged but fixable. And the queen's, the N°160? "It is now safe with us and in good condition," Deena Lawi, one of the museum's officers recently reported.

News of the Marie-Antoinette's re-appearance was kept quiet for the second half of 2006 and for almost all of 2007. During that time, the L. A. Mayer Museum of Islamic Art informed the police, negotiated with the insurers, and embarked upon the restoration of the watches for their exhibition in 2008. Breguet could sponsor it. But, as of the end of 2007, the museum still had not allowed the Breguet company to come and examine the watch. So some doubt might still linger as to its authenticity.

Marie-Antoinette, Queen of France, as painted by Élisabeth Vigée-LeBrun, 1785 version of the 1783 "with rose" painting.

1

▶▶ 1 *Patek Philippe, Graves*
*The "Graves" pocket watch required eight years of work
from Patek Philippe, including three years of preliminary research
in astronomy, mathematics and mechanics.*

▶▶ 2-3 *Leroy 01*
*A watch to rival the Graves, the Leroy 01 was ordered from
the famous French watchmakers Leroy, of Besançon,
by a Portuguese doctor in 1896. Its twin-faced case integrates
20 additional indications linked to time measurement.*

Complications in your pocket

If one name says it all in the matter of complicated watches, it has to be Patek Philippe. In 1925, a New York banker and art collector, Henry Graves Junior, asked the Geneva watchmaker to make him the most complicated watch ever. The Graves pocket-watch took Patek Philippe eight years to complete, three of them for initial astronomical and mechanical calculations. It was delivered to the American tycoon in January 1933 for 16,000 dollars. Comprising more than 900 parts, the double-faced watch combines 24 complications, including a grand strike in passing on a carillon of four gongs, with a fifth gong for the alarm. One face features a split-seconds chronograph and a perpetual calendar; on the other side it indicates sidereal time, the equation of time, the times of sunrise and sunset in New York and well as a mobile representation of the night sky over Henry Graves jnr's home. In 1999 the Graves watch smashed all records for a horological item at auction by selling to a bid of 11,002,500 dollars. The Graves' claim to be the world's most complicated watch has long been challenged by another horological monument, the Leroy 01 of 1904. The prominent French watchmakers, Leroy of Besançon were commissioned to make it by a Portuguese physician in 1896. Its double-faced case displays 20 different ways of measuring time, including the equation of time, the chronograph, the night sky in the northern and southern hemispheres and a grand strike in passing. Also incorporated are five non-horological instruments: a hygrometer, a thermometer, barometer, altimeter and compass. If these are tallied as complications then the Leroy 01 claims 25, against the 20 complications of the Graves.

Settling the issue

In 1989, Patek Philippe put the issue to rest by unveiling the Calibre 89, to mark its 150th anniversary. With 33 com-

2

3

Patek Philippe, Calibre 89
Marking 150 years of the Manufacture of Patek Philippe, the Calibre 89 currently constitutes the most complicated watch in the entire history of watchmaking, thanks to its 33 complications and 1,728 pieces.

plications and comprising 1,728 parts, this watch today represents the most complicated portable timepiece in the history of watchmaking. It might be portable, but it is hardly wearable, with a diameter of 88.2mm, 41.07mm thick and weighing more than a kilogram. Development and construction of the Calibre 89 took nine years. Aside from such classic complications as the calendar, chronograph, chime, and astronomical complications (see box), it features some highly unusual devices, notably a secular calendar operating on a cycle of 400 years that will indicate the dates without adjustment until the 28th century. A patented mechanism indicates the date of Easter, a moveable feast determined by an elaborate system of calculation. The Calibre 89 is also fitted with a celestial chart in sapphire crystal displaying the Milky Way as well as 2,800 northern hemisphere stars in their various magnitudes. Among the exclusive devices is a mechanism to halt the chime before its spring runs out. Only four Calibre 89s were ever, and will ever be made. The first, in yellow gold, fetched 3.2 million dollars at an auction in Geneva held by Antiquorum. Three other examples, respectively in pink gold, in white gold and in platinum left the Patek Philippe workshops in the early 1990s. All four now belong to the same person, while the company keeps the cherished prototype.

THE PATEK PHILIPPE CALIBRE 89 IN FIGURES

- **Project duration: 9 years, including 5 for research and 4 for manufacturing and assembly;**

- **Number of parts: 1,728, including 2 dials, 8 discs, 24 hands, 61 bridges, 129 rubies, 184 wheels, 332 screws, 415 pegs and 429 mechanical components;**

- **Case dimensions: diameter 88.2mm, thickness 41 mm;**

- **Weight: 1,100 grams;**

- **33 complications:**
  The hours, minutes and seconds of sidereal time
  Time in a second time zone
  Times of sunset and sunrise
  Equation of time
  Tourbillon escapement
  Perpetual calendar
  Secular calendar
  Date, day and month
  Century, decade and year
  Four-year cycle
  Sun hand (seasons, equinoxes, solstices and houses of the Zodiac)
  Celestial chart
  Phases and age of the moon
  Date of Easter
  Chronograph
  Split seconds with flyback
  12-hour elapsed time indicator
  30-minute elapsed time indicator
  Grand carillon in passing
  Small carillon in passing
  Minute-repeater
  Alarm
  Power-reserve indicator for the movement
  Power-reserve indicator for the chime
  Mechanism to halt the chime
  Twin-barrel winding system
  Four-way setting system by the winding crown
  Winding crown position indicator.

1
▲

2
▲

Mechanical poetry

In 2000, Patek Philippe once more rose to watchmaking prominence with the double-faced Star Caliber 2000 pocketwatch. The idea was not to put as many complications together as possible, but to "select those that express time in the most poetic way." This essentially means astronomic indications: the course of the stars and the sun, the changing face of the moon, the cycle of the seasons. It recalls the days when people measured time by the recurrence of natural phenomena. Also the product of nine years of research and development, the Star Caliber 2000 comprises 21 complications. The front dial, dedicated to our sun, displays its setting and rising and its path over 24 hours, as well as the solar time running against mean time to provide the equation. The back dial features the night sky with a rotating celestial chart carrying the stars and the moon as well as the phases of the moon, while a golden ellipse terminates the visible sky from a given point of observation. The movement comprises 1,100 parts, and represents six patented horological innovations, covering the carillon chime, the astronomical indications, and the way the cover opens. It is housed in an elegant half-hunter case with the back cover in engraved openwork in Renaissance style. Unlike the Calibre 89, the Star Caliber is available in the Patek Philippe catalogue—provided you have a respectable watch budget and a bit of patience.

Even without aiming for the Guinness Book of Records, other major producers and watchmakers have recently come out with watches to demonstrate extreme mechanical sophistication. The Grande Complication Savonnette from Audemars Piguet combines, under the yellow-gold cover of its case, a perpetual calendar, a minute-repeater and a split-seconds chronograph. The Breguet N° 5, a replica of an antique piece, encloses automatic winding, a power reserve of 60 hours, moon-phase

▶▶ *3*   *Breguet, n°5*
Breguet's N° 5, recreation of a former model, combines automatic winding, a 60-hour power reserve, a moonphase display and a quarter repeater "à toc," which means that the hammer strikes the inside of the case to produce a muffled sound.

▶▶ *4*   *Vincent Bérard, Quatre Saisons Carrosse*
The artisan watchmaker Vincent Bérard has chosen to reinterpret "carriage" watches ¥in creating the "Quatre Saisons Carrosse" collection .This piece, completely handmade and produced in four versions with different colors of gold, combines a perpetual calendar, quarter repeater, automata on the dial, power reserve indicator and a thermometer. The version shown is the "summer" model.

▶▶ *5*   *Vincent Bérard, Quatre Saisons Carrosse*
The caseback of the "spring" piece in Vincent Bérard's "Quatre Saisons Carrosse" series.

3 ▲

indication and a "dumb" quarter-repeater, striking against the case instead of on a gong.

Watchmaker Vincent Bérard has rediscovered the old coaching watches in his Quatre Saisons Carrosse. Entirely crafted by hand, this 90mm-diameter timepiece features a perpetual calendar, a quarter-repeater, and automatons on the dial, a power-reserve indicator and a thermometer. Only four are made, dedicated to the four seasons—green gold for spring, yellow gold for summer, pink and white gold for fall and winter, with a design in fired enamels for each season. The automata on the dial are also matched to the time of year—two swallows fly in summer and leaves denote the fall.

4 ▲

5 ▲

▶▶ 1 *Gérald Genta, Octo Grande Sonnerie*
Over 1,000 pieces compose the
movement of Gérald Genta's Grande
Sonnerie, which has a diameter
of 30mm and a thickness of 8.4mm.

▶▶ 2 *Blancpain, 1735*
In 1991, Blancpain presented the 1735
(a tribute to the founding year of the
Manufacture), which combines the six
"masterpieces of horology": ultra-thin
movement, moonphases, perpetual
calendar, split-seconds chronograph,
tourbillon and minute repeater.

The wristwatch exploit

The advent of wristwatches with the 20th century forced watchmakers to curtail their ambitions in the matter of complications, given the limited volume of the cases. Nevertheless wristwatches also provoked them to find clever ways of miniaturizing mechanisms and assembling them into exceptional timepieces. Since the revival of mechanical watchmaking in the 1980s, ultra-complicated wristwatches have multiplied and the contest for the world's most complicated wristwatch is in full swing. In 1991, Blancpain introduced the 1737 (the year of its origins), which consists of the six "masterworks of horology": an extra-thin movement, moon phases, perpetual calendar, split-seconds chronograph, tourbillon and minute-repeater. This watch, which took six years to complete, has a movement of 745 parts in a plain round case in the understated Blancpain style. It is noted for its slimness, given its number of complications. In 1994, Gerald Genta challenged Blancpain with its Grande Sonnerie, a tourbillon clockwatch with grand and small strike in passing on a four-gong Westminster carillon, a minute-repeater, perpetual calendar, a second time zone, twin, selfwinding mainspring barrels, as well as the power-reserve indicators for the movement and the carillon. The 1,000-part movement goes into a case of 30mm diameter for a thickness of 8.4mm. As always for appearance's sake, Gerald Genta designed a highly distinctive octagonal

3

▶▶ *3*   *Patek Philippe, Celestial Réf.5102*
Patek Philippe's Celestial model builds
upon the principle of a sky chart seen
in the Sky Moon Tourbillon, but gives it
a place of honor on the front of the case.

▶▶ *4*   *Patek Philippe, Sky Moon Tourbillon*
This double-faced timepiece
combines—in an unprecedented way—
the twelve complications considering
the most rare and the most fascinating,
including a minute repeater with
"cathedral" chime, a perpetual
calendar with a retrograde date hand,
and, of course, a tourbillon.

4

case with eight steps for his Grande Sonnerie. The original styling stood in stark contrast to the prevailing traditional styling of grand complications.

New Peaks

Patek Philippe had to re-establish its supremacy and introduced the Sky Moon Tourbillon in 2001—the firm's most complicated wristwatch to date. The double-faced watch is an unprecedented combination of the 12 most rare and fascinating complications, including a minute-repeater on cathedral gongs, a perpetual calendar with retrograde dates, and, of course, the tourbillon. The back dial displays a most unusual function in a wristwatch—a celestial chart in motion that precisely tracks the movement of the stars, the moon and her changing phases. Patek Philippe devised this celestial ballet with three superimposed discs of sapphire crystal, rotating at different speeds according to precisely calculated gear ratios. This patented mechanism is derived from the system developed for the Star Caliber 2000. Patek Philippe Celestial watch also adopts the celestial chart, but gives it place of honor on the face of the watch.

In 2005, Vacheron Constantin celebrated its 250th anniversary by producing—alongside other exceptional pieces—an ultra-com-

▶▶ *1-2* *Vacheron Constantin, Tour de l'Ile*
Presented as "a wristwatch in the most
complicated series in the world," the
Tour d'Ile is a double-faced watch with
a 47mm diameter, 17.8mm thick which
contains no fewer than 16
complications in its 834-part movement.

▶▶ *3* *Zenith, Grande Class Traveller Répétition*
Minutes El Primero
The Grande Class Traveller Répétition
Minutes has a triangular aperture and
an openworked design in platinum that
reveal the strike mechanism.

plicated model named, Tour de l'Ile, a reference to the historical building that was the company's home in Geneva from 1834 to 1875. Presented as "the most complicated series-production wristwatch in the world." the double-faced watch demonstrates no fewer than 16 complications comprising 834 parts in a case measuring 47mm wide and 17.8mm thick. Functions include minute-repeater, tourbillon, the age and phases of the moon, perpetual calendar, equation of time, the times of sunrise and sunset and a celestial chart. The Tour de l'Ile was produced in a single series of seven watches. On April 3, 2005, one of the watches fetched more than 1.7 million dollars at an Antiquorum auction and all the others quickly found buyers. The Tour de l'Ile was won the Golden hand award, the supreme prize at the prestigious Grand Prix d'Horlogerie in Geneva.

Also in 2005, Zenith upgraded its foray into the complications front from a skirmish with its tourbillon to a full-scale offensive backed by its Grande Class Traveler Répétition Minutes El Primero, with a triangular window and openwork baseplate revealing the chiming mechanism. Assembled from 744 parts, it brings together minute-repeater, alarm (ringing or vibrating), a

1 *Franck Muller, Aeternitas Mega 4*
Unveiled in 2007, the Aeternitas Mega
4 unites in an elegant tonneau case 15
complications, including grand and
small strike minute repeaters with a
Westminster chime, a "secular"
perpetual calendar with retrograde date,
an equation of time, a tourbillon,
a split-seconds chronograph and two
supplementary time zones.

2 *Jaeger-LeCoultre, Reverso Grande
Complication à triptyque*
This exceptional timekeeper features
three faces for three dimensions of
time, due to its famous reversible case,
created in 1931.

second time zone, a large instantaneous date as well as the power-reserve indications for the movement and the chime. On top of all this are the El Primero chronograph functions.

In 2006, Jaeger-LeCoultre raised the bar with the Reverso Grande Complication à triptyque a novel variation using the make's trademark reversible case devised in 1931. This remarkable time-piece has in fact three faces for three dimensions of time. At the front of the reversible case is the time of day, regulated by a new type of precision detent escapement in an ultra-light tourbillon cage in titanium. On the other side are sidereal time, sky chart, zodiac calendar, equation of time, and the times of sunset and sunrise. Finally, a complete perpetual calendar finds its place in the frame of the reversible case. The brand reckons a total of 18 complications and six patented devices, including the clever way the energy in the movement is transmitted to the frame.

Franck Muller's Aeternitas Mega 4, produced in 2007, packs some 15 complications into an elegant tonneau case, among them grand and small strike and minute-repeater on a Westminster carillon, a secular perpetual calendar with a retrograde date, an equation of time, a large tourbillon, a split-seconds chronograph and two extra time zones.

Patchy prowess

These few star watches, with up to four hand-counts of complica-tions, should however not blind us to other watchmaking cre-ations with more modest pretensions that nevertheless present some remarkable achievements. In this context, "grand compli-cation" has now come to mean a watch with three or four addi-tional functions, especially if they express the traditional areas of watchmaking expertise: the chime, calendars, chronographs and tourbillons. In 2005, a new brand, Jean Dunand, co-founded by the movement constructor, Christophe Claret, (secret purveyor

Jean Dunand, Grande Complication
In 2005, the young brand Jean Dunand—co-founded by the
renowned complicated-movement maker Christophe Claret—
presented an 827-piece wristwatch baptized Grande Complication.

to the most select brands), produced a wristwatch named Grande Complication. The 827-part construction in integrates all the complications on one plate, including a single-button split-seconds chronograph, a tourbillon, minute-repeater, a perpetual calendar with retrograde dates and days, and host of other clever mechanical solutions. After the costly Tourbillon Orbital (see the Tourbillon chapter), the same Jean Dunand brand again drew attention in 2007 by launching the Shabaka, named after the first pharaoh of the 25th dynasty. The distinguishing features are its novel mechanisms and the extraordinary construction of its dial—a stunning display of Art Deco meets ancient Egypt. Shabaka combines a minute-repeater on cathedral gongs with a complete perpetual calendar. Its originality lies in the way the days, dates and months are indicated—on cylinders instead of discs at 10:00, 12:00 and 2:00 respectively. Unlike in most other calendars, the dates, days and months jump instantaneously at midnight, when a sprung mechanism is released. The leap-year cycle is indicated most ingeniously between 6:00 and 9:00 by a white plate passing beneath the dial. The moon phases, at between 3:00 and 6:00, have dark discs progressively moving over the face of the moon like the shadow of the Earth; the moon wanes as they advance from the left and waxes as they retreat from the right.

As an offshoot of the prestigious Tour de l'Ile of its 250th anniversary, Vacheron Constantin's Patrimony Traditionnelle Calibre 2755 brings together the three main areas of mechanical complication—minute-repeater, tourbillon and perpetual calendar—in an elegant round case. The flagship of Cartier's private Paris collection is the Rotonde à Grande Complication, which amalgamates a tourbillon, a perpetual calendar, a single-button chronograph and an eight-day power-reserve indicator. It all comes in a generously proportioned case in platinum with a dial in the typical Cartier graphic style.

Deep among the stars

Astronomical complications are at the source of watchmaking as an art. They also form the classic repertoire of all the ultra-complicated pieces that have appeared to date. Ulysse Nardin put them in the forefront in a trio of extraordinary pieces named the Trilogy of Time. Ludwig Oechslin, the brand's consultant watchmaker and director of the international museum of watchmaking in La Chaux-de-Fonds, who designed the three wristwatches, drew his inspiration from Renaissance astronomy and astrology. The first watch, the Astrolabium Galileo Galilei, indicates the functions of an astrolabe, a navigational instrument that aided great discoveries. It shows the respective positions of the sun, the moon and the stars as viewed from Earth. The Planetarium Copernicus gives a permanent display of the month, the house of the zodiac and the astronomical positions of the planets and the Earth relative to the sun on a dial consisting of seven rings. The third piece, the Tellurium Johannes Kepler, with a dial in cloisonné enamels depicting the Earth viewed from above the North Pole, indicates in particular the times of sunrise and sunset in zones of dark and light, as well as the solar and lunar eclipse: the universe on your wrist.

A. LANGE & SÖHNE

DATOGRAPH-PERPETUAL - REF. 410.025

This model is driven by a manually-wound Lange movement: Calibre L952.1. It is a flyback chronograph with a precisely jumping minute counter as well as perpetual calendar with outsize date, moonphase display, day-of-week, month, leap-year display, small seconds hand with stop seconds, and day/night indicator. The plates and bridges made of untreated German silver, balance cock engraved by hand. The three-part platinum case features anti-reflection-coated sapphire-crystal glass and caseback, main pushpiece for simultaneously advancing all calendar displays as well as recessed pushpieces for separately advancing the calendar displays; two chronograph pushpieces. The hand-stitched crocodile strap is fitted with a solid-platinum buckle. The luminous two-part dial in rhodium-plated solid silver is equipped with a tachometer scale.

A. LANGE & SÖHNE

TOURBOGRAPH - REF. 702.025

The Tourbograph Pour le Mérite houses the manually wound Caliber L903.0 and is the world's first one-minute tourbillon in wristwatch format with a fusée-and-chain transmission, chronograph rattrapante functions, and power-reserve indicator. The mainspring and the fusée are interconnected with a delicate chain consisting of more than 600 parts. While the watch is being wound, the chain is wound up on the tapered fusée and the spring in the barrel is tensioned. The spring's power is delivered to the movement via the fusée, and thereby with constant torque. A planetary gear train composed of 38 parts keeps the movement running even while the mainspring is being wound. Without the chain, the movement consists of 465 parts and 43 jewels, two of which are diamond endstones. The three-part platinum case is equipped with sapphire crystal and caseback. It is created in a limited series of 51 pieces; a re-edition of 50 gold pieces is planned.

AUDEMARS PIGUET

JULES AUDEMARS PERPETUAL CALENDAR AND CHRONOGRAPH "ARNOLD ALL STARS"
REF. 26094OR.00.D002CR.01

Crafted in 18K pink gold, this Jules Audemars "Arnold All Stars" houses the self-winding caliber 2326/2839 with 21K gold rotor. This limited edition of 100 pieces features the functions: hours, minutes, small seconds, date, day, month, 4-year leap-year cycle, astronomical moon indication (with no manual adjustments required until the year 2010) and chronograph. It offers a power reserve of 40 hours and beats at 28,800 vibrations per hour. The sapphire caseback is stamped with the "Arnold All Stars" Foundation logo.

JULES AUDEMARS PERPETUAL CALENDAR AND CHRONOGRAPH "ARNOLD ALL STARS"
REF. 26094BC.00.D095CR.01

Crafted in 18K white gold, this Jules Audemars "Arnold All Stars" houses the self-winding caliber 2326/2839 with 21K gold rotor. This limited edition of 100 pieces features the functions: hours, minutes, small seconds, date, day, month, 4-year leap-year cycle, astronomical moon indication (with no manual adjustments required until the year 2010) and chronograph. It offers a power reserve of 40 hours and beats at 28,800 vibrations per hour. The sapphire caseback is stamped with the "Arnold All Stars" Foundation logo.

AUDEMARS PIGUET

JULES AUDEMARS GRANDE COMPLICATION CHRONOGRAPH RATTRAPANTE
REF. 25866PT.00.D002CR.01

The Jules Audemars Grande Complication houses the self-winding Caliber 2885 with 654 components. The watch offers perpetual calendar with 52-week indication, astronomical moon, minute repeater, and split-second chronograph. It is housed in a platinum case and features five correctors and a slide for the repeater on the side. The month and four-year cycle are positioned at 6:00 and the moonphase and date are shown at 12:00. This watch is also available in rose, yellow, white gold or platinum with sapphire caseback, on crocodile strap with double-blade AP deployment clasp in corresponding metal. Made to order.

AUDEMARS PIGUET

JULES AUDEMARS TOURBILLON CHRONOGRAPH - REF. 26010BC.00.D002CR.01

This Jules Audemars Tourbillon with Chronograph houses the exclusive Audemars Piguet tourbillon. The rhodium-plated movement features the Côtes de Genève pattern and circular graining. It offers chronograph function with 30-minute counter at 3:00 and a center sweep-seconds hand. The new hand-wound Caliber 2889 is equipped with 70-hour power reserve and the tourbillon has a progressive recoil click enabling fast winding of the watch. The titanium lever's low inertia eliminates 99% of the characteristic jumps made by the seconds hand when the chronograph is activated. This watch bears a sapphire crystal caseback and applied gold numerals riveted to the engine-turned dial. Its large-scale crocodile strap is secured with a gold AP folding clasp. This timepiece is also available in rose gold.

AUDEMARS PIGUET

JULES AUDEMARS MINUTE REPEATER TOURBILLON WITH CHRONOGRAPH
REF. 26050OR.00.D002CR.01

Cased in 18K rose gold, the Jules Audemars Minute Repeater Tourbillon with Chronograph is powered by the manual-winding Caliber 2874. The watch's minute repeater device strikes on request—and two notes—the hours, quarter hours and minutes, transcribing time that we see into time that we hear. The chronograph has a 30-minute counter and small seconds along the tourbillon axis. Limited production.

AUDEMARS PIGUET

MILLENARY MC12, LIMITED EDITION - REF. 26069PT.00.D028CR.01

Cased in 950 platinum, this tourbillon and chronograph houses the manual-winding Caliber 2884 that beats at 21,600 vibrations per hour and bears 30 jewels. This complication features a twin barrel tourbillon chronograph mounted in carbon base plate, secured by anodized aluminum bridges, cased in platinum with off-center displays, exposed by openwork dial. The Millenary MC12 displays hours and minutes, carbon 30-minute counter at 12:00, chronograph, and 10-day power-reserve indication. This edition is limited to 150 pieces and commemorates the partnership between Audemars Piguet and Maserati with the MC12.

AUDEMARS PIGUET

POCKET WATCH GRANDE COMPLICATION CHRONOGRAPH RATTRAPANTE

REF. 25712BA.00.0000XX.01

Cased in 18K yellow gold, the Classique Pocket Watch Grande Complication is powered by the manual-winding Audemars Piguet Caliber 2860 with minute repeater, perpetual calendar and split-seconds chronograph. The watch has a hunter-type design with a sapphire crystal and has been in production since 1875. Also available in platinum. Made to order.

AUDEMARS PIGUET

ROYAL OAK CHRONOGRAPH TOURBILLON - REF. 259770R.OO.D002CR.01

This Royal Oak Chronograph Tourbillon houses a manual-winding Caliber 2889.The dial features an engine-turned "Grande Tapisserie" pattern with applied riveted numerals. The watch is crafted in 18K pink gold with a transparent sapphire caseback. This Royal Oak Chronograph tourbillon also offers a 70-hour power reserve.

AUDEMARS PIGUET

ROYAL OAK HAND-WOUND TOURBILLON WATCH WITH CHRONOGRAPH

REF. 26116BC.ZZ.D002CR.01

Bearing 430 brilliant-cut diamonds, this white-gold Royal Oak Hand-Wound Tourbillon Chronograph houses the self-winding caliber 2889. The diamond-pavé dial in mother-of-pearl is fitted with a sapphire caseback. The bezel and lugs sets are composed with 48 baguette-cut diamonds.

AUDEMARS PIGUET

ROYAL OAK HAND WOUND TOURBILLON WATCH WITH CHRONOGRAPH
REF. 26039BC.ZZ.1205BC.01

Crafted in an 18K white-gold case and bracelet, the Royal Oak Wound Tourbillon Chronograph features a bezel set with 40 diamonds and a diamond-pavé dial with mother-of pearl counters on a transparent sapphire caseback. The movement features a manual-winding Tourbillon with a titanium lever eliminating the phenomenon of the jumping chronograph hand. Gemstone certificate is supplied. Limited production.

AUDEMARS PIGUET

ROYAL OAK OFFSHORE SELFWINDING PERPETUAL CALENDAR CHRONOGRAPH

REF. 25854TI.OO.1150TI.01

Crafted in a titanium case and bracelet, this Royal Oak Offshore perpetual calendar indicates the day, date, moonphases, months, leap years and small seconds at 12:00. This Royal Oak Offshore houses the self-winding Caliber 2226/2839. The movement features a 21K gold oscillating weight segment, rhodium-plated Côtes de Genève.

AUDEMARS PIGUET

ROYAL OAK GRAND COMPLICATION - REF. 25865BC.OO.1105BC.01

The Royal Oak Grand Complication houses the self-winding Caliber 2885 and features a split-seconds chronograph, astronomical moon, a minute repeater and a perpetual calendar with day of the week indication. A subdial for the seconds is offered at 9:00. Cased in 18K gold, the movement beats at a steady 19,800 vibrations per hour. Twelve indicators are on the dial, including current year, leap-year indicator and moonphase readout. The movement is a labyrinth of 654 parts. Made to order.

AUDEMARS PIGUET

ROYAL OAK TOURBILLON CHRONOGRAPH - REF. 25977BA.001205BA.02

Crafted in yellow gold, this Royal Oak Tourbillon Chronograph houses the manual-wind Caliber 2889 with 70-hour power reserve. The movement vibrates at 21,600 beats per hour and houses 25 jewels. The watch, with sapphire caseback, displays hours and minutes, subseconds dial and chronograph functions. This timepiece is also available in stainless steel.

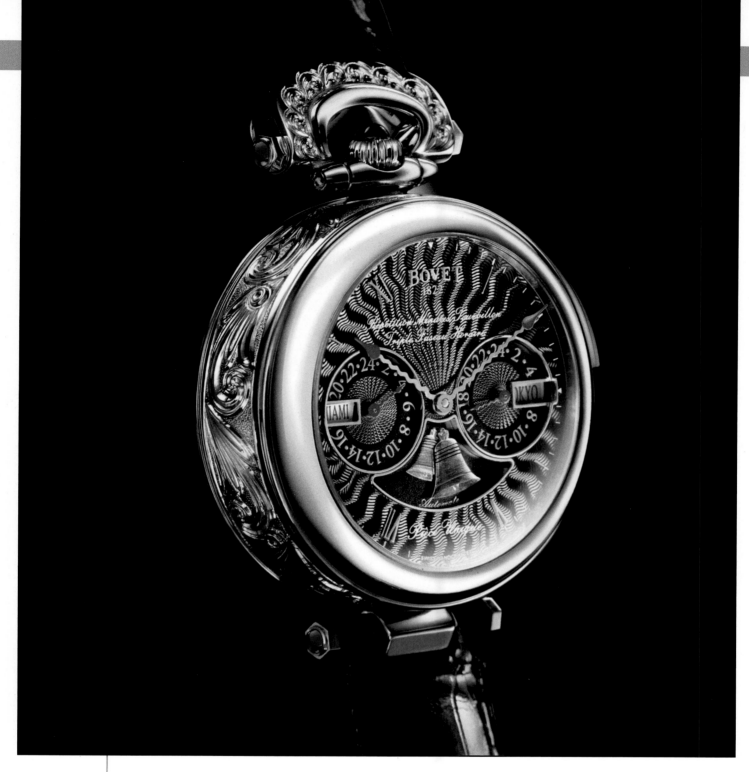

FLEURIER MINUTE REPEATER, TOURBILLON, TRIPLE TIME ZONE AND AUTOMATON

BOVET presents one of the most spectacular technical achievements of 2007 in this hand-wound Minute Repeater, Tourbillon, Triple Time Zone and Automaton Fleurier 44mm wristwatch. The BOVET Haute Horlogerie movement, made of more than 600 different components, is visible through the backside of the case thanks to the transparent sapphire crystal glass. The cathedral gongs of the minute repeater have been attached to the case to provide a clearer sound to the fortunate owner of this magnificent piece of art. The handmade guilloché dial adorns itself with two independent time zones offering to the traveller the indication of 40 cities. Less than 10 pieces of this model will be produced every year, in white or rose gold.

BOVET

FLEURIER MINUTE REPEATER WITH TOURBILLON AND REVERSED HAND FITTING

This single watch encompasses everything BOVET is about. The 44mm 18K white-gold case houses a minute repeater with tourbillon and reversed hand-fitting movement of 365 components visible through a crystal sapphire. The unique feature of this hand-wound caliber is that the movement is shown side up meaning the hand-fitting has to be reversed so that the hands turn clockwise dial-side. The BOVET minute repeater presents two different cathedral chiming gongs, a low-pitch first striking the hours, followed by a combination of high- and low-pitch gongs chiming the quarters and then the minutes.

FLEURIER SELF-WINDING PERPETUAL CALENDAR WITH RETROGRADE DATE
AND SECOND TIME-ZONE INDICATION

Rather than pairing the perpetual calendar with the conventional moonphase indicator, BOVET has bestowed the more practical second time-zone function upon this attractive new 42mm model shown in 18K white gold. The perpetual calendar and 24-hour indication (at 6:00) are combined within an exclusive mechanism constructed by BOVET. In black or white and gold, the dial displays the day, month and leap-year cycle in apertures framed by the arc of the retrograde-date scale. BOVET demonstrates its graphic skills in the creation of an uncluttered dial that conveys seven indications of time with the utmost clarity. This model is also available in 18K red gold.

CLASSIQUE GRANDE COMPLICATION - REF. 1907BA/12

This Classique Grande Complication pocket watch is crafted in 18K yellow gold and features a grand strike and tourbillon. The hand-engraved and hand-wound movement has a 2-way rotating crown and features an off-centered chapter ring and center minute hand on a silvered gold dial, hand-engraved on a rose-engine. The caseback is protected by a sapphire crystal.

CLASSIQUE GRANDE COMPLICATION - REF. 3755PR/1E/9V6

This Classique Grande Complication open-worked wristwatch is crafted in a platinum water-resistant case. Its hand-wound movement in pink gold is engraved by hand and features include a tourbillon, with small seconds on the tourbillon shaft, and a perpetual calendar showing the day, date, month and leap years, and a compensating balance-spring with Breguet overcoil.

BREGUET

MARINE - REF. 5837BR/92/5ZU

This Marine tourbillon with chronograph is crafted in 18K rose gold and houses a hand-wound movement, featuring a tourbillon with small seconds on the tourbillion carriage. Its black rhodium-plated 18K gold dial, engine-turned in a wave pattern, displays a chapter ring with pink gilt applied Roman numerals and luminous dots and a 12-hour totalizer at 6:00. Its Breguet hands are luminous, open-tipped and 18K rose gold. Its case is enhanced with a sapphire caseback and complemented with a rubber strap with folding clasp.

BVLGARI

ASSIOMA MULTICOMPLICATION - REF. AA48PLTBSK

Encased in 48mm of polished platinum, this automatic tourbillon with perpetual calendar and GMT two time zones is powered by the in-house manufactured Caliber BVL 416 (Ø 27.4x7.57mm) consisting of 416 pieces and visible through the caseback. It features an exclusive hanging tourbillon bridge, a black-gold hand-finished back with perlage treatment, an 18K white-gold skeletonized rotor with applied 18K yellow-gold engraved ring, a 64-hour power reserve, 39 jewels, and beats at 21,600 vph. Beneath the curved antireflective scratch-resistant sapphire crystal lies an in-house manufactured dial with four hand-applied levels, enriched by opalin and azuré treatments and horizontal and vertical brushings. This Assioma is presented on a pre-curved rebordé black alligator strap with platinum three-blade folding buckle.
Water resistant to 30 meters, the model is limited to 20 numbered pieces.

BVLGARI

ASSIOMA MULTICOMPLICATION - REF. AA48C5PLTB

The in-house manufactured, automatic-winding Caliber BVL 416 operates the Assioma Multicomplication's automatic tourbillon, perpetual calendar and GMT dual time zone. Visible through the caseback, BVL 416 consists of 416 pieces, an exclusive hanging tourbillon bridge, a black-gold hand-finished back with perlage treatment, an 18K white-gold skeletonized rotor with applied 18K yellow-gold engraved ring, a 64-hour power reserve, 39 jewels, and beats at 21,600 vph. The watch's 48mm, curved, polished platinum case is water resistant to 30 meters and fitted with a curved, antireflective scratch-resistant sapphire crystal and in-house manufactured dial with minute circle, GMT display and date counter decorated with guilloché, Clou de Paris and striate motives, hand-applied anthracite minute circle and indexes. Its pre-curved rebordé black alligator strap has a platinum three-blade folding buckle and this version is available in a limited edition of 25 pieces with number engraved on the case side.

GERALD GENTA

ARENA TOURBILLON PERPETUAL CALENDAR MOON PHASE

REF. ATM.X.75.860.CN.BD

The Arena Tourbillon Perpetual Calendar Moon Phase features a Gérald Genta exclusive tourbillon automatic manufacture movement, offering a 64-hour power reserve. It is coated in antique gold and decorated with a concentric circular-graining. It is housed in a Ø 41mm platinum case with fluted caseband and palladium bezel. The black, red and satin-finish metallic skeleton dial offers original indications for moonphase, leap years and months, days of the month, small seconds and days of the week.

GERALD GENTA

OCTO TOURBILLON PERPETUAL CALENDAR WWT - REF. OTW.Y.50.930.CN.BD

The Octo Tourbillon Perpetual Calendar Moon Phase World Wide Timer offers an entirely hand-decorated Gérald Genta in-house tourbillon movement with perpetual calendar, phases of the moon, and global time on a rotating bezel (WWT). It is housed in a Ø 42.5mm octagonal platinum case with tantalum bezel, enhanced by a white-gold guilloché and cloisonné ivory and black ceramic dial and beaded crown with Falcon-eye cabochon. This model is water resistant to 10atm and is also available in a red-gold case with a red-gold guilloché and cloisonné black and red ceramic dial.

HUBLOT

BIGGER BANG ALL BLACK

Cased in 44.5mm of micro-blasted black ceramic topped with a matching bezel secured by six H-shaped titanium screws, the manual-winding HUB1400CT powers this Bigger Bang's flying tourbillon and chronograph with direct coupling on the cage (which does not have ball bearings and is raised 2.8mm above the base of the bottom plate for maximum visibility on the skeleton dial). The movement also boasts a 120-hour power reserve, beats at 21,600 vph with a Gyromax regulating inertia-block, and is visible through a sapphire crystal caseback. Water resistant to 5atm, Bigger Bang All Black is fitted on an adjustable, smooth natural black rubber with Hublot logo and deployant clasp in black PVD-coated steel. Limited to 28 individually numbered pieces.

HUBLOT

BIGGER BANG PLATINUM DIAMONDS

REF. 308.TX.130.RX.094

Crafted in platinum PT950, this Bigger Bang's skeleton dial is framed by a bezel holding 48 white baguette diamonds and a round-diamond-pavé case. Total diamond weight is 3.9 carats and this version is limited to just 3 pieces. It is powered by the new chronograph / flying tourbillon HUB1400CT movement, visible through a sapphire crystal caseback.

IWC

GRANDE COMPLICATION - REF. 377019

This self-winding IWC caliber 79091 (Valjoux 7750 modified base + IWC calendar and repeater modules) offers perpetual calendar (date, day, month, four-digit year, moonphase), minute repeater, and chronograph with three counters. The most impressive complications—perpetual calendar, repeater and chronograph—are combined in this historical watch, a highly valuable timepiece that allows automatic calendar updating until the year 2499; the digits representing 2200 to 2500 are stored in a small glass tube, supplied with the watch. The four-digit year display and the new repeater system with a reduced number of mobile components (some of which have special new designs) are witnesses of a superior class. The Ø 42mm case is waterproof and antimagnetic.

IWC

GRANDE COMPLICATION - REF. 377015

This Grande Complication offers chronograph, perpetual calendar, perpetual moonphase indicator, four-digit year indicator, minute repeater and small seconds with stop device. It houses the caliber 79091 movement with 75 jewels and 44 hours of power reserve. The watch beats at 28,800 vibrations per hour.
ALTERNATE VERSION: 9270 IN PLATINUM WITH PLATINUM BRACELET

JAEGER-LECOULTRE

GYROTOURBILLON I

Jaeger-LeCoultre's patented GyroTourbillon I houses the Caliber 177 complete with a built-in running equation-of-time mechanism, as well as a host of other functions and indications. The exquisite escapement is a first in the history of the tourbillon due to its spherical design, whose technically advanced multi-dimensional rotation is fascinating. The complex caliber is comprised of 512 parts. In addition to depicting the hours and minutes, its dial also indicates the remaining power reserve, date, month and true solar time as part of the equation-of-time function. The perpetual calendar will not require manual intervention until February 28, 2100. The spherical tourbillon features an aluminum case and an inner titanium and aluminum carriage that is oriented at a 90-degree angle to the outer case and rotates 2.5 times faster than its companion. The total weight of the nearly 100 components that comprise this spherical wonder is just 0.33 grams.

JAEGER-LECOULTRE

REVERSO SQUADRA CHRONOGRAPH GMT BLACK

The Reverso Squadra Chronograph GMT Black immediately asserts its sporting nature through its chronograph functions in keeping with the finest Jaeger-LeCoutre traditions. The hour and minutes are shown on the main dial, and the second time zone on a 24-hour display appears through an aperture at 6:00. Two additional square counters enable readings of the chronograph indications—minutes at 3:00 and hours at 9:00. The large date window at 12:00 is linked to the first time zone. Visible through a transparent caseback, Jaeger-LeCoultre Caliber 754, with its 65-hour power reserve, 39 jewels and 28,800 vph, is housed within a stainless steel or 18K pink-gold case that is water resistant to 5atm.

JAEGER-LECOULTRE

MASTER COMPRESSOR DIVING PRO GEOGRAPHIC

The Master Compressor Diving Pro Geographic, which is recognizable by its 46.3mm diameter and its characteristic appearance due to the presence of the depth gauge, houses a new *Geographic* sports movement. The user must simply position the city symbolizing a given time zone in the aperture at 6:00 and the corresponding time is automatically shown on a 24-hour subdial at 9:00. This indication highlights the "rack" required to transmit the depth indication, read off by a pointer on the logarithmic scale of the depth gauge shown on an outer dial ring. The date appears in an aperture at 3:00 and the luminescent movement-operating indicator is located in the lower part of the dial. Equipped with the automatic Jaeger-LeCoultre Calibre 979 and water resistant to 300 meters, the Diving Pro Geographic model is available in satin-brushed grade-5 titanium.

JAEGER-LECOULTRE

REVERSO GRANDE COMPLICATION À TRIPTYQUE

This Reverso model displays three dimensions of time on three faces: civil, sidereal and perpetual time, made possible by a specially adapted, manually wound mechanical Jaeger-LeCoultre movement. The watch's front dial has a tourbillon endowed with an ellipse isometer escapement, which does away with the traditional Swiss pallet. Its back dial features a zodiacal calendar with an astronomical chart, while the third dial is remarkable for its unique location: a perpetual calendar in the Reverso carriage. A highly original, patented mechanism makes it possible to transmit energy from the movement to the carriage. In total, the timepiece boasts 18 complications, and has six patents pending.

JAEGER-LECOULTRE

MASTER COMPRESSOR EXTREME LAB

The revolutionary Master Compressor Extreme LAB is an exceptional achievement. Operating without any form of lubricant, the new Jaeger-LeCoultre Calibre 988C powering this watch is fully capable of running smoothly for years without any wear of its parts or deterioration of its performances—even at extreme temperatures of -40°C, when the oils or grease in a classic watch freeze and bring the movement to a halt, to +60°C. A new geometry of the balance, the use of new lighter and more resistant materials in the escapement, and a latest-generation tourbillon regulator, converge in this automatic movement. Clothed in 45mm of high-tech carbon and titanium, this watch is a concentrated blend of technology and inventiveness, for which six patents have been filed, and will be released in an exclusive and limited production. Functions include: tourbillon; dual time zone; patented jumping date display linked to local time; 48-hour power reserve. It is water resistant to 10atm.

JEAN DUNAND *PIÈCES UNIQUES*

SHABAKA

The Shabaka minute repeater and perpetual calendar with moonphases is Jean Dunand's impressive new Pièce Unique, offering a dramatic display of calendar information. Cylinders on 90-degree transmissions show dates, days and months that advance instantaneously at midnight. The leap-year cycle is indicated by a white plate illuminating cut-out figures on the dial, while the state of wind is revealed ingeniously by exposing the mainspring against a scale. The repeater chimes on cathedral gongs that circle the movement twice. The displays are integrated in the Art Deco design of the dial, engineered on four levels and set with pyramids of gold. Produced by Thierry Oulevay and manufactured by Christophe Claret, the Shabaka takes its name from the first Pharaoh of Egypt's 25th Dynasty and is water resistant to 3atm.

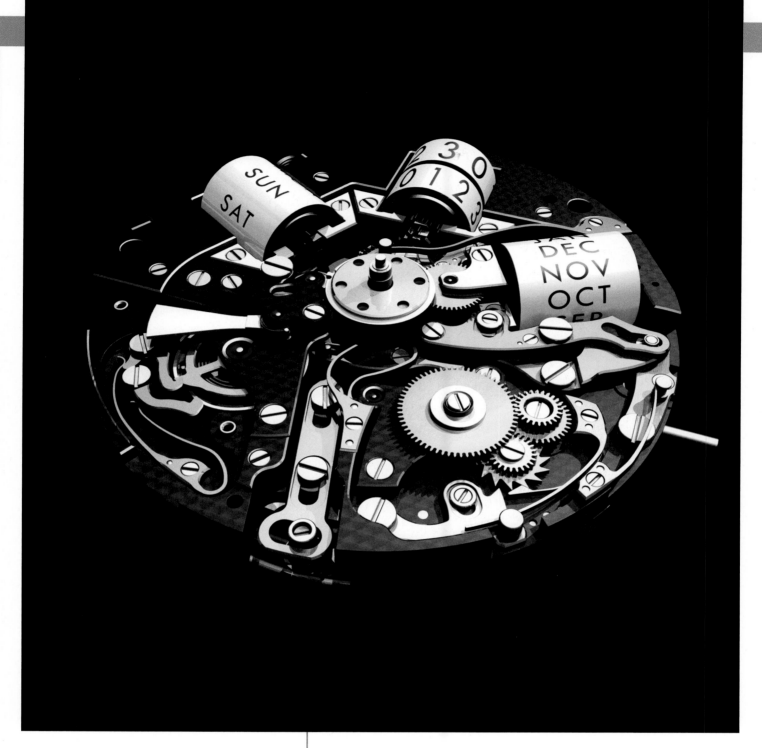

JEAN DUNAND *PIÈCES UNIQUES*

SHABAKA - CALIBRE CLA88RMQP

Christophe Claret's manually wound Calibre CLA88RMQP operates the Shabaka minute repeater with moonphase and instantaneous perpetual calendar featuring days, dates and months on four cylinders. Claret's 721-part movement includes 54 jewels, holds 45 hours of power reserve and beats at 18,000 vph with a swan's neck index and adjusting screws on an overcoil spring. This movement and the watch's outstanding design unite to define Jean Dunand's "super watches" of the 21st century: extreme technical innovation, precision engineering, exceptional manufacturing, and one-of-a-kind timepieces.

PARMIGIANI FLEURIER

TECNICA CHRONO SKELETON

This unique piece is a manual-winding, 43 jeweled tourbillon that features a minute repeater with 2 cathedral chimes. The bridges are engraved by hand according to the theme with chamfering and hand polished backing, steel set lengthways with stones. Beating at 21'600 vibrations per hour, the PF353 movement offers 48 hours of power reserve. The watch's functions include hours, minutes, minute repeater and chronograph. The 44mm case is crafted in 950 platinum and is water resistant to 30 meters. Each watch is individually numbered on the back.

TORIC CORRECTOR MINUTE REPEATER AND PERPETUAL CALENDAR

A world premiere timepiece, this Toric houses the mechanical manually wound Parmigiani Fleurier caliber with retrograde perpetual-calendar module entirely crafted in-house. The 33-jeweled movement vibrates at 21,600 beats per hour and offers 45 hours of power reserve. The movement consists of hand-beveled bridges and the Côtes de Genève decorative motif. It offers hours, minutes, day, retrograde date, month, leap year and a high-precision moonphase indicator, as well as the minute-repeater mechanism that strikes on two gongs. The watch is offered in platinum or 18K pink gold with a pushpiece that instantly corrects all perpetual calendar and moonphase functions. The dial is silvered 18K gold with barely corn guilloché motif.

PATEK PHILIPPE

CHRONOGRAPH PERPETUAL CALENDAR - REF. 3970E

This model's manual-winding movement with Geneva Seal (Patek Philippe caliber CH 27-70 Q, CH 27-70 base + calendar module) offers perpetual calendar (date, day, month, four-year cycle, moonphase) and chronograph with two counters.

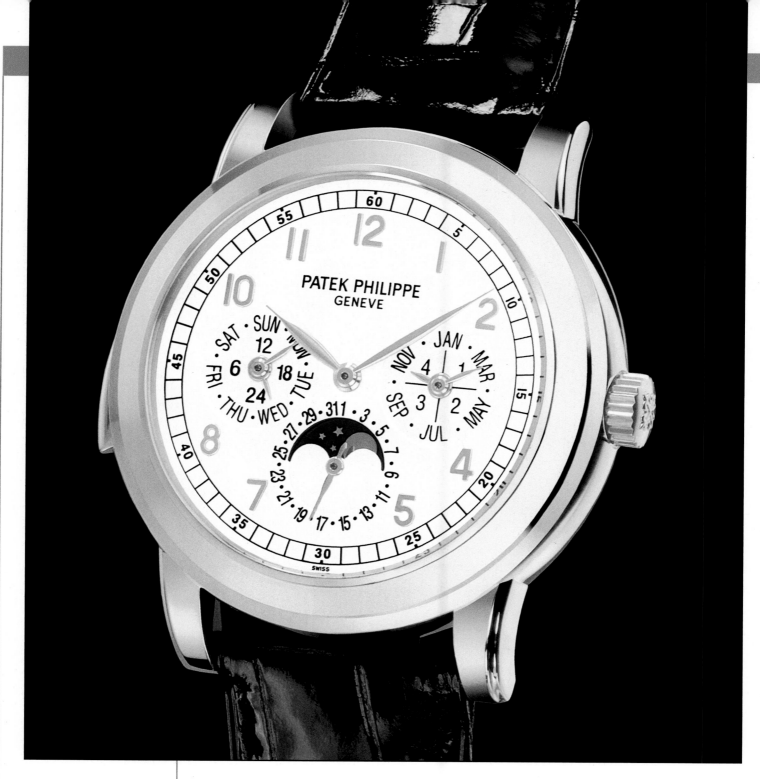

PATEK PHILIPPE

PERPETUAL CALENDAR MINUTE REPEATER - REF. 5074

This self-winding, 467-part movement with Geneva Seal (Patek Philippe caliber R 27 Q, R 27 PS base + calendar module) offers perpetual calendar (date, day, month, four-year cycle, moonphase) and minute repeater. The Ø 40mm case houses the repeater-perpetual movement realized by Patek Philippe long ago by combining the automatic base including a minute repeater (R 27 PS caliber without seconds) and the most classic calendar module with 24-hour indications. This model, presented in 2001 with only with the repeater, is meant for connoisseurs. The case size assures a particularly clean amplification of the Cathedral sonnerie. The gong is realized with a special alloy and undergoes several rotations. The full and long-lasting sound thus obtained recalls the bells of ancient cathedrals. The special alloy used for the acoustic gongs, which assures an extraordinary resonance, was developed by Patek Philippe in cooperation with the metallurgy experts of the Federal Swiss Institute of Technology of Lausanne.

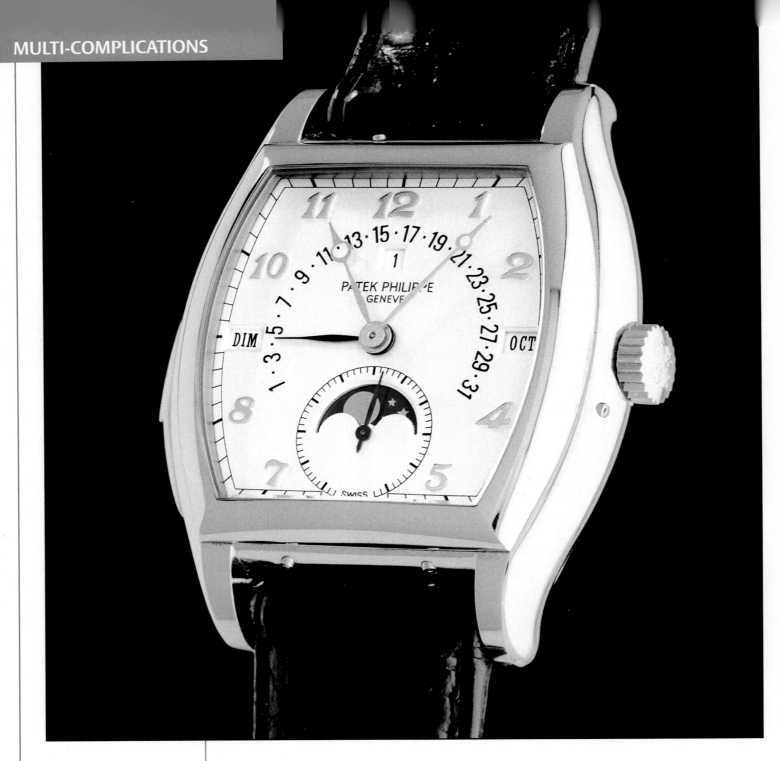

PATEK PHILIPPE

PERPETUAL CALENDAR REPEATER TONNEAU - REF. 5013

This self-winding movement with Geneva Seal (Patek Philippe caliber R 27 PS QR, R 27 PS base + 126 calendar module) offers perpetual calendar (retrograde date, day, month, four-year cycle, moonphase) and minute repeater. The elegant tonneau-shaped case with sapphire crystal caseback has a repeater slide and four small, integrated pushers on its middle for fast calendar correction. The dial shows the analog indications of hour, minute, small second and date (the latter with a retrograde hand), while the day of the week, the month and the four-year cycle are digitally displayed in small windows.

PATEK PHILIPPE

SKY MOON

This self-winding movement with Geneva Seal (caliber 240 CL LU, 240 base + 165 module) offers a sky chart and moonphase. Without further complications, but provided with the thin 240 automatic movement with its integrated micro-rotor, Patek Philippe's Sky Moon model reproduces the portion of the sky visible from a certain place (in this piece, the city of Geneva) enclosed in an ellipsis (representing the horizon) on the main dial. It indicates the positions and sidereal hours of Sirius and the Moon, as well as the moonphase in an additional window. These indications are displayed by sapphire disks controlled by a complexity of gears totaling 301 components. The Sky Moon Tourbillon's astronomic mechanism (686 components) is protected by a patent.

PATEK PHILIPPE

SKY MOON TOURBILLON - REF. 5002J

This manual-winding movement with Geneva Seal (Patek Philippe caliber RTO 27 QR SID LU CL) offers tourbillon, minute repeater, perpetual calendar, (retrograde date, day, month, four-year cycle, moonphase) and astronomic functions. On the sky map, the moon (with phases) and the Sirius star's sidereal positions are indicated on a 24-hour scale. The sidereal day is determined by two subsequent passages of a star on a meridian (here, the one of Geneva). The sidereal time indication is useful to determine the longitude from a certain place. The ellipsis moves and displays, at any moment, the part of the sky visible from that place (in this case, Geneva). The variations of astronomic indications by a few seconds each century are the slightest ones ever obtained by a mechanical watch.

RICHARD MILLE

RM 003-V2

The RM 003-V2 Tourbillon houses the mechanical, hand-winding movement 003-V2. In addition to the spline screws in grade-5 titanium for the bridges and case, many details exemplify Mille's technical approach to watchmaking such as the fast-rotating barrel with new involute tooth profile, central bridge in ARCAP, variable inertia PVD-treated balance wheel with overcoil balance spring and jewels set in white gold chatons. The finely finished pushbutton, located at 9:00, advances the second time zone in one-hour increments by utilizing a rotating disk of sapphire that allows the time zone to be visible at 3:00.

RICHARD MILLE

RM 008-V2 TOURBILLON SPLIT SECONDS CHRONOGRAPH

Representing a totally new design of spilt-seconds chronograph movement with tourbillon escapement, this watch was the result of many years of development. Built on a carbon nanofiber baseplate, it offers hours, minutes, seconds at 6:00, 30-minute counter, split seconds, power-reserve indicator and a torque indicator in dNmm. The column wheel and other parts of the movement are crafted from titanium; the exceptional movement can be seen through the sapphire glass caseback. The unusual pushbutton layout was designed to optimize practical use of the chronograph and split seconds function. The RM 008-V2 is offered in titanium, 18K red or white gold and platinum.

ULYSSE NARDIN

SONATA CATHEDRAL DUAL TIME - REF. 670-88/213

Housed in an 18K white-gold 42mm case, the Sonata Cathedral Dual Time is powered by Caliber UN-67. The watch is equipped with a chiming 24-hour alarm with countdown indicator. It also features a dual time system with instant time-zone adjustor. The Sonata is also available in 18K rose gold, with various dial combinations, and on a bracelet.

ULYSSE NARDIN

TELLURIUM - REF. 889-99

Crafted in platinum, the 43mm Tellurium houses Caliber UN-88. This astronomical masterpiece boasts a perpetual calendar with moonphases, solar and lunar eclipses. The part of the Earth lit by the sun indicates the time and place of sunrise/sunset. The Tellurium is also available in 18K yellow gold.

ULYSSE NARDIN

TRIPLE JACK - MINUTE REPEATER - REF. 736-61/E2

An Animated Jaquemarts Minute Repeater, the 42mm Triple Jack is powered by the Caliber UN-73 and its repeater functions on two distinct gongs. Limited to 50 pieces and shown in 18K rose gold, the Triple Jack is also available in platinum, with several dial combinations, and on a bracelet. Price available upon request.

VACHERON CONSTANTIN

MALTE PERPETUAL CALENDAR MINUTE REPEATER - REF. 30040/000R

Crafted and accented in 18K pink gold, this Malte Perpetual Calendar Minute Repeater offers minute repeater and perpetual calendar with day, date, month, year, and moonphase. Powered by the extra-flat, mechanical manual-winding Vacheron Constantin Caliber 1755 QP, the model was released in a 30-piece limited edition. With a perpetual calendar module, the 30-jeweled movement measures 4.9mm thick, is finished and decorated by hand, and is visible through a sapphire caseback. The silvered dial is guilloché with a basket-weave pattern.

VACHERON CONSTANTIN

PATRIMONY TRADITIONNELLE CALIBRE 2755 - REF. 80172

Based on the exceptional and truly striking showpiece of the 250th anniversary, the Tour de l'Ile, the Patrimony Traditionnelle "Calibre 2755" watch required over three years to create and is now the most complicated model in the Manufacture's collection. The new caliber 2755 comprises 602 components and powers a trifecta of complications—the Tourbillon, the Minute Repeater, and the Perpetual Calendar, with its day, month, date and leap year indications—making this a "Grande Complication." The 2755's power reserve is innovatively displayed on a bridge on the back of the movement and thus seen through the watch's display back. The 2755 is, of course, stamped with the prestigious Geneva hallmark. It is housed in a 44mm 18K pink gold case, giving the minute repeater chime a remarkable resonance.

ZENITH

GRANDE CLASS TRAVELLER RÉPÉTITION MINUTES

Housing the new El Primero 4031 movement with minute repeater, alarm function (with vibrating alert or buzzer), dual time, large date and three power-reserve indicators at 6:00 (movement reserve level is shown on left side of aperture, alarm reserve on right; when the minute repeater's reserve is low, a red light comes on under the alarm indicator), this Grande Class Traveller Répétition Minutes contains 744 components and 63 jewels. Offering 50 hours of power reserve, it beats at 36,000 vibrations per hour and measures short time intervals to 1/10 of a second. The watch's 44mm platinum18K rose-gold case is water resistant to 50 meters and holds a curved sapphire crystal and sapphire crystal caseback.

DEFY XTREME TOURBILLON EL PRIMERO

Incorporating the date into the tourbillon carriage near 12:00, this Defy Xtreme Tourbillon El Primero one-minute tourbillon houses the 4035 SX automatic chronograph with 332 components. The movement's train-wheel bridge, chronograph and lower cage bridges are crafted in shock-absorbing Zenithium Z+. The watch is built with an Incabloc® anti-shock device and beats at 36,000 vibrations per hour; with automatic winding in both directions, it offers 50 hours of power reserve and times to 1/10 of a second. The heavy metal oscillating weight has carbon-fiber inserts, and the case, pushers, crown and screw-in caseback are black titanium. A helium escape valve ensures water resistance to 1,000 meters.

ZENITH

GRANDE CHRONOMASTER XXT QUANTIEME PERPETUAL EL PRIMERO

This 45mm platinum 950 PT Grande ChronoMaster XXT Quantième Perpetual is framed with 60 baguette-cut Top Wesselton diamonds. Vibrating at 36,000 beats per hour, its 321-part El Primero 4003 caliber is a COSC-certified chronometer chronograph that times to within 1/10 of a second. This Grande ChronoMaster XXT offers perpetual calendar, moonphase indication, and a power reserve of 50 hours on a mother-of-pearl dial with 11 diamond indexes. The diamond-set version is available on a black leather strap accented with a strip of satin.

ZENITH

GRANDE CHRONOMASTER XXT TOURBILLON EL PRIMERO CONCEPT

This limited-edition, 45mm 18K white-gold Grande ChronoMaster XXT Tourbillon El Primero Concept houses the new El Primero 4005 C automatic chronograph movement with one-minute tourbillon (revealed at 11:00). The new main plate is uniquely worked with a special design. The watch movement consists of 319 components, including 35 jewels, and beats at 36,000 vibrations per hour. The power reserve is more than 50 hours. The chronograph measures to 1/10 of a second, and offers 30-minute and 12-hour counters.

ZENITH

GRANDE CHRONOMASTER XXT TOURBILLON EL PRIMERO

This Grande ChronoMaster XXT Tourbillon El Primero houses the El Primero 4005 automatic chronograph movement with one-minute tourbillon at 11:00. The 319-part movement with 35 jewels beats at 36,000 vibrations per hour and offers 50 hours of power reserve. The chronograph measures short time intervals to 1/10 of a second. With bidirectional automatic winding, the watch features a central rotor on ball bearings and a 22K gold guilloché oscillating weight. The date indication is positioned around the tourbillon carriage. The 30-minute counter is at 3:00 and the 12-hour counter is at 6:00. With sapphire crystal and caseback, this version is shown in 18K rose gold and available in white gold. It is water resistant to 30 meters.

ZENITH

GRANDE CLASS TOURBILLON

Housing the El Primero 4035 automatic chronograph movement with one-minute tourbillon, this Grande Class Tourbillon is comprised of 325 components. Beating at 36,000 vibrations per hour, it measures short time intervals to 1/10 of a second. The Grande Class Tourbillon offers hours, minutes, tourbillon, center seconds, 30-minute and 12-hour counters. It is crafted in 18K gold and water resistant up to 50 meters.

ZENITH

GRANDE PORT-ROYAL TOURBILLON EL PRIMERO

Beating at 36,000 vibrations per hour, the 35-jeweled El Primero 4007 automatic chronograph movement powering this Grande Port-Royal Tourbillon consists of 298 components and offers 50 hours of power reserve. On an 18K white-gold dial, the chronograph features center seconds hand, 30-minute counter at 3:00, and 12-hour counter at 6:00. The case is black titanium with a curved, antireflective sapphire crystal and sapphire caseback. Water resistant to 50 meters, the watch is presented on a carbon-fiber integrated strap lined with calfskin.

STAR TOURBILLON EL PRIMERO

This Star Tourbillon houses the El Primero 4029 automatic chronograph movement. The 292-part tourbillon movement consists of 35 jewels, features a central rotor on ball bearings and a 22K white-gold oscillating weight with 0.3 carat of diamonds. El Primero 4029 beats at 36,000 vibrations per hour and offers 50 hours of power reserve. The 30-minute and 12-hour counters are each symbolized by a Zenith star. The 18K white-gold case, bezel and horns are set with 112 baguette-cut diamonds weighing 8.8 carats. The dial is 18K gold and mother of pearl, set with diamonds, and positioned on a black Ottoman strap.

ZENITH

GRANDE CLASS TRAVELLER RÉPÉTITION MINUTES

Cased in platinum and water resistant to 50 meters, this Grande Class Traveller Répétition Minutes houses the El Primero 4031 automatic chronograph movement with minute repeater, alarm function (with vibrating alert or buzzer), dual time, large date and three power-reserve indicators at 6:00 (movement reserve level is shown on left side of aperture, alarm reserve on right; when the minute repeater's reserve is low, a red light comes on under the alarm indicator). The chronograph offers central seconds hand, 30-minute counter and 1/10-of-a-second counter while the minute repeater functions are controlled by the single pushbutton on the crown. The incredibly complex El Primero 4031 consists of 744 components, including 63 jewels. It beats at 36,000 vibrations per hour and offers over 50 hours of power reserve. The 22K white-gold oscillating weight is engraved with a Grain d'Orge guilloché pattern.

ZENITH

GRANDE CLASS TRAVELLER RÉPÉTITION MINUTES

The Grande Class Traveller Répétition Minutes houses the El Primero 4031 automatic chronograph movement with minute repeater, alarm function (with vibrating alert or buzzer), dual time function, large date and triple power-reserve indicators (movement, alarm and minute repeater). The chronograph offers central seconds hand, 30-minute counter and 1/10-of-a-second counter while the minute repeater functions are controlled by the single pushbutton on the crown. The incredibly complex El Primero 4031 consists of 744 components, including 63 jewels. It beats at 36,000 vibrations per hour and offers over 50 hours of power reserve. The 22K white-gold oscillating weight is engraved with a Grain d'Orge guilloché pattern. The platinum watchcase is water resistant to 50 meters.

Minute Repeaters
and Sonneries

Co-president of Chopard

Karl-Friedrich Scheufele

L.U.C Strike One

There was a time when Chopard built silent watches. Then, a model with a musical complication took its place in the catalog. Available in a limited edition, the L.U.C Strike One opens up new territory to the Manufacture, already renowned for the extreme care it brings to its production.

"The L.U.C prefigures other striking watches by Chopard"

Visible between 12:00 and 1:00 through a cutout in the dial, the hammer strikes the circular gong once an hour, which transforms the passing time into a note. For its first "musical" piece, Chopard has played upon a studied sobriety by displaying the key components of the caliber in a delicate arrangement that marries technique and elegance.

Limited to 100 pieces in rose gold and 100 pieces in white gold, the L.U.C Strike One offers an original complication that makes it beautiful to the ear. "It took two years of research and development at the Manufacture in Fleurier," explains Karl-Friedrich Scheufele, co-president of Chopard, "to perfect and to ensure the reliability of this new movement, called L.U.C 96 SH. To allow the hammer to strike the bell with sufficient force, the engineers designed a system of mechanical winding that stores energy for several minutes before the complication is triggered. On the hour, all that energy is transmitted at once to the piece which then hits the gong precisely. "The Manufacture's engineers have worked a lot on regulating the mechanism to produce a crystalline, clear sound," points out Scheufele. To guarantee the perfection of its product, Chopard chose to have the L.U.C 96 SH movement stamped with the prestigious Geneva Seal. The movement is also a COSC-certified chronometer, proof of its extreme precision.

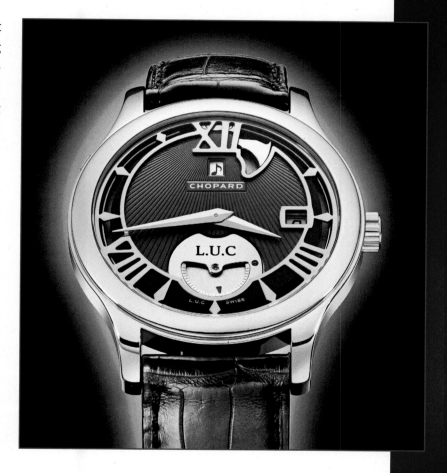

FACING PAGE
Karl-Friedrich Scheufele, co-president of Chopard.

THIS PAGE
The L.U.C Strike One in rose gold and its L.U.C 96 SH movement. It will be followed by other striking watches from Chopard.

Refinement and elegance are the hallmark of Chopard's L.U.C watches, such as in this new 2008 version of the ultra-thin L.U.C XP with anthracite dial.

As well as a hammer and a gong, the L.U.C Strike One displays the date at 3:00, while small seconds have been placed at 6:00. Shown through a rotating disk engraved with a small red arrow, the seconds follow a semicircle of indexes. In a small touch of refinement typical of Chopard, when the user wishes to see whether the watch is set to strike, a small eighth-note appears in a window at 12:00, either in full or crossed out. Just like the movement, the rest of the watch demonstrates superlative quality and impeccable execution. For visual pleasure, the L.U.C Strike One has a rotor in 22-karat gold. The movement, for its part, is decorated with Côtes de Genève and visible through the sapphire crystal caseback.

TOP LEFT
A particularly difficult complication to master, the chronograph entered Chopard's collection with the L.U.C 10 CF caliber. The picture shows the Chrono One model housing this movement.

TOP RIGHT
A blend of technique, design and aesthetic with the new L.U.C Tech Twist, powered by the L.U.C 96 TB movement.

RIGHT
The famous L.U.C Lunar One perpetual calendar with orbital moonphase houses the L.U.C 96 QP calendar.

"It is through the expertise that the Chopard Manufacture in Fleurier has acquired over more than ten years that we have been able to perfect this striking movement," states Scheufele. The Manufacture has already introduced many exceptional movements, including the L.U.C 96 QP, which powers the L.U.C Lunar One perpetual calendar with orbital moonphase, and the Caliber L.U.C 4T, a four-barrel tourbillon movement, as well as the famous chronograph Caliber L.U.C 10 CF. Founded in 1996 under Scheufele's guidance, the development and production center in Fleurier has enabled the brand to become inde-

pendent and to propel itself into the ranks of the great names of haute horology. Housing more than 15 different specialties, the Manufacture also plays the role of an educational center, regularly taking on apprentices. It is behind 25,000 watches released every year, and also produces several thousand components stamped L.U.C, a label of quality and expertise recognized the world over. All evidence points to more surprises to come from Chopard Manufacture in Fleurier, destined to delight lovers of beautiful watchmaking. When asked if the L.U.C Strike One prefigures other striking watches from Chopard, Scheufele responds affirmatively: "The L.U.C Strike One is L.U.C's first striking watch, and it will naturally be followed by others."

CEO of
Romain Jérôme

Yvan Arpa

Titanic-DNA
The White Star
Tourbillon

The brand Romain Jérôme has gotten people talking all over the world with its use of elements from the RMS Titanic in its watches. Bezels in rusted steel, dials powdered with coal taken from the wreckage of the storage rooms—never had a watchmaker gone to look for its primary materials twelve and a half thousand feet under the sea. But the brand cannot be reduced to a genius stroke of marketing. In its mastery of complications like the tourbillon, Romain Jérôme brings a new perspective to haute horology.

"The tourbillon was a smash hit"

Some might have thought of it, but Yvan Arpa actually did it. In using materials from the Titanic's wreckage, Arpa, CEO of Romain Jérôme, has succeeded in bringing exceptional visibility to his company in record time. This former math teacher, who crossed the Republic of Guinea on foot before setting his sights on horology, with stints at Sector, Baume & Mercier and Hublot, had to find the mother lode, the approach that would land them in virgin territory. He decided to explore the idea of "legends."

A piece of metal recovered from the ship by a diver, before the site was protected in 1994, gave Arpa his opening. Well aware that his was a young brand, Arpa listed the gripping legends that had marked the last century and would anchor Romain Jérôme to history. Among these legends, the Titanic loomed large; this is why, when the chance appeared to link his brand to the history of the luxury liner, Arpa didn't hesitate for an instant, and acquired the relic.

There was an obstacle: the material was not usable as it was, as it didn't meet standards and contained too much nickel, an allergenic substance. The solution lay in fusion. Under legal supervision, Arpa fused his historic material with steel from the Belfast shipyard Harland & Wolff, the same one that had constructed the Titanic. Ingots were cast

FACING PAGE
Yvan Arpa.

THIS PAGE
The White Star
Tourbillon from the
Titanic-DNA
collection...and its
diamond-set cage!

FACING PAGE
TOP RIGHT
The hours-minutes-seconds version of the T-oxy Concept Watch.

TOP LEFT
The Tourbillon T-oxy Concept is sold under a glass bell filled with argon. If the bell is removed, the watch will oxidize even further.

FACING PAGE
TOP LEFT
The Titanic-DNA rusted steel T-oxy III Chronograph.

TOP RIGHT
Titanic-DNA Five Black I Tourbillon.

and brought back to Switzerland in armored trucks, to be worked there. Arpa also recovered some coal from the Titanic, which he pulverized and used for the dials.

A luxury legend for haute horology

"The Titanic embodies the ideal of absolute luxury," explains Arpa. "By using steel taken from its wreckage, we've brought some of its prestige into our watches. We had to make sure, then, that the watches' mechanics would be of the same standing. This is why we chose to incorporate the tourbillon into our collections." Arpa had no idea of the success that would follow. "The tourbillon was a smash hit! That is why we took in the absolutely stunning number of orders that we did."

According to Arpa, these added values also appealed to a clientele hungry for benchmarks, for guidelines. "I've come across affluent collectors who still didn't know all the mechanical refinements incorporated in the watches they were buying. On the other hand, they immediately knew the value of a piece made out of metal from the Titanic. So we had to combine these two worlds. Now the client is completely aware that not only is

he wearing a piece of history on his wrist, but also that it houses a refined complication."

The solution of a whole new category allowed the brand to find its audience. "When I started at Romain Jérôme," recalls Arpa, "I thought we would sell watches for around eight thousand dollars. Today, some are worth twenty times that, and we're not finished. Working with the tourbillon has helped us become a high-end watchmaker." Romain Jérôme has also produced a truly one-of-a-kind tourbillon. The White Star Tourbillon is the first watch to feature a tourbillon cage set with diamonds. "All the stones must have exactly the same weight, and all the incisions must be absolutely identical," emphasizes Arpa, underscoring the accomplishment by the contractor BNB, who performed the work.

Pushing the concept of the Titanic-DNA collection to the extreme, Arpa has also launched a tourbillon and an hours-minutes-seconds model under the name T-oxy Concept. Crafted in non-stabilized rusted steel from the Titanic, these watches aren't for wearing! They are carefully protected under a glass bell filled with argon. If the bell should break, oxidation will follow its natural course.

Future anterior
For this year, in addition to variations on current

collections, limited to nine pieces each, Arpa is announcing the release of two tourbillon watches, one of which has two cages which are linked by a differential gear and interlock in turn. The brand is also extending its reach to writing instruments, producing a pen with "surprising" ink, according to Arpa. Finally, Romain Jérôme will introduce its "Safe of Legends," a chest with six drawers, one per complication, including those yet to come. Owning a piece of Romain Jérôme haute horology is a prerequisite for purchasing the chest, which contains, in each drawer, a sealed envelope containing the name of the next legend, for Arpa will not stop at the Titanic, revealing, "Starting in 2009, we will explore a new legend."

Minute Repeaters
and Sonneries

Now that tourbillons are commonplace, minute repeaters
are becoming the new standard-bearers of Swiss
watchmaking. Several recent innovations and
reinterpretations seem to confirm its comeback—yet
there is little chance that we will be swamped by them,
for these jewels of fine watchmaking require expertise in
both micromechanics and acoustics. As such, minute
repeaters are among the most difficult complications to
produce. As for the grand- and small-strike
clockwatches that chime the time in passing, they
remain the preserve of a few highly skilled craftsmen.

Ding-dong bell

Mechanisms that strike the hours appeared on early pocket-watches. There were already reports at the end of the 15th century of watches that chimed in passing like the church tower-clocks. At the end of the 17th century, quarter-repeating watches that struck the hours and quarters on demand, appeared. These repeaters, in which hammers struck tiny bells, were most useful for telling the time in the dark. English watchmaker Thomas Mudge is credited with developing the minute repeater in around 1750. At the end of the century, Abraham-Louis Breguet had the idea of replacing the bells with gongs made of tempered steel rods coiled around the movement. This led to much thinner watches and greater clarity of tone.

▲ 1

▲ 2

▶▶ *1–2 Jaeger-LeCoultre, Master Minutes
Repeater Antoine LeCoultre
Jaeger-LeCoultre's Master Minute
Repeater Antoine LeCoultre has a new
system of transmitting sound: it is sent
directly to the outside by the watch's
sapphire crystal.*

▶▶ *3 Audemars Piguet, Tourbillon Répétition
minutes Chronographe Jules Audemars
The Brassus manufacture has specially
developed new striking systems, which
are found in its Jules Audemars
Tourbillon Minute Repeater Chronograph*

▶▶ *4 Roger Dubuis, Excalibur RD08
The minute repeater mechanism
of the Excalibur RD08 is activated
by rotating the bezel.*

▲ 3

The music of time

In the 20th century, chiming mechanisms, reduced to wrist-watch size, became the highest demonstration of the watch-making art. Exceptional skills are required to craft the complex mechanical memory with the racks that drop onto the snail cams to read the hours, quarters and minutes, and then rise to activate the gathering pallets that cause the hammers to strike the gongs. One needs a good ear to tune the gongs like a musical instrument, especially if there's a carillon of three or more gongs or in the case of so-called cathedral gongs that coil twice around the movement.

There are basically two types of chiming watches: the clock-watches that strike the time in passing and the repeaters that chime on demand. Clockwatches generally feature a grand strike, which chimes the hours before each quarter and a small strike, which chimes the hours on the hour, and the quarters only. Minute repeaters usually have two gongs—a low note for the hours and a high note for the minutes. Double strikes—high, low—mark the quarters.

Striking developments

Watchmakers recently decided to revive the interest in minute repeaters by exploring new technical and aesthetic possibilities. In 2005, Jaeger-LeCoultre launched the Master Minute Repeater Antoine LeCoultre, with an unprecedented way of transmitting sound through the sapphire-crystal glass of the watch, on which are soldered the heels of the steel gongs. The result is a sound of unparalleled intensity and clarity. Other companies have developed new striking systems, such as that in Audemars Piguet's Jules Audemars minute repeater with tourbillon and chronograph, or, like Roger Dubuis, novel ways of operating the repeater. In its Excalibur RD08 caliber, the repeater is activated by turning the rotating

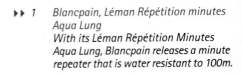

bezel. Blancpain has successfully tackled one of the great drawbacks of minute repeaters—their lack of water resistance due to the sliding bolt that activates the chime. It's an Achilles' heel that can be fatal in a humid climate. Its Léman Répétition Minutes Aqua Lung is water resistant to 100 meters, due to an ingenious link consisting of a rack, intermediary wheels and gaskets, between the outside slide and the inside winding arm. This minute-repeating movement claims to be the thinnest and the smallest in diameter. At the risk of upsetting purists, one should also mention the unusual combination between a quartz movement and a minute repeater in the Eco-Drive Minute Repeater Perpetual by the Japanese Citizen brand. Its battery-free Eco-Drive system draws its energy from natural or artificial light.

A symphony for the eye

The only thing that identifies the conventional minute repeater is the slide or bolt on the side of the case. Today, however, most watchmakers like to reveal the complex mechanism by opening up the dial. Examples include the Zenith Grande Class Traveller Répétition Minutes El Primero (see Multi-Complications chapter) or the Kalpa XL Répétition Minutes by Parmigiani Fleurier, with its large circular aperture. Harry Winston's Westminster Tourbillon combines a flying tourbillon with a minute repeater that copies the Westminster chimes of Big Ben. The absence of a dial reveals

▶▶ 1   *Blancpain, Léman Répétition minutes Aqua Lung*
With its Léman Répétition Minutes Aqua Lung, Blancpain releases a minute repeater that is water resistant to 100m.

▶▶ 2   *Citizen, Eco-Drive Minute Repeater Perpetual*
Citizen's Eco-Drive Minute Repeater Perpetual has no battery, drawing all its energy from natural or artificial light with its Eco-Drive system.

▶▶ 3   *Zenith, Grande Class Traveller Répétition Minutes El Primero*
Today, most watchmakers prefer to show the movement by opening up the dial, as with the Zenith Grande Class Traveller Répétition Minutes El Primero.

4

6

5

▶▶ **4** *Vacheron Constantin, Maîtres Cabinotiers Skeleton Minute Repeater*
The 3.3mm-thick movement of Vacheron Constantin's Maîtres Cabinotiers Minute Repeater contains more than 330 pieces, most of them openworked.

▶▶ **5** *Parmigiani Fleurier, Kalpa XL Répétition minutes*
Parmigiani Fleurier also highlights the complexity of its movement by cutouts on the dial.

▶▶ **6** *de GRISOGONO, Occhio Ripetizione Minuti*
Based on the principle of the reflex camera, the watch dial is made up of twelve ceramic blades that open up to reveal the movement and minute repeater mechanism, then close as soon as the chiming stops.

▶▶ **7** *Harry Winston, Westminster Tourbillon*
The Westminster Tourbillon by Harry Winston combines a flying tourbillon with a minute repeater that mimics the chime of Big Ben.

the four hammers striking on four cathedral gongs. Vacheron Constantin also aims for maximum transparency and thinness in its Répétition Minutes Squelette Maîtres Cabinotiers, unveiled in 2006. The 3.3mm-thick movement comprises more than 330 parts, most of which are open-worked, decorated and engraved. Instead of a dial, de GRISOGONO's Occhio Ripetizione Minuti has a diaphragm like that of a reflex camera; when the repeater is engaged, 12 ceramic leaves open to reveal the movement during the strike on cathedral gongs.

7

1

2

3

New rhythms

Other watchmakers offer variations on the frequency and type of chime. Chopard's L.U.C Strike One, for example, fitted with a proprietary Geneva Seal chronometer movement, strikes once on the hour. An aperture at 12:00 on the dial allows you to see the tiny hammer at work. This watch is issued in a limited series of 100 in white or pink gold. In 2005, Finnish watchmaker Kari Voutilainen demonstrated his inventiveness in a unique piece: the Masterpiece N° 6. It's a minute repeater that strikes the hours, tens of minutes and minutes instead of the hours, quarters and minutes. The 10-minute strike is said to be easier to grasp. The Japanese brand Seiko has brought back the ancient hourly strike in a new upscale model called the Credor Spring Drive Sonnerie. The strike has three modes: the hourly strike, striking thrice every three hours (12:00, 3:00, 6:00 and 9:00) and strike silent. The exclusive Seiko Spring Drive system ensures that the hands advance "as regularly and as silently as time itself."

Summit in sound

The supreme striking mechanism combines the repeater and the chime in passing in the same movement. Philippe Dufour, one of today's leading independent watchmakers, created the first minute-repeating wristwatch with grand and small strike in 1992. François-Paul Journe, another high-flying horologist, went a step further with his Sonnerie Souveraine. This wristwatch, which took six years to develop, is noted for its extreme functionality. Journe developed a number of sys-

▶▶ *1   Kari Voutilainen,
          Masterpiece N° 6
          Kari Voutilainen's
          Masterpiece N° 6 houses a
          minute repeater that strikes
          not the hours/quarter hours/
          minutes, but the hours/ten
          minutes/minutes, a system
          that allows for a more
          intuitive reading of time.*

▶▶ *2   Chopard L.U.C, Strike One
          On its L.U.C Strike One,
          Chopard presents a
          mechanism that strikes once
          (hence the name) at the
          passage of each hour.*

▶▶ *3   Seiko, Credor Spring Drive
          Sonnerie
          The Japanese company Seiko
          has brought back the "hour
          repeater" in this new top-of-
          the-line model.*

▶▶ 4
Philippe Dufour, Grande Sonnerie
Philippe Dufour, one of the
greatest watchmaker-artisans
working today, created in 1992
the first minute-repeater wristwatch
with grand and small strike.

▶▶ 5
Ulysse Nardin, Genghis Khan
The Genghis Khan is the first watch
with minute repeater, tourbillon
and jaquemarts that features a
Westminster chime.

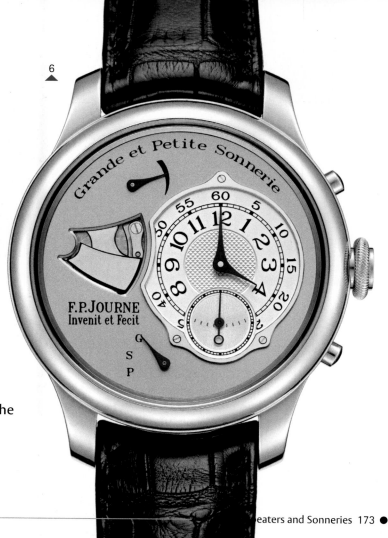

Time with action

To delight the eye and the ear, Ulysse Nardin continues its tradition of watches with automata. Among several noteworthy creations is the Genghis Khan model, the first tourbillon minute repeater with a Westminster carillon and striking jacks on the dial. The gold case encloses four gongs with different notes (E, C, D, G) and strikes the hours in G, the minutes in E and the quarters on all four gongs, changing the sequence for each quarter. The black onyx dial features hand-engraved gold figurines that move in perfect time with the strikes of the gongs.

tems to make the watch safe and easy to use, notably a device that prevents user-damage caused to the watch when changing the time while the strike is operating. He also limited the energy use to enable the grand strike in passing to function for a full 24 hours. The watch is protected by no fewer than 10 patents. A notable feature is its steel case—unique in the Journe collection—for a more resonant chime. The Sonnerie Souveraine won the 2006 Golden Hand award at the Geneva watchmaking Grand Prix, and it was also named "watch of the year" in Japan.

AUDEMARS PIGUET

JULES AUDEMARS JUMPING HOUR MINUTE REPEATER - REF. 26151OR.OO.D002CR.01

Shown here in an 18K pink-gold case, this Jules Audemars combines two in-house specialties: the minute repeater and the jumping hours. This marvel of precision and harmony perpetuates Audemars Piguet's supreme expertise in the field of complicated watches. With its case and dial featuring a new take on classical styling, it gives a fresh boost to the Jules Audemars collection. The delightful new model will be music to the ears of connoisseurs the world over. Also available in platinum (Ref. 26151PT.OO.D028CR.01).

BOVET

FLEURIER MINUTE REPEATER

This 44mm, 18K white-gold BOVET case houses a minute repeater finished with the highest standards of Swiss watchmaking. The mother-of-pearl dial features a miniature hand-painted "Madonna della Sedia." The steel screws and cathedral chiming gongs blued by fire are BOVET trademarks. The BOVET minute repeater has two different cathedral chiming gongs. The hammers first strike the low-pitch gong to count the hours from 1 to 12, then a combination of high- and low-pitch gongs from 0 to 3 chime the quarters, and then 0 to 14 high-pitch gongs chime the minutes after the quarter. The chiming work of the minute repeater can be seen through the sapphire crystal.

BVLGARI

BVLGARI-BVLGARI - REF. BBW40C6GLRM

The Bvlgari-Bvlgari Ref. BBW40C6GLRM, features a completely hand-made, mechanical, manual-winding Vaucher Caliber 9950 movement, with 31 jewels, and a vibration rate of 21,600 vph. It offers the functions of hours, minutes, seconds and minute repeater. The 40mm, polished platinum case, which is fitted with an antireflective, scratch-resistant, sapphire crystal and a snap-on back displaying the movement through a sapphire crystal, is engraved with a limited-edition number on the caseback and is water resistant to 30 meters. The blue satiné dial, embellished with Côtes de Genève and stippling, has a blue galvanic lower-level minute circle, a small seconds counter, hand-applied indexes and displays hours, minutes and seconds. The hand-sewn brown alligator strap has a platinum triple-fold-over buckle. Limited edition of 15 pieces.

CHOPARD

L.U.C STRIKE ONE - REF. 161912-1001

The L.U.C Strike One houses the L.U.C 96 SH caliber, which measures 33mm in diameter and is 5.7mm thick, offers 65 hours of power reserve (Twin Technology—two spring-barrels). It provides an hour-strike function with on/off function and a small seconds indicator at 6:00. The movement bears the Geneva Seal quality hallmark and is chronometer-certified. The bridges are decorated with straight-line Côtes de Genève pattern. Limited edition of 100 timepieces in 18K white gold.

DANIEL ROTH

ELLIPSOCURVEX MINUTE REPEATER - REF. 308.Y.60.152.CN.BD

This elegant 18K white-gold timepiece features an entirely hand-decorated in-house patented manual-winding minute-repeater movement. The 18K white-gold guilloché dial displays a black enamel hour indication encircled with a white-gold ring, a tiny striking indicator aperture above and power-reserve sector below the hours and minutes hands, as well as small seconds at 7:00. This movement with two hammers, a flat balance-spring and escapement lever, is housed in an Ellipsocurvex white-gold case, the repeating pushpiece is located on the case at 9:00. The watch is fitted with a sapphire caseback and is water resistant to 3atm.

DANIEL ROTH

LA GRANDE SONNERIE - REF. 607.X.60.166.CN.BD

In this extraordinary timepiece, Daniel Roth has succeeded in accommodating within its famed double-ellipse case a Grande Sonnerie mechanism complete with minute repeater, grand- and small-strike system, a four-hammer Westminster chime, a tourbillon and two power-reserve indicators—one for the striking mechanism (sector between 12:00 and 3:00) and the other for the movement (sector between 3:00 and 6:00). Five patented systems protect the movement and the functions during handling.

DeWITT

MINUTE REPEATER ROSE GOLD - REF. AC.8801.53.M750

To reproduce a sound of the utmost purity, a master watchmaker, artist and musician worked together to create this model's infinitesimal strike-hammers. The watch's repeater chimes the hours, quarters and minutes with an innovative strike-function activator located mysteriously below the bezel. The small seconds are displayed at 9:00 and the opening at 6:00 reveals the mechanism. Limited edition of 50 pieces.

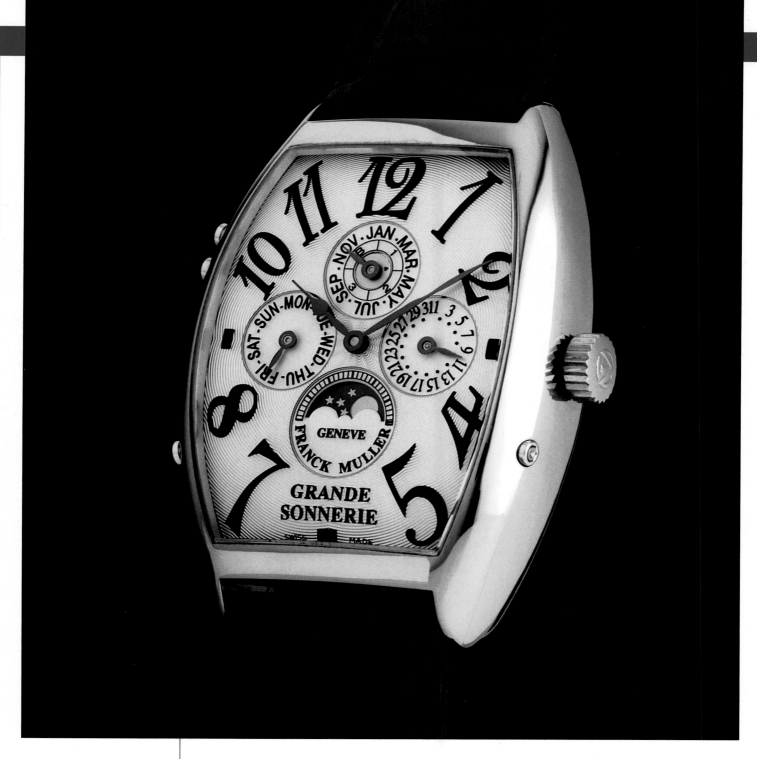

FRANCK MULLER

CINTRÉE CURVEX GRANDE AND PETITE SONNERIE PERPETUAL CALENDAR

The manual-winding Franck Muller caliber RFM 7850 offers repeater, grande and petite sonnerie, and perpetual calendar. Along with the classic minute repeater, it is provided with the rare sonnerie "au passage," function. The grande sonnerie indicates the hours through a sequence of low tones, and strikes the hours and quarters at the passage of the quarters (the latter with two tones, one high- and one low-pitched). The petite sonnerie strikes only the hours. On the case's left side is the slide for the actuation of the hour, quarter and minute repeater, and the cursor for the selection of the sonnerie modes (grande, petite and mute). The 500-part movement has 50 jewels and two barrels that allow bidirectional crown winding: counterclockwise for the movement, clockwise for the sonnerie.

GERALD GENTA

ARENA GRANDE SONNERIE - REF. GS1.X.60.529.CN.BA

The Arena Grande Sonnerie features a manual-winding in-house tourbillon Grande and Petite Sonnerie movement with minute repeater and double power reserve. This Grande Sonnerie, presented for the first time in 1994, was improved and the new version presented for the 30th anniversary of the Gérald Genta brand. The very limited space of this wristwatch's movement with off-center hour display, tourbillon and two barrels also houses the repeater mechanisms and the "au passage" strike-work with a four-hammer Westminster chime. Located on the caseback of this extraordinary piece are subdials for the power reserves (one for the Sonnerie and one for the movement), as well as for the sonnerie mode selection (grande, petite, mute).

GERALD GENTA

OCTO GRANDE SONNERIE - REF. OGS.Y.60.930.CN.BD

The Gérald Genta Octo Grande Sonnerie offers an entirely hand-decorated automatic Grande sonnerie tourbillon movement, with grand and small strike on four Westminster chime gongs. It also presents retrograde hours in the purest tradition of the Gérald Genta brand, as well as revolving minutes disk and minute repeater functions. It offers a power reserve of 48 hours for the movement and 18 hours for the striking mechanism, shown on two separate displays. This amazing movement is housed in a Ø 42.5mm octagonal white-gold case and enhanced by a white-gold guilloché and cloisonné black and red ceramic dial.

GERALD GENTA

OCTO MINUTE REPEATER - REF. ORM.Y.50.785.CN.BD

The Octo Minute Repeater features a Gérald Genta exclusive automatic manufacture movement with 37 jewels, oscillating at 21,600 vibrations per hour and offering a 42-hour power reserve. This two-gong minute repeater mechanism is combined with a jumping hour and retrograde minutes. It is housed in an octagonal 5N red-gold case with open back, sporting a unique ceramic cloisonné dial on an engraved red-gold base as well as a falcon-eye cabochon-set pearl-beaded crown. This model is presented on a hand-stitched black folded alligator strap with circular-grained gold folding clasp. It is water resistant to 3atm.

IWC

PORTUGUESE MINUTE REPEATER - REF. IW524204

The Portuguese Minute repeater houses the 95290 caliber with 54 rubies and beating at 18,000 vibrations per hour. It offers 43 hours of power reserve and features a stunning minute repeater function with small second and stop device. It is offered in limited editions of platinum and two colors of gold.

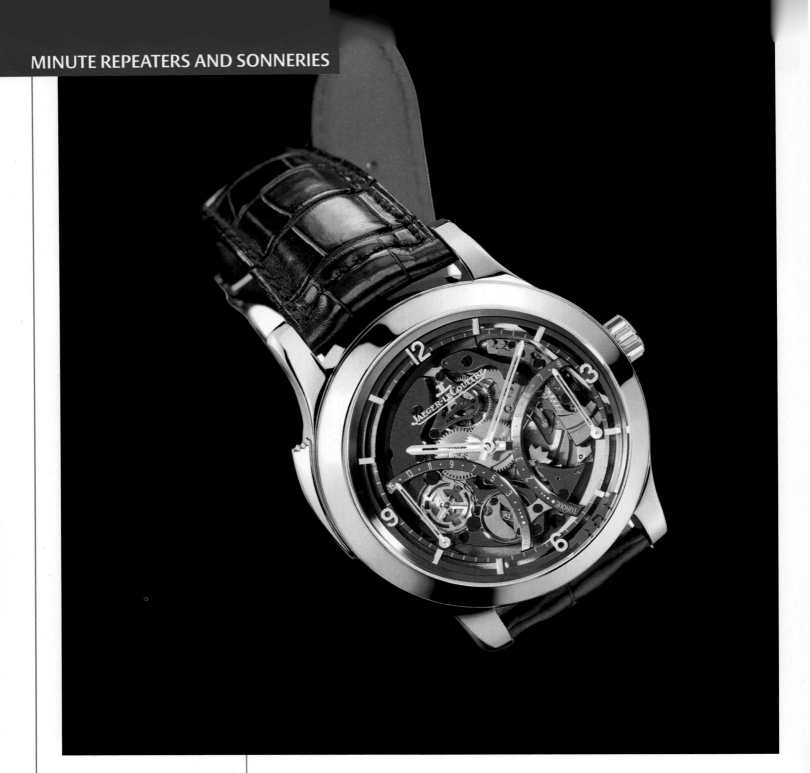

JAEGER-LECOULTRE

MASTER MINUTE REPEATER ANTOINE LECOULTRE

Crafted in titanium, the acoustical qualities of this timepiece surpass all expectations and offer a new standard for repeaters. Its crystalline chime, which has exceptional purity of sound, is the fruit of a collaborative effort between a musical conductor and the watchmakers and technicians at Jaeger-LeCoultre. The materials used for transmitting the vibrations at greater speed are new: the gongs are made of steel and sapphire crystal acts as the sound transmitter. The manually wound caliber 947 mechanism is endowed with 360 hours (15 days) of power reserve—indicated on the dial. Created in a limited edition of 200 pieces, the Master Minute Repeater Antoine LeCoultre houses 41 jewels and beats at 21,600 vibrations per hour.

PARMIGIANI FLEURIER

KALPA XL MINUTE REPEATER - REF PF600449.01

The Kalpa XL Minute Repeater features an open window on the dial that showcases the skill of this master watchmaker. The mechanical hand-wound Caliber PF350 movement has hand-beveled bridges with a "Geneva stripes" decoration and is entirely crafted in-house. This Minute Repeater sounds every hour, quarter-hour and minute with two chimes. The case is offered in platinum or 18K rose gold with an Hermès alligator strap and ardillon buckle.

ULYSSE NARDIN

FORGERONS - MINUTE REPEATER - REF. 719-61/E2

This 42mm Forgerons Minute Repeater is encased in platinum. Housing Caliber UN-71, the exquisite timepiece features Animated Jaquemarts that move with the repeater, which functions on two distinct gongs. It is built in a limited edition of 50 pieces and also available in 18K rose gold, with various dial combinations, and on a bracelet. Price available upon request.

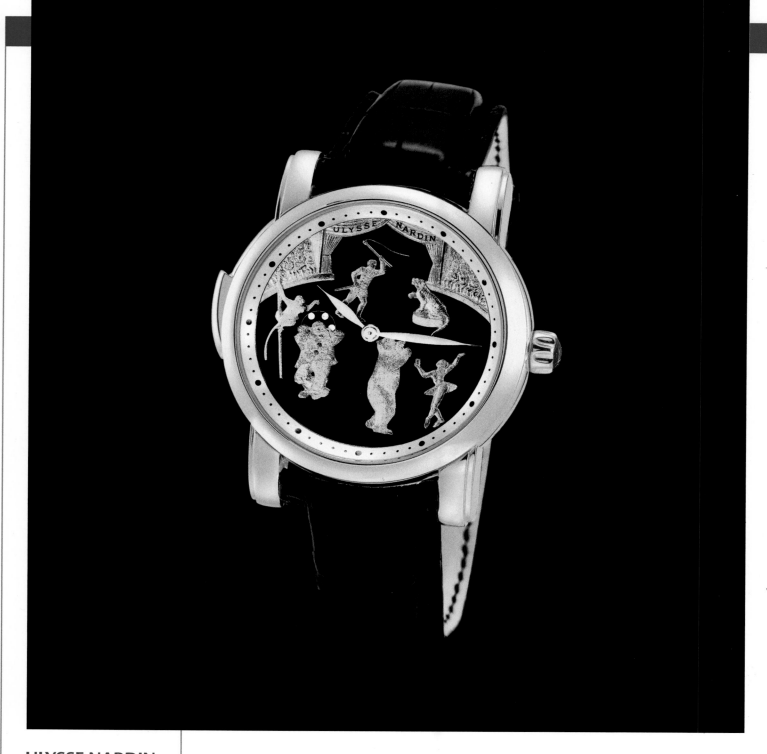

ULYSSE NARDIN

CIRCUS - MINUTE REPEATER - REF. 746-88

Also available in platinum and on a bracelet, this captivating Circus Minute Repeater houses the Caliber UN-74 within its 42mm 18K rose-gold case. The minute repeater chimes on two distinct gongs, activating the Animated Jaquemarts. Circus was created in a limited edition of 30 pieces. Price available upon request.

ULYSSE NARDIN

HOURSTRIKER - SONNERIE EN PASSANT - REF. 759-80/E2

The 42mm Hourstriker Sonnerie en Passant is encased in platinum. Visible through an exhibition caseback, Caliber UN-75 operates the automatic chime activation and the Animated Jaquemarts. The Hourstriker is also available in 18K rose gold and with various dial combinations.

ULYSSE NARDIN

HOURSTRIKER - EROTICA - REF. 769-80-P0-02

Fitted with Caliber UN-76 (visible through an exhibition caseback) with automatic chime activation and Animated Jaquemarts, this platinum 42mm Hourstriker is also available on a bracelet.

ULYSSE NARDIN

TRIPLE JACK - MINUTE REPEATER - REF. 736-61/E2

An Animated Jaquemarts Minute Repeater, the 42mm Triple Jack is powered by the Caliber UN-73 and its repeater functions on two distinct gongs. Limited to 50 pieces and shown in 18K rose gold, the Triple Jack is also available in platinum, with several dial combinations, and on a bracelet. Price available upon request.

VACHERON CONSTANTIN

PLATINUM SKELETON MINUTE REPEATER - REF. 30030/000P

Fully skeletonized, this Platinum Skeleton Minute Repeater is fitted with the manually wound, extra-flat Vacheron Constantin Caliber 1755 SQ. This exceptional 30-jeweled movement is 3.3mm thick and is entirely decorated and chased by hand. The repeater is operated via a slide on the left of the case. The Platinum Skeleton Minute Repeater was created in a limited edition of just 15 numbered pieces.

Tourbillon

CEO
of Richard Mille

Richard Mille

RM 012

A visionary with a decidedly offbeat approach to his profession, Richard Mille regularly shakes up the watchmaking planet with his futuristic watches. In 2007, his RM 012 model with its tubular structure earned him an award he regards as the watchmaking Oscar: the Golden Hand in the Geneva Watchmaking Grand Prix. Known for his positive attitude and his insatiable appetite for new technologies, this Breton by adoption leads his brand by blending style and panache with rigorous standards.

"I'm a pack leader"

"I'm a pack leader", says Richard Mille with just a hint of provocation in his tone. He considers himself the front-runner of a set of passionately dedicated watch lovers. CEO of his own brand, the entrepreneur handles his activities from his manor house nestling in the countryside of Brittany. Cell phones and high-speed internet connections enable him to run from a distance a company composed of various partners operating as a network. For while the captain resides in France, all the artisans who create, develop and produce Richard Mille watches are dotted across the Swiss Jura region..

Tubular architecture

One of them is the Audemars Piguet (Renaud & Papi) movement design engineering firm in Le Locle. Recognized among connoisseurs for its undeniable expertise, this workshop developed the RM 012, the watch that earned Richard Mille the Golden Hand in the 2007 edition of the Geneva Watchmaking Grand Prix. Pursuing the structural approach that governed the creation of the RM 009 Felipe Massa, Richard Mille completely rethought the entire morphology of the skeleton movement in order to give it a contemporary interpretation more reminiscent of the Atomium in Brussels than of a traditional watch model. The entire going train as well as the flying tourbillon are in fact completely integrated within a tubular

THIS PAGE AND FACING PAGE
The RM 012 is made up of tiny tubes made of Invar and joined to each other. This entirely novel construction makes the movement extremely resistant to shocks, to torsion and to variations in temperature.

FACING PAGE
Passionately dedicated to technologies, Richard Mille constantly seeks to incorporate a maximum dose of innovation into each of his watches.

TOP
By using Alusic, a material borrowed from the aeronautical industry, Richard Mille created the world's lightest watch, weighing less than 40 grams.

BOTTOM
Close-up view of the earth in the planetarium-tellurium currently in the making.

structure that takes over the functions usually handled by the baseplate. The totally unprecedented movement is composed of a set of assembled microtubes made of Invar, a stainless and highly stable steel. Developing this architecture called for considerable research in order to achieve maximum rigidity, while compensating for the absence of matter... The real challenge lay in joining these tiny tubes together with incredibly precise pivoting angles, rigorously perpendicular axes and micron-level tolerances. In all, the RM 012 required two years of development and four prototypes before reaching a final version that is truly remarkable for its resistance to shocks, corrosion and variations in temperature. Moreover, the sheer complexity of the caliber considerably prolonged the production time for each watch, since simply assembling the movement takes several months. The world-first RM 012 is produced in a platinum limited edition of 30.

Golden Hand

Having won Richard Mille the famous Golden Hand, the RM 012 already ranks as a watchmaking masterpiece. For the CEO, the award is far more than a symbolic trophy. "This prize is a seal of approval and a confirmation", he explains. "It is a token of recognition from the watchmaking com-

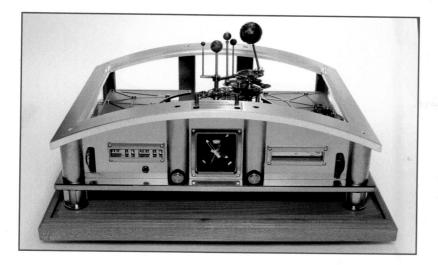

munity. "When I launched my brand, I wanted to create something completely off the beaten track. I never once imagined that my work might represent a turning point in watchmaking history." Nonetheless, his stubborn determination to systematically focus on innovation, even if that has meant changing the manufacturing method or the material used for a component during the actual production process, has borne fruit. A fervent devotee of the aviation and automobile worlds, Richard Mille has forged his identity and earned the esteem of his peers by incorporating the most cutting-edge technologies within his products. The RM 009 Felipe Massa is an eloquent example of this approach, since this watch – the lightest in the world at under 40 grams – features a case middle in alusic, an ultra-resistant and ultra-light material used in the aerospace industry.

Planetary-tellurium watch and new releases
During the summer of 2008, Richard Mille will be putting up for sale his planetary-tellurium watch, a one-of-a-kind model such had not been made since the 19th century. A three-dimensional representation of the movements of the earth and four other heavenly bodies including the moon, this creation took a full ten years to research, develop and fine-tune. "Each part made us sweat blood", Richard Mille remembers. "And even though I'm really pleased with the result, there won't be any others. Its sheer complexity makes it one of the most difficult horological constructions to make, a true technical paroxysm. It represented a challenge for me and I'm glad that we were able to rise to it." Richard Mille now prefers to concentrate on his collections and to launch into other projects. He has indeed just completed a daring interpretation of an historical genre by presenting his very first pocket-watch, the RM 020. It will be followed later in the year by another new release.

CEO of Hublot

Jean-Claude Biver

Bigger Bang All Black

Jean–Claude Biver, Hublot's CEO, has continued to build this brand around the idea of fusion. Its main example is the unlikely combination of such materials as rubber and gold. But it also has its mechanical counterpart in a spectacular mix of complications, starting with the tourbillon.

"I like watches that steal the show"

"The tourbillon takes center stage at Hublot because it is one of the few complications that you always see in motion," explains Biver. "Other complications, like the chronograph or the minute-repeater, only react on demand. The perpetual rotation of the tourbillon gives a watch its life and mystery."

Devised in around 1795 by the brilliant Abraham-Louis Breguet to counter the effects of gravity on the balance, the tourbillon has become the right of passage into luxury watchmaking for the brands. Its main attraction is that it displays the beat and the rotation of the movement. "Technically, the tourbillon isn't all that complicated," says Biver. "Its popularity is mainly due to its unique architecture. It allows you to get to the essence of the movement and that's what consumers want. It's that demand that explains the general popularity of the tourbillon."

Nevertheless the tourbillon isn't tamed easily. "The adjustment is the real issue at stake with the tourbillon," Hublot's boss explains. "And there are few craftsmen that can adjust them properly. They are rarer than watchmakers on the job market."

Personally, Biver likes the tourbillon because he

The stylistic gearing of carbon wheels screwed to the face recalls the film Modern Times.

FACING PAGE
Jean-Claude Biver, Hublot's CEO.

THIS PAGE
The movement of the Bigger Bang
All Black has been designed for
maximum display.

FACING PAGE
TOP
The slightly recessed lower part of
the dial allows the tourbillon
carriage to stand proud.

BOTTOM
The Big Bang Platinum Mat
Diamonds features a bezel set
entirely with baguette diamonds.

prefers "watches that steal the show. When I wear a chronograph, I keep it running because I hate seeing the hands stand still. I pay particular attention to animations that give a watch its soul."

The Hublot tourbillons

A number of Hublot models feature the tourbillon, either alone or combined with another complication. The Bat Bang Tourbillon All Black and the Big Bang Platinum Mat Big Date each have one at 6:00. The first, which evokes Charlie Chaplin's movie Modern Times, is dressed entirely in black. A carbon bridge cut out in a train of wheels reaches over the face divided by an arc at its center. This configuration of shapes in relief, with a decorative structure on the upper part of the dial and a recessed lower part, is designed to highlight the tourbillon. It fits in nicely with the overall styling of the watch, thanks to other elements in black. The only notes of color are the ruby jewels. The Big Bang Platinum Mat Big Date has the same face layout with the lower part recessed to make the tourbillon stand out. Fitted with a power-reserve indicator and a large date display, this model is available only in sandblasted platinum with a PVD coating. Bridges in solid carbon sustain the wheels of the manually wound caliber HUB1050GD movement.

Having created the first watch entirely in black from the hands to the band, Biver took the All Black concept further by incorporating a movement with two complications, a chronograph and tourbillon, with the basic timekeeping functions. The Bigger Bang All Black is where the ultimate in engineering is applied to create a show, where traditional watchmaking snatches the future. The movement was designed to catch the eye with delightful movement. For example, the column-wheel of the chronograph has been turned over so that it appears at the back of the watch. One can watch the chronograph engage with the tourbillon carriage. An openwork dial reveals the rest of the movement, where ruby stars glow in a dark, metallic universe.

Parmigiani
Fleurier

Jean-Marc Jacot

Kalpa Tourbillon 30 Secondes Chiaroscuro

"Though the Parmigiani Fleurier brand celebrated its tenth anniversary in 2006, Michel Parmigiani, its founder and very soul, has been a talented watchmaker for thirty years," explains Jean-Marc Jacot, horology spokesman for the Sandoz Foundation (Parmigiani Fleurier and Vaucher Manufacture).

"The Kalpa collection allowed Parmigiani Fleurier to reach a wider public. We are continuing down this path with our new Pershing collection"

"We wanted to pay tribute to those thirty years by presenting two exceptional pieces: the Kalpa XL Tourbillon 30 secondes Chiaroscuro and the Kalpa XL hebdomadaire squelette." It is a well-known fact that Michel Parmigiani, a native of Fleurier, had helped restore exceptional historic timepieces and worked quietly for the most prestigious brands before launching Parmigiani Fleurier, with the help of the Sandoz Family Foundation. Since then, moving forward at a controlled, moderate pace, the Parmigiani brand has made a remarkable journey, becoming a full-fledged Manufacture, a step that makes it one of the most respected brands in the Swiss watchmaking industry.

Occasionally philosophical, demanding, exacting, and as attentive to detail as he is to the whole picture, Parmigiani is an emblematic figure of the best of today's horological art, and the Kalpa XL Tourbillon 30 secondes model that the brand introduced to mark his 30 years of watchmaking experience is a watch in his image. The model marries the aesthetic and technical qualities that have helped Parmigiani Fleurier make a name for itself in the crowded world of Swiss haute horology. Its movement, the Caliber PF 501, has a double barrel offering a seven-day power reserve. Its bottom plate and skeletonized bridges are beveled by hand and jeweled from end to end.

FACING PAGE
Jean-Marc Jacot.

THIS PAGE
TOP
Tour de l'Ile, billed "the world's
The Kalpa XL Tourbillon 30
secondes Chiaroscuro.

RIGHT
The sapphire caseback of the
Kalpa XL Tourbillon 30 secondes
Chiaroscuro is reveals the house
movement, Caliber PF 501, which
offers a seven-day power reserve.

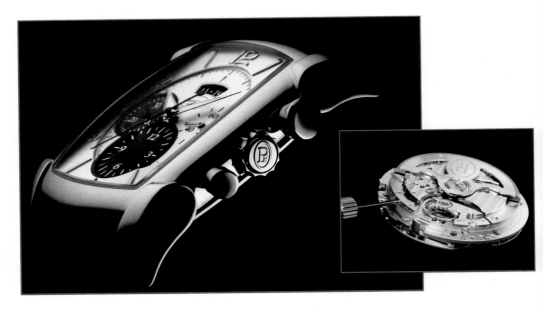

Following the current trend for watches with a sapphire crystal dial that reveals the watch's mechanical complexity and the finishing of the components, the Tourbillon Kalpa 30 Secondes Chiaroscuro is characterized by its visible movement and its skeletonized bottom plate and bridges. These components are highlighted by a PVD colorization process. The originality of the piece comes from the variation of metallic hues—original colors developed by Parmigiani Fleurier—that form a mosaic in nuances of pink, purple, light brown and gray. The transparent sapphire-crystal dial is decorated with a rhodium-plated minute area, and the upper part of the dial contains the rhodium-plated indexes, the power-reserve indicator and the Parmigiani Fleurier cartridge.

"Our other anniversary model," explains Jacot, "the Kalpa XL hebdomadaire squelette, shows what Michel Parmigiani has been doing for more than thirty years, his painstaking care with the delicacy of the decorations and finishings on all of the components. In order to keep this celebration one-of-a-kind, the piece was entirely crafted in solid 18-karat gold. Completely skeletonized, the Caliber PF 110 was renamed Caliber PF 118. Each bridge is engraved and beveled by hand. All parts are also chamfered

and drawn out with a file along their surface. The sinks are polished and the screws are mirror-polished and chamfered. Both barrels as well as several wheels are also skeletonized to give greater depth to the movement.?The transparent sapphire crystal enables one to gaze at length at the exquisite beauty of the workmanship, since only the black transferred markers of the hour zone, the power reserve and the small seconds are present. With 30 examples of each model produced—in a platinum 950 case for the tourbillon and a solid palladium 950 case for the skeleton—these two anniversary models are offered on a Havana-colored Hermès alligator leather strap with folding clasp.

"Beyond these anniversary models, the arrival of the Kalpa collection allowed Parmigiani Fleurier to reach a wider audience," underscores Jacot. "We produced 4,800 pieces last year, but we know that in order to maintain the brand's image and fame, and to meet the demand that we haven't yet confronted, we will have to produce about 10,000 timepieces per year." The group of Parmigiani Fleurier and Vacher Manufacture, established by the Sandoz Foundation, now employs about 550 workers, to which about 50 more will be added in 2008. At the same time, to ensure a rise in production, the group—which counts among its clients Richard Mille and Corum

as well as its partner Hermès—has undertaken the construction of a new production site at Fleurier over an area of 43,000 square meters (463,000 square feet). "One of the things of which we are proudest," affirms Jacot, "is that thanks to Michel Parmigiani, we have been able to restart the watchmaking industry in the Fleurier region."

2008, the year of Pershing

Parmigiani Fleurier will address 2008 on a resolutely sporty note. Through a partnership with the Italian naval construction group Ferretti and its Pershing brand, Parmigiani Fleurier will introduce a new aquatic and sports collection that will include a chronograph, an automatic-winding model and a tourbillon. "We have a lot of common values with the Ferretti group," explains Jacot. "Like Parmigiani Fleurier, the Ferretti group was created by the passion of one man, it is independent and working at the peak of its art, pushing luxury and sophistication to the extreme. These shared values make for a natural partnership, and we understood each other very quickly. The alliance between Parmigiani Fleurier and Pershing will be a boon for all involved."

President of Parmigiani Fleurier North America

Michelle Veyna

"Parmigiani Fleurier matches up perfectly with the expectations of American aficionados, who demand authenticity, exclusivity, expertise and passion from a brand," affirms Michelle Veyna, president of Parmigiani Fleurier North America. According to her, the personality of Michel Parmigiani, as well as the time that the brand has put into becoming a long-term leading brand, are elements that attract a loyal clientele.

"We're building the brand for the long term"

FACING PAGE
Michelle Veyna, president of Parmigiani Fleurier North America.

THIS AND FACING PAGE LEFT
Two variations on the latest addition the Parmigiani Fleurier, the Kalpa Hémisphères.

"For several years, we've approached the market as a true brand, and we are recognized as such by retailers as well as by direct clients. Parmigiani Fleurier has a major asset: its Manufacture. At a time when many brands run into difficulty explaining how they produce their pieces, the fact that we have this operational industrial facility and that we are almost entirely autonomous in the production of movements and other components is important not only in terms of flexibility and being able to react to the demands of the market, but also in terms of a long-term guarantee for our clientele."

"The Sandoz Family Foundation, which owns Parmigiani Fleurier, keeps telling us, 'You work for future generations,'" reveals Veyna. "This perspective of building a brand over the long term is a fundamental argument that lets us avoid being opportunists and leads us to favor relationships that are long-lasting, strong and sincere." From this perspective, Parmigiani Fleurier is enjoying its ongoing development in the United States, and collectors appreciate the independence and long-term vision that are tied to the company.

Veyna also emphasizes another element that she finds essential: customer relations and service. "We are making an effort to develop this relationship with our clientele, a relationship we see as essential. We're not just talking about post-purchase customer service here—that's only one element of it—but a true service of advising and supporting our clients in all of their dealings with the brand."

On the product side, Veyna underscores the success of the Kalpa collection, which offers very recognizable timepieces that reveal an undeniable expertise. Ladies' watches are also enjoying growing success, and soon the market will welcome the new GMT model and sport collection that will complete the array of these exceptional watches.

manager of watchmaking activities at Jacob & Co

Claude Sanz

The Quenttin

Seven barrels with a vertical tourbillion, a world premiere in the history of watchmaking. In 2006, the jeweler from New York, Jacob & Co, presented the Quenttin, its first foray into the world of fine timepieces. The model immediately set the brand sailing and propelled it to the rank of respectable maison. This recognition has opened the way to new, very accomplished models that will be available when the spring fairs open their doors.

"A gamble"

"A gamble!" exclaims Claude Sanz, manager of watchmaking activities at the New York jeweler, Jacob & Co. In 2006, when he presented the Quenttin, an exceptional watch that displays the hour on cylinders and is equipped with seven barrels, Claude Sanz knew he was playing for high stakes. "Until then, Jacob & Co had offered timepieces that were very advanced in terms of the exterior but technically quite basic. To give the brand stature, it had to test fate and create something extraordinary, taking on all the risks entailed. It was double or quits." The market welcomed this timepiece with enthusiasm, and thus the metamorphosis came about.

But it hasn't always been plain sailing. In 2002, after several years spent working with rare stones to create exceptional jewels, Jacob Arabo, a Russian-born jeweler, decided to introduce time into his universe. A series of rather inconclusive experiences made his initial efforts difficult until the day he crossed paths with Claude Sanz, who at the time also managed Bunter, a company specialized in setting beads in fine timepieces. This meeting marked the beginning of a fruitful business relationship in which two gem specialists decided to make a name for themselves in the world of fine watchmaking.

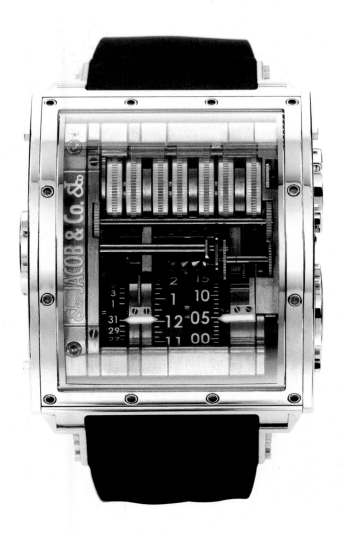

FACING PAGE
Claude Sanz, manager of watchmaking activities at Jacob & Co Watches.

THIS PAGE
The Quenttin marked a major turning point in the history of Jacob & Co by elevating it to the rank of a genuine watch brand.

The Quenttin machine

The Quenttin model marks a decisive turning point in the history of the brand. "When it was launched, we were congratulated by several big players in the traditional watchmaking sector, proof that we had truly won our bet." And there was good reason. The Quenttin is the first watch in the world to offer a 31-day power reserve. To make this possible, the movement, developed exclusively by the manufacturer BNB, aligns seven barrels, a feat never seen before. "From the design to the technical aspects through to the concept itself, we have fine-tuned every detail to extremes. We wanted to shake up the sector by setting it a veritable challenge." The size of the crystal, one of the largest on the market, confirms this exceptional status. It covers a case that is equally imposing and required numerous adjustments in order to guarantee its water resistance. Crafted in white or rose gold, or in blue, red or black magnesium, it boasts an impressive size and yet the watch weighs in at 360 grams.

The risk taken by Jacob Arabo and Claude Sanz is paying off. This mechanical UFO has generated global interest: "Until then, our clients knew the brand for its striking arrangements of dia-

monds and precious stones. Today, the brand enjoys genuine legitimacy in fine watchmaking. Suddenly, we are reaching a wider and more discriminating clientele."

Despite its $360,000 price tag, the Quenttin quickly found buyers. Of the 136 pieces created in all, more than half have already been sold. In addition to connoisseurs and collectors, traditional buyers who often come from the American jet-set, such as 50 Cent, Jay-Z, Brad Pitt or Jessica Alba, have also shown interest. Incidentally, the first Quenttin adorned the wrist of famous soccer player David Beckham.

Reading comfort amidst a waltz of tourbillons

2008 is a rich year for Jacob & Co. Allied with the manufacturer of movements, Concepto SA, which it in part financed, the brand is reaping the fruits of this agreement. It now presents two series of chronographs, the Chrono Epic One with round cases and the Chrono Epic Two with square cases. "These two lines were directly inspired by the Quenttin, explains Claude Sanz. We transposed its ADN into more affordable models." Lamenting the generally difficult-to-read dials of chronographs, Claude Sanz has striven to make them as legible as possible. "With this complication, design always tends to overtake functionality. Here, the concept was reversed, resulting in sophisti-

cated dials that can be read equally well during the day or at night."

Two tourbillion models add to the list of new creations. The Octopus, in a limited edition of 180 pieces, features a bridge on the front cut to form the brand initials. Making a break from usual decorations, its upper plate is engraved with Clous de Paris. Moreover, the logo of the brand appears to be set in on the back of the caliber. The totally unprecedented New Quadra, the ultimate new creation, looks like a watch to be reckoned with in the family of spectacular complications. Equipped with four tourbillions and a unique winding system located at the rear of the watch, this newcomer will be hard to come by as it is a limited edition of only 18 pieces.

Tourbillon

Invented at the start of the 19th century to compensate for the effects of gravity on the rate of pocket-watches, the tourbillon has, for a number of years, known unprecedented popularity. With its tiny mobile carriage comprising some 60 or 70 parts for a weight of less than a gram, the tourbillon represents the peak of the watchmaking art, leading brands to produce increasing numbers of exclusive tourbillon movements. Watches that focus on the aesthetics of display configure elaborate settings for the mechanism. Watchmakers also develop new constructions such as multiple and multi-axis tourbillons that are better suited to wristwatches, even though the attraction of this queen of complications lies more in its technical sophistication and its mechanical show than in any real improvement in precision.

A Most Sophisticated Mechanism

In the days when they were worn in vest pockets, watches spent most of their time in the same vertical position. But the Earth's attraction has a negative effect on the rate of the movement, acting especially on the balance and spring, which determine the precision of the watch. To counter these irregularities, Abraham-Louis Breguet (1747-1823) had the idea of enclosing the heart of the watch—the balance, spring and escapement—in a tiny carriage that rotated about its axis once a minute. Rotating the balance through all vertical positions thus averaged out the positional errors in its rate. The overwhelming adoption of the wristwatch in the 20th century could have led to the demise of the tourbillon, for this device loses a great deal of its effectiveness in a watch that is never stationary. But the revival of mechanical watchmaking in the 1980s propelled the tourbillon into the top rank of horological complications as a supreme demonstration of Swiss watchmaking skills.

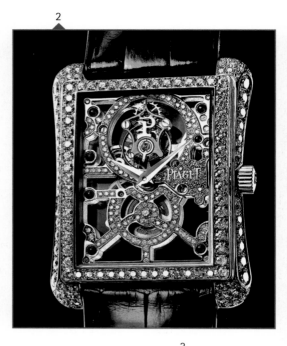

Mighty Comeback

Tourbillon fever has taken hold since the start of the millennium. In 2004 alone, total production reached some 2,500 pieces—more than all the tourbillons made between 1805 and 1980. More than 50 Swiss brands have a tourbillon wristwatch in their catalog, which is remarkable considering that only a handful of artisans are said to be capable of building the device. Faced with this relative abundance, the major watchmaking companies are making a point of offering proprietary tourbillons with innovative solutions. In 2002, Piaget created the thinnest tourbillon form movement, the 3.5mm-high caliber 600P, for its rectangular Emperador models. In its jeweled skeleton Emperador, the company has produced a totally ethereal version of the tourbillon with the gems set directly in the movement. The same caliber 600P beats within the square Altiplano Tourbillon, which is a modern version of the fob watch. In 2003, Chopard presented its L.U.C 1.02 4T caliber with four mainspring barrels that provide an eight-day power reserve. It has since been released in a new case that is both technical and modern. Zenith recently launched two tourbillon watches in its new Academy collection, one of which, with an asymmetrical dial, is combined with a chronograph and a perpetual calendar. Jaeger-LeCoultre presented its Master Tourbillon with much fanfare in the spring of 2006.

▶▶ **1**   *Piaget, Altiplano Tourbillon*
The Calibre 600P beats at the heart of the
square Altiplano Tourbillon pocket watch,
a contemporary reinterpretation of the form.

▶▶ **2**   *Piaget, Emperador Tourbillon Squelette Serti*
On the Emperador Tourbillon Squelette Serti,
Piaget presents a totally ethereal version of
the complication, with diamonds and
sapphires set directly in the movement blank..

▶▶ **3**   *Zenith, Academy Tourbillon El Primero
Quantième perpétuel*
Zenith recently relaunched two tourbillons
in its new Academy collection, one paired
with a chronograph and perpetual calendar.

▶▶ **4**   *Chopard, L.U.C Tourbillon*
In 2003, Chopard presented its Calibre L.U.C
1.02 4T, with four barrels that provide a
power reserve of eight days.

The proprietary movement is notable, not only for its technical features but also for its price, which is significantly more affordable than that of competitive products. To give the devil his due, the Swatch Group's Breguet company, run by Nicolas Hayek himself, has also decided to honor the finest jewel of its heritage. In 2007, its Tradition collection included a model displaying a spectacular tourbillon mechanism with a fusée and chain. This transmission device with differential gearing delivers constant torque to the escapement, whatever the state of wind of the mainspring. In a more playful mode, Girard-Perregaux offers a most original model called the Vintage 1945 Jackpot Tourbillon, with a slot machine fitted with a chiming mechanism. Also remarkable is Harry Winston's Tourbillon Glissière because of its automatic winding system, which consists of two sliding weights acting on the winding ratchet.

Visibility Above All

With its mobile carriage turning on its axis like a planet, the tourbillon lends itself to a variety of display formats. Girard-Perregaux set the theme in its legendary tourbillon on three gold bridges. In Ulysse Nardin's Royal Blue Tourbillon, the bridges and baseplate

8

▶▶ *1–2 Jaeger-LeCoultre, Master Tourbillon*
Jaeger-LeCoultre made a big splash in the spring of 2006 with its Master Tourbillon, housing a House-made movement that was notable not only for its technical perfection, but its price as well, which is much more "approachable" than competing products.

▶▶ *3 Girard-Perregaux, Vintage 1945 Jackpot Tourbillon*
Girard-Perregaux's Vintage 1945 Jackpot Tourbillon houses a slot machine with a chiming mechanism!

▶▶ *4 Harry Winston, Tourbillon Glissière*
Harry Winston's Tourbillon Glissière stands out for its unusual winding system, equipped with two sliding blocks that engage the winding ratchet.

▶▶ *5 Breguet, Tradition 7047 Tourbillon à fusée*
This model features differential gears that allow it to beat at a constant rate, whatever the level of winding.

▶▶ *6 Ulysse Nardin, Royal Blue Tourbillon*
In the Royal Blue Tourbillon by Ulysse Nardin, the sapphire bridges and bottom plates give the impression that the rotating cage is floating in mid-air.

▶▶ *7 Vincent Calabrese, Regulus*
For his Regulus model, Vincent Calabrese created a flying tourbillon completely isolated in space.

▶▶ *8 MB & F, Horological Machine N°1*
The Horological Machine N°1 by MB & F gives the tourbillon a central place in an unusual three-dimensional design, with two separate dials for the hours and minutes, and four barrels providing a power reserve of seven days.

▶▶ *9 Breguet, Tourbillon Messidor*
Launched in 2007, Breguet's Tourbillon Messidor also provides a "weightless" construction, with a particularly airy cage and bridges with a whirling feeling to their geometry.

▶▶ *10 Girard-Perregaux, Tourbillon sous trois ponts d'or*
With its cage spinning on its axis like a planet, the tourbillon creates beautiful plays of composition and transparency. Girard-Perregaux sets the tone in its famous Tourbillon under three gold bridges.

in sapphire crystal give the impression that the carriage is rotating in space. Vincent Calabrese designed a similar flying tourbillon, rotating apparently unsupported in his Regulus watch. Launched in 2007, Breguet's Tourbillon Messidor also has a "floating" tourbillon with a particularly open carriage and swirling bridges. The Horological Machine N° 1 by MB & F puts the tourbillon in the center in an unprecedented three-dimensional design with two separate dials for the hours and minutes, and four mainspring barrels that give a running time of seven days.

1 **Richard Mille, RM012**
   In Richard Mille's RM012, all the gears, as well as the flying tourbillon, are completely integrated into a tubular structure that serves the functions normally provided by the bottom plate.

2 **Richard Mille, RM009 "Felipe Massa"**
   With its case/movement combination composed of extremely avant-garde materials, the RM009 "Felipe Massa" is the lightest wristwatch in the world (less than 30g).

3 **Richard Mille, Tourbillon RM015 Perini Navi Cup**
   Inspired by nautical themes, the Tourbillon RM015 Perini Navi Cup stands out for its bottom plate in carbon nanofibers, its winding system with a variable-inertia pendulum and its rapid-rotation barrel.

4 **Ulysse Nardin, InnoVision**
   The Innovision by Ulysse Nardin also functions without lubrication, thanks to ten technological innovations in the realm of silicon and its use.

Silicon Valley

In the past few seasons the venerable tourbillon has been rejuvenated in novel constructions and high-tech materials. In Richard Mille's RM012, the entire going train as well as the flying tourbillon are integrated within a tubular structure that takes the place of the traditional baseplate. With its case and movement in advanced materials, the RM009 "Felipe Massa" claims the title of the lightest wristwatch at less than 30 grams. The nautically inspired Tourbillon RM015 Perini Navi Cup is notable for its baseplate in carbon nano-fibers, its free-sprung balance and its fast-rotating mainspring barrel. The Breguet Marine Tourbillon Chronographe features the latest technical developments in isochronism with a balance-spring, escape-wheel and pallet-lever entirely in silicon, and the tourbillon carriage in titanium. In 2007, Jaeger-LeCoultre made a real breakthrough with its Master Compressor Extreme Lab, claiming it as the first dependable and accurate oil-free watch. Its novel balance-wheel configuration, new low-weight materials and the latest generation tourbillon with a magnesium cage contribute to this achievement. As a worthy successor to the 2001 Freak watch, in which the entire movement rotates as well as the tourbillon, the 2007 Ulysse Nardin InnoVision also functions without lubrication thanks to a dozen technical advances in silicon technology as well as new production processes.

▶▶ 5   *Breguet, Marine 5837 Tourbillon Chronographe*
The Breguet Marine Tourbillon Chronographe
brings together the very latest technological
advances in isochronism, with a spiral, an escapement
wheel and an anchor in silicon, as well as a
tourbillon with bridge and pillars in titanium.

▶▶ 6   *Jaeger-LeCoultre, Master Compressor Extreme LAB*
The Master Compressor Extreme LAB is the first
mechanical watch to function precisely and reliably
without any lubrication.

2

1

3

In Three Dimension

The past few years have seen the advent of a new generation of tourbillons rotating on more than one axis. The idea is to increase the precision of wristwatches by increasing the number of positions the balance wheel can occupy. Launched in 2004, Jaeger-LeCoultre's Gyrotourbillon I has two carriages, one inside the other. The outer cage turns on its axis once a minute; the inner carriage, set at 90° to the first, turns at 2.5 revolutions a minute. Greubel Forsey created a similar system, but with the two planes of rotation at 30°, for the Harry Winston Opus VI. The company is named after the two watchmakers who have been constructing innovative tourbillons based on different planes and speeds of rotation. The Double Tourbillon 30° has an inner carriage rotating once a minute and an outer carriage with a four-minute rotation. In 2007, the "Secret" version came out in which the mechanical ballet is only visible through the back of the watch, save for a hand on the dial turning with the four-minute tourbillon. The Tourbillon 24 Secondes Incliné, where the carriage rotates two and a half times as fast as a conventional tourbillon, needed special conical gearing as well as customized alloys. The Quadruple Tourbillon "à différentiel," unveiled in 2005 as an experimental prototype, is scheduled to go into production in 2008. Thomas Prescher emphasizes the three dimensions in his transparent round watch with a triple-axis tourbillon. Panerai assumed the coronet of its rise up the aristocracy when it presented the Luminor 1950 Tourbillon GMT with an "in-house" movement having two innovations especially conceived for the wristwatch: the tourbillon cage rotates twice a minute and at a right-angle to the plane of the balance-wheel. In addition, three barrels ensure a going time of six days, and a small hand at 9:00 on the dial runs directly off the tourbillon.

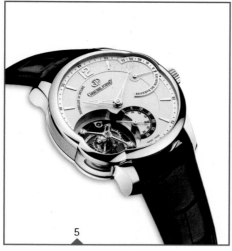

4

5

6

7

▶▶ 1 *Thomas Prescher, montre ronde avec tourbillon à trois axes*
Thomas Prescher plays with reliefs and transparency in his round watch with a three-axis tourbillon.

▶▶ 2 *Jaeger-LeCoultre, Gyrotourbillon I*
Launched in 2004, Jaeger-LeCoultre's Gyrotourbillon I contains two nested cages: the exterior cage makes a full rotation in 60 seconds; the interior cage, placed on an axis at 90° to the first, rotates 2.5 times per minute.

▶▶ 3 *Harry Winston, Opus VI*
Designed by Greubel Forsey, Harry Winston's Opus VI also combines two tourbillons, one inside the other.

▶▶ 4 *Greubel Forsey, Quadruple Tourbillon à différentiel*
The launch of the Quadruple Tourbillon à Différentiel is slated for 2008. The picture shows a glimpse of the movement.

▶▶ 5 *Greubel Forsey, Tourbillon 24 Secondes Incliné*
In the Tourbillon 24 Secondes Incliné, the 25° cage, which turns two and a half times faster than an ordinary tourbillon, obliged its creators to turn to a new kind of inclined gear, as well as specific alloys.

▶▶ 6 *Panerai, Luminor 1950 Tourbillon GMT*
Panerai has crowned its ascent to high-end watchmaking by presenting the Luminor 1950 Tourbillon GMT, with a "proprietary" movement featuring two innovations invented for wristwatches: the tourbillon's cage turns at a right angle to the axis of the pendulum, and it performs two rotations per minute.

▶▶ 7 *Greubel Forsey, Double Tourbillon 30°*
The Double Tourbillon 30° possesses an interior cage making a one-minute rotation and an exterior cage that rotates over the course of four minutes.

▶▶ 1 *Jean Dunand, Tourbillon Orbital*
With its Tourbillon Orbital, Jean Dunand offers
a sophisticated system in which the tourbillon
performs a complete rotation in one minute,
while completing a full revolution around the
dial in one hour.

▶▶ 2 *Piaget, Polo Tourbillon Relatif*
The principle of double revolution shows up
in Piaget's Polo Tourbillon Relatif, one of 2006's
big surprises.

▶▶ 3 *Blu, Blu Majesty T3*
Bernahrd Lederer, chief designer of Blu, invents
a new way of telling time by combining three
rotation speeds in his piece "Blu Majesty T3."

2
▲

Merry-go-rounds

Instead of rotating in three dimensions, Jean Dunand's Tourbillon Orbital offers extreme mechanical sophistication on one plane—the tourbillon orbits the dial once an hour while rotating once a minute on its own axis. Piaget adopts the same principle in its Polo Tourbillon Relatif, one of the big surprises of 2006 and since produced in a gem-encrusted version. Suspended on the end of the minutes hand, the revolving carriage of the flying tourbillon seems disconnected from the movement that drives it—a fine example of engineering prowess applied to create an optical illusion. In his Blu Majesty T3, Bernhard Lederer, the watchmaker behind the Blu brand, has invented a new way of telling the time by combining three rates of revolution: the tourbillon turns on its own axis once a minute; it is housed in a carriage that rotates once an hour to indicate the minutes; and the carriage goes around the dial in 12 hours to mark the hours.

1. **Antoine Preziuso, 3Volution**
   For its 3Volution, Antoine Preziuso imagined a system with a plateau turning in two minutes fifteen seconds, upon which are placed three tourbillons rotating in one minute.

2. **Breguet, Double tourbillon tournant**
   In 2006, Breguet introduced a Double Tourbillon Tournant protected by several patents.

3. **Parmigiani Fleurier, Kalpa XL Tourbillon Diamants**
   Bernahrd Lederer, chief designer of Blu, invents a new way of telling time by combining three rotation speeds in his piece "Blu Majesty T3."

4. **Piaget, Polo Tourbillon**
   Piaget's Polo Tourbillon clothes its precious mechanism in mother-of-pearl and a refined geometrical motif composed of round- and baguette-cut diamonds.

5. **Zenith, Star Tourbillon El Primero**
   Zenith's Star Tourbillon features a diamond star as a tourbillon bridge; the watch is set with more than 280 diamonds and the mother-of-pearl dial is adorned with large twirling numerals.

A Whirlwind of Tourbillons

In another effort to make tourbillons more technical and attractive, watchmakers have been combining several in one watch. In 2006, Breguet launched its "Double tourbillon tournant," protected by a number of patents. Two independent tourbillons, linked by differential gearing are mounted on a baseplate that rotates in 12 hours. They thus cancel out one another's tiny differences in rate to obtain greater precision. Antoine Preziuso conceived for his 3Volution a plate that completes a revolution in two minutes and 15 seconds while carrying three one-minute tourbillons. The tourbillons are close enough together to be synchronized by the effect of resonance, making them even less sensitive to positional errors.

Ms. Tourbillon

Combining jewelry with sophisticated engineering, major watch brands have also designed a few tourbillon watches for women. Zenith's La Star Tourbillon El Primero has a diamond star as the tourbillon bridge, the watch is encrusted with more than 280 diamonds and fancy numerals whirl on the dial. The Kalpa XL Tourbillon Diamants by Parmigiani Fleurier combines a two-rpm tourbillon with a weeklong power reserve. Audemars Piguet's Tourbillon Chronographe Dame Jules Audemars sparkles with 251 brilliant-cut diamonds and 68 baguette diamonds. Piaget has dressed its Polo Tourbillon's valuable mechanism in inlaid mother-of-pearl and a geometric regalia of round and baguette diamonds.

Audemars Piguet, Tourbillon Chronographe Dame Jules Audemars
The Jules Audemars Ladies' Tourbillon Chronograph by Audemars Piguet sparkles with 251 brilliant-cut diamonds and 68 baguette-cut diamonds.

AUDEMARS PIGUET

EDWARD PIGUET SKELETON TOURBILLON - REF. 25947OR.00.D002CR.01

Created in 18K pink gold, this Edward Piguet Skeleton Tourbillon houses the manual-winding Caliber 2881 SQ. The elegant timepiece is equipped with a one-minute tourbillon with small seconds along the tourbillon axis. This complication features an elaborate hand-hollowed and -engraved rose-gold finished movement. The watch features a sapphire caseback revealing the exquisite movement.

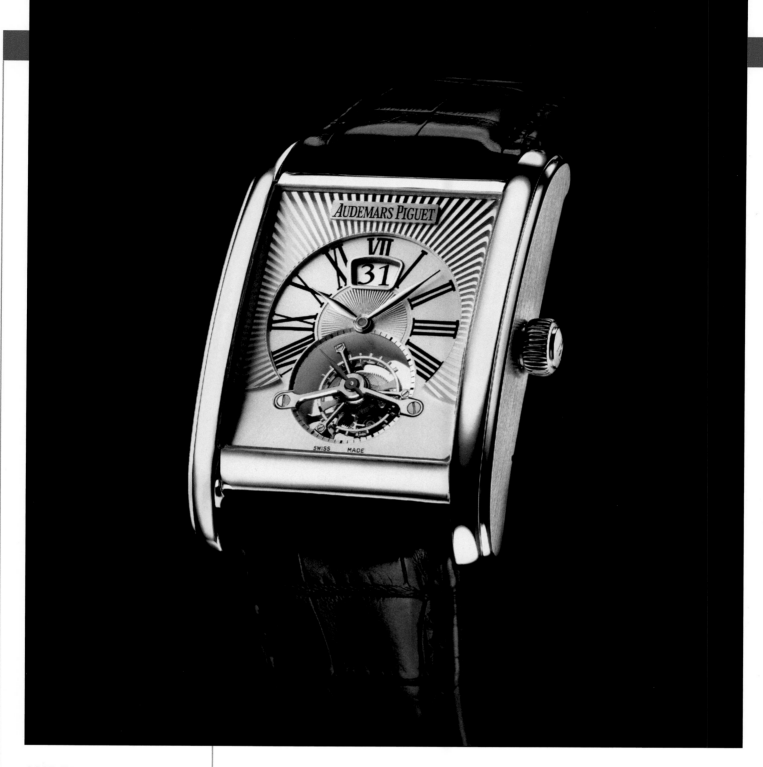

AUDEMARS PIGUET

EDWARD PIGUET TOURBILLON WITH LARGE DATE DISPLAY

REF. 26009BC.OO.D002CR.01

This 18K white-gold Edward Piguet Tourbillon with Large Date Display features a manual-winding movement with tourbillon, hours, minutes, large date, and small seconds along the tourbillon axis. The dial features an engine-turned pattern with applied riveted numerals and hands in gold. This watch's case is glare-proof and has a sapphire crystal and caseback. Limited production.

AUDEMARS PIGUET

JULES AUDEMARS 10-MINUTE REPEATER WITH TOURBILLON
REF. 26072TI.00.D002CR.01

Crafted in titanium, this Jules Audemars features a minute repeater device that strikes on request—on two notes—the hours, 10 minutes, and minutes, with small seconds along the tourbillon. The dial is engine-turned with a sun pattern and riveted gold numerals with gold hands. The timepiece is equipped with an antireflective sapphire crystal and antireflective sapphire crystal caseback. Also available in rose gold.

AUDEMARS PIGUET

LADY JULES AUDEMARS TOURBILLON - REF. 26084OR.ZZ.D016CR.01

This Lady Jules Audemars Tourbillon houses a manual-winding rhodium-plated movement with Côtes de Genève decorative pattern and circular graining. The movement's bridges are hand-engraved with a "dancing spirals" motif. This 18K pink-gold Jules Audemars has a white mother-of-pearl dial engraved with a spiral flinqué design, polished Roman numerals, diamond hour-markers and polished 18K white-gold leaf-shaped hands. Its bezel holds 56 brilliant-cut diamonds, and the caseback is made of antireflective sapphire crystal that reveals the entire mechanism. Supplied with gemstone certification.

BELL & ROSS

BR01 INSTRUMENT TOURBILLON

The mechanical manual-winding BR01 TOURBILLON movement contains carbon-fiber mainplates and a black-gold tourbillon carriage. It is housed inside a 46mm XXL case, crafted in glass-bead-blasted titane with DLC (Diamond-Like Carbon) virtually scratchproof coating. The dial is in black carbon fiber; the numbers, hands and indexes have photoluminescent coating for nighttime reading. Hours can be read in a counter at 12:00, a trust index is positioned at 3:00, and the 120-hour power-reserve indicator is at 9:00. A central hand displays the minutes. The timepiece is fitted on a rubber or alligator leather strap and is water resistant to 100 meters. Limited edition of 60 pieces.

BELL & ROSS

BR01 INSTRUMENT TOURBILLON PHANTOM

Created in a limited edition of just 18 pieces, the BR01 INSTRUMENT TOURBILLON PHANTOM has a black carbon-fiber dial and is encased in glass-bead-blasted titane with DLC. It is powered by a mechanical manual-winding BR01 TOURBILLON with carbon-fiber mainplates and a black-gold tourbillon carriage. The hours are shown in a counter at 12:00, the trust index is positioned at 3:00, and the 120-hour power-reserve indicator is at 9:00. A central hand displays the minutes. Water resistant to 100 meters.

BOVET

FLEURIER MANUALLY WOUND 8-DAY TOURBILLON - LIMITED EDITION

This model was designed to celebrate BOVET's 185th anniversary, in combination with the acquisition of DIMIER 1738, Manufacture of Haute Horlogerie Artisanale. For better reliability and performance, the tourbillon cage was lightened and framed in a solid, yet harmonious and rounded bridge. Shown here in a platinum case set with 107 baguette-cut diamonds (12.89 carats) with a dial fully paved with 451 round-cut diamonds and 6 baguette-cut diamond indexes (1.24 carats), this limited edition is really a "Case for Art," a tribute to the watchmaking crafts that have been the essence of BOVET watches for 185 years. Also available with automatic movement.

BOVET

FLEURIER MANUALLY WOUND 8-DAY TOURBILLON - LIMITED EDITION

This Fleurier manually wound 8-day Tourbillon's movement is a true work of art. The main plate is entirely hand-engraved in BOVET's *fleurisanne* style and observed here through the caseback.

BOVET

FLEURIER MANUALLY WOUND 8-DAY TOURBILLON - LIMITED EDITION

This model was designed to celebrate BOVET's 185th anniversary, in combination with the acquisition of DIMIER 1738, Manufacture of Haute Horlogerie Artisanale. For better reliability and performance, the tourbillon cage was lightened and framed in a solid, yet harmonious and rounded bridge. The back of the movement is a true piece of art, with its main plate entirely hand-engraved in BOVET's *fleurisanne* style. The rose-gold case is fitted with a black enamel dial with an aperture at 3:00, also hand-engraved in *fleurisanne* style. Also available with automatic movement.

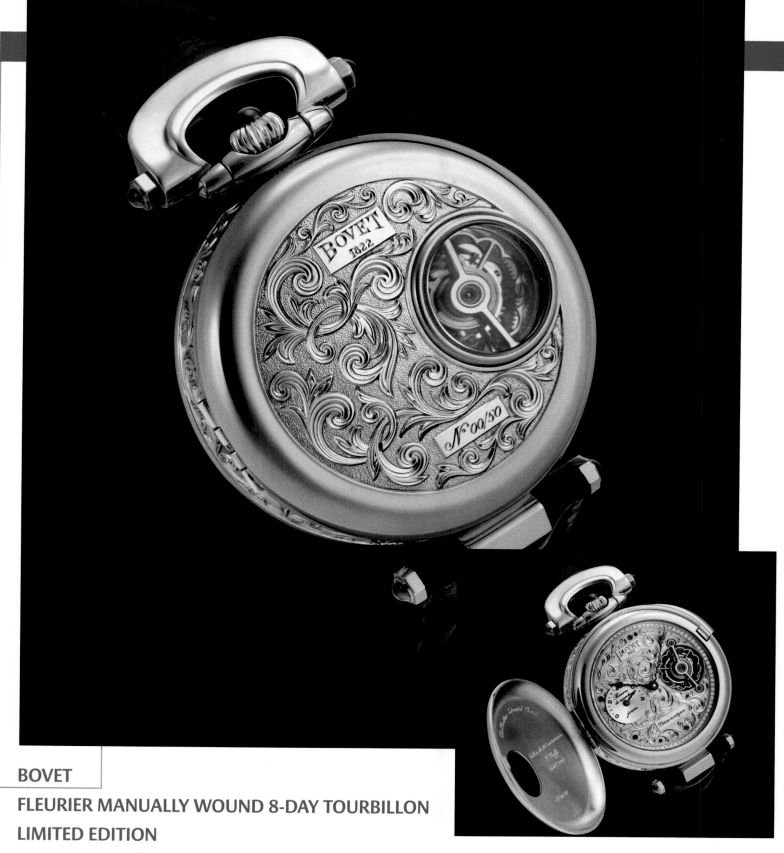

BOVET

FLEURIER MANUALLY WOUND 8-DAY TOURBILLON

LIMITED EDITION

This model was designed to celebrate BOVET's 185th anniversary, in combination with the acquisition of DIMIER 1738, Manufacture of Haute Horlogerie Artisanale. For better reliability and performance, the tourbillon cage was lightened and framed in a solid, yet harmonious and rounded bridge. The back of the movement becomes a true piece of art, with its main plate being entirely hand-engraved in BOVET's *fleurisanne* style. This "Hunter Case" version is in white gold with the dial and front cover fully hand-engraved in *fleurisanne* style. Also available with automatic movement.

BOVET

FLEURIER BUTTERFLY TOURBILLON

The tourbillon embodies all the ingenuity, precision and beauty of fine horology. This magnificent 44mm 18K white gold timepiece reveals the astonishing workmanship of the original tourbillon construction—wolf's teeth and curved spokes on every wheel, blued steel serpentine jumper springs, blue spinels, and the entire surface of the movement's 18K gold structure is blackened. The inner bezel adorns itself with applied Roman numerals. The hand-wound Haute Horlogerie BOVET caliber 12BM05 has a power reserve of 110 hours.

BREGUET

CLASSIQUE GRANDE COMPLICATION - REF. 5347PT/11/9ZU

This Classique Grande Complication wristwatch is crafted in platinum and houses a hand-wound movement, featuring a center plate engine-turned by hand including two apertures for the tourbillons, which rotates in step with the passing hours, and Breguet overcoils. Its ring-shaped dial forms a flange in silvered 18K gold and displays a chapter ring with Roman numerals. The hour hand is an extension of the bridge supporting the two tourbillon carriages. The water-resistant case has a sapphire caseback, bearing a hand-engraved drawing representing the solar system.

BREGUET

CLASSIQUE GRANDE COMPLICATION - REF. 3355PT/00/986

This Classique Grande Complication openworked wristwatch is crafted in platinum and includes a tourbillon. The hand-wound movement is engraved by hand and features a small seconds on the tourbillon shaft and is enhanced by a compensating balance-spring with Breguet overcoil. The hour and seconds chapter rings are made of engine-turned and silvered gold. The movement is protected by a water-resistant case with sapphire crystal caseback.

BREGUET

CLASSIQUE GRANDE COMPLICATION - REF. 5359BB/6B/9V6 DD00

This Classique Grande Complication is crafted in 18K white gold and houses a hand-wound movement featuring a tourbillon with small seconds on the tourbillon shaft and a compensating balance-spring with Breguet overcoil. Its silvered gold dial is hand-engraved on a rose-engine and paved with 356 diamonds (approximately 0.5 carat). The bezel, lugs and caseband are paved with 134 baguettes (approximately 10.37 carats) and the case is water resistant.

BREGUET

TRADITION - REF. 7047BA119ZU

Housed in 18K yellow gold and visible through a sapphire crystal caseback is a hand-wound movement with tourbillon and fusée-chain transmission, Breguet overcoil, and a power-reserve indicator on the barrel drum. The off-centered silvered-gold dial is hand engraved on a rose-engine.

BREGUET

TOURBILLON MESSIDOR - REF. 5335BR429W6

From the Grande Complications collection, this 18K rose-gold Tourbillon Messidor features pink-gold ornaments set into the sapphire crystal, off-centered at 12:00. Visible through a sapphire crystal caseback, the openworked hand-wound movement is engraved entirely by hand and bears a tourbillon regulator. Running seconds are displayed on the tourbillon carriage at 6:00, itself secured by two sapphire crystals. Tourbillon Messidor is also available in 950 platinum.

BREGUET

CLASSIQUE GRANDE COMPLICATION - REF. 5317PT/12/9V6

This Classique Grande Complication wristwatch is crafted in platinum or 18K yellow gold and houses a self-winding movement engraved by hand, featuring a tourbillon with a small seconds on the tourbillon shaft, a 5-day power-reserve indicator and compensating balance-spring with Breguet overcoil. Its silvered gold dial is hand-engraved on a rose-engine and the water-resistant case is enhanced with a sapphire crystal caseback.

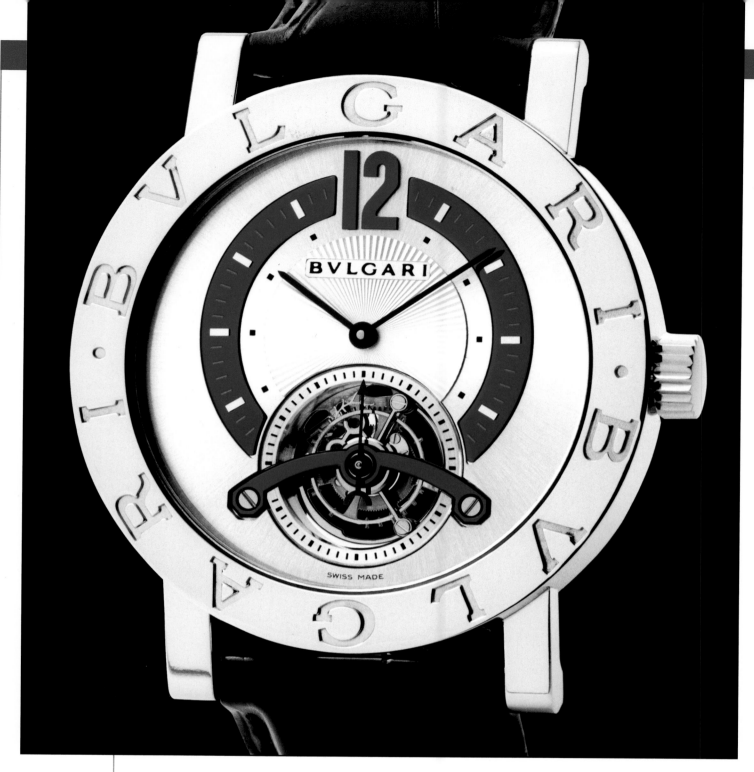

BVLGARI

BVLGARI-BVLGARI TOURBILLON - REF. BB40C6PLTB

The Bvlgari-Bvlgari Tourbillon features an in-house manufactured, mechanical, manual-winding Caliber 052 with tourbillon device; the movement offers a 64-hour power reserve, contains 20 jewels, has a vibration rate of 21,600 vph (3Hz) and is finished and decorated with Côtes de Genève and satiné soleil treatments. The Ø 40mm case is crafted in polished platinum and is fitted with a double-sided, antireflective, scratch-resistant, sapphire crystal, a bezel with engraved logo and a snap-on back, displaying the movement through a sapphire crystal. The limited edition number is engraved on the side of the case, which is water resistant to 30 meters. The silver dial is decorated with guilloché and satiné soleil treatments, blue applied minute track and numeral 12, and hand-applied, rhodium-plated indexes. The tourbillon is visible at 6:00 and has a blue bridge. The display includes off-center hours and minutes, a small seconds at 6:00 on the tourbillon cage and a power-reserve indicator on the back. The strap is made of hand-sewn black alligator and has a platinum triple-fold-over buckle. Limited edition of 20 pieces.

BVLGARI

BVLGARI-BVLGARI TOURBILLON - REF. BB38GLTB

Shown here in yellow gold, the Bvlgari-Bvlgari Tourbillon is powered by the proprietary, manual-winding Caliber 052 with 64-hour power reserve (indicated on back). The small seconds display is integrated with the tourbillon aperture at 6:00. Water resistant to 30 meters, this Ø 38mm case is enclosed with an antireflective scratch-resistant sapphire crystal and a snap-on sapphire crystal caseback that reveals the Côtes de Genève and satiné soleil treated movement. The silver, guilloché dial bears applied gold-plated indexes and is rimmed with an engraved bezel. Also available in white gold with an anthracite dial on a black alligator strap, the yellow-gold version (on a brown hand-sewn alligator strap with yellow-gold triple-fold-over clasp) is limited to 25 pieces.

BVLGARI

RETTANGOLO - REF. RT49PLTB

The Rettangolo features a mechanical, manual-winding Claret Skeleton with tourbillon device, 100-hour power reserve, 19 jewels and a vibration rate of 21,600 vph. The polished platinum 49mm case is fitted with an antireflective, scratch-resistant, sapphire crystal, a snap-on back, displaying the movement through a sapphire crystal, shows the limited-edition number engraved on the case side and is water resistant to 30 meters. The display shows hours and minutes, with small seconds at 6:00. The hand-sewn brown alligator strap has a platinum triple-fold-over buckle. Limited edition of 20 pieces.

CHANEL

BLACK J12 TOURBILLON

Created in a 38mm case of high-tech ceramic and white gold, this J12 Tourbillon houses the manual-winding Chanel movement 0.1-T.1. It offers 100 hours of power reserve and is water resistant to 50 meters. Vibrating at 21,600 rotations per hour, it is equipped with 17 rubies. This J12 Tourbillon is adorned with baguette-cut diamonds (5.3 carats). Only five pieces will be produced and each bears its edition number engraved on the back of the case.

CHANEL

BLACK J12 TOURBILLON - CASEBACK

A world premiere, both aesthetically and technically: a black ceramic bottom plate.

CHOPARD

L.U.C TOURBILLON STEEL WINGS CLASSIC - REF. 161906-1001

The L.U.C 4T Quattro Tourbillon houses the L.U.C 1.02 caliber, which measures 29.1mm in diameter and is 6.1mm thick, offers 9 days of power reserve and features the tourbillon escapement, with aperture at 6:00. The carriage completes one full revolution around its axis once per minute. The 222-part L.U.C 1.02 caliber includes the variable inertia four-arm Variner-type balance with integrated inertia blocks. The movement features 33 jewels and beats at a frequency of 28,800 vibrations per hour. The exceptional movement is certified by the Geneva Seal hallmark. Limited series of 100 timepieces in white gold.

DANIEL ROTH

TOURBILLON LUMIERE

The Daniel Roth 780 tourbillon manual movement is entirely developed and manufactured by Daniel Roth. The skeletonization process involves touching up each part and finishing it with straight graining, beveling or hand chasing. The bridge and bottom plate are in red gold with special hand decoration and movement finishing. The movement provides a 64-hour power reserve, and is housed in a 44mm case in red gold, which rests on a hand-stitched double-face alligator strap with gold folding claps. This model is part of a limited edition of 50 pieces.

DANIEL ROTH

TOURBILLON 8-DAY POWER RESERVE - REF. 197.X.40.223.CC.BA

The new Tourbillon 8-Day Power Reserve features an in-house manufacture double-face manual-winding tourbillon movement with high-end finishing (stippled main plate, Côtes de Genève, beveled, hand-drawn and smoothed flanks and surfaces). This movement is housed in a flip-over pink-gold case with upper face presenting off-centered hours and minutes, extra-large tourbillon aperture with gold guilloché Clous de Paris background, traditional tourbillon with small seconds on its axis moving over triple-level segment. The lower face shows the 200-hour power reserve and date. This timepiece offers the possibility of personalized engraving on the caseback lid.

DANIEL ROTH

TOURBILLON RETROGRADE DATE - REF. 196.X.70.362.CM.BA

The Tourbillon Retrograde Date offers an in-house manufacture double-face manual-winding tourbillon movement with high-end finishing (stippled main plate, Côtes de Genève, beveled, hand-drawn and smoothed flanks and surfaces). This movement is housed in a platinum case with the 64-hour power reserve visible on the caseback, while the dial presents off-centered hours and minutes and retrograde date display, as well as a tourbillon carriage opening with small seconds on tourbillon axis moving over a dedicated ring. This model is water resistant to 3atm.

DeWITT

TOURBILLON DIFFERENTIEL SPORT - REF. AC.8002.28A.M954

DeWitt combined an incredible blend of noble and avant-garde materials such as titanium, red gold and black rubber with a complicated movement to enhance this model's tourbillon, mastered to perfection by Dewitt watchmakers. The exclusive Dewitt caliber DW8002 and the tourbillon with a patented spherical differential system for the winding of the power reserve ("IRM" 2005 patent)—equipped with a fast, flat planetary winding—allows for exceptional time saving (2/3) in the winding speed. The case is engraved with the signature DeWitt Imperial Columns. Limited edition of 250 pieces.

F.P. JOURNE

TOURBILLON SOUVERAIN WITH INDEPENDENT SECONDS

This platinum world-exclusive tourbillon timepiece is fitted with the manually wound F.P. Journe caliber FPJ1403 with tourbillon, power-reserve indicator, hours, minutes and an independent seconds subdial. It is equipped with a remonitoir, or constant force device, and is now enriched with the independent, or deadbeat seconds dial. In a deadbeat seconds watch, the seconds hand remains motionless for as long as the second has not actually elapsed. The hand only indicates the second once it has passed. In the Tourbillon Souverain with Independent Seconds, the watch is equipped with a natural deadbeat seconds device mounted on one of the wheels of the constant-force device. The movement beats at 21,600 vibrations per hour with a dedicated 4-arm balance with inertia adjustment.

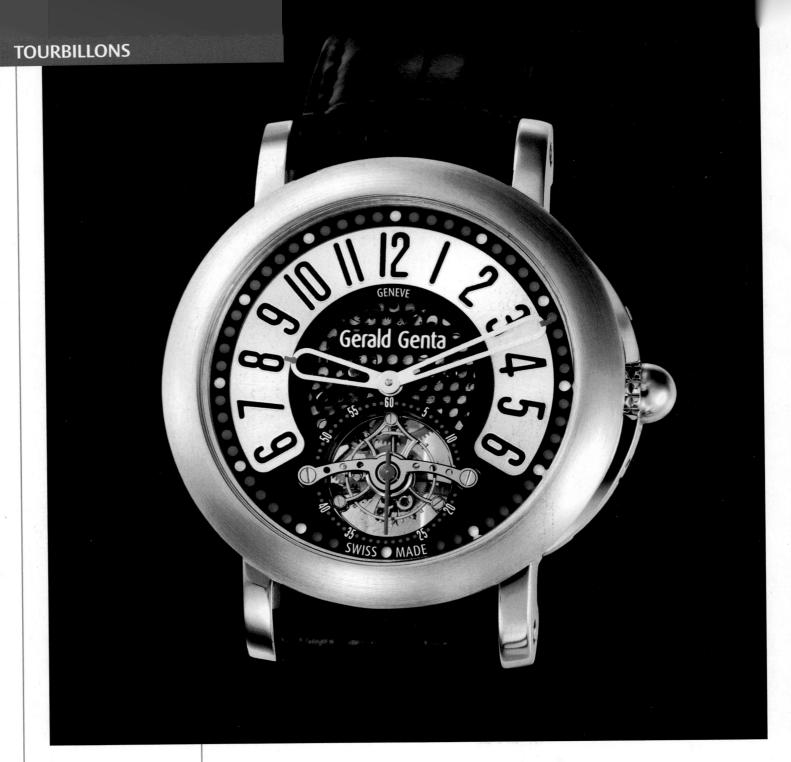

GERALD GENTA

ARENA TOURBILLON RETROGRADE HOURS - REF. ATR.X.75.860.CN.BD

From the Arena collection, this 41mm watch is offered in platinum case with fluted caseband and palladium bezel, enhanced by a black and satin-finish metallic net-like dial displaying the tourbillon cage at 6:00, fixed with a sapphire bridge. It is equipped with an entirely hand-decorated in-house automatic tourbillon movement with retrograde hours, central minutes and seconds on the tourbillon axis. This model, offering a 64-hour power reserve, is water resistant to 10atm.

GERALD GENTA

OCTO TOURBILLON BLACK SPIRIT - REF. OTR.Y.76.999.CN.BD.S61

The Octo Tourbillon Black Spirit offers an exclusive Gérald Genta in-house tourbillon movement, entirely hand-decorated, black gold finish, featuring retrograde hours, central minutes hand and a transparent sapphire tourbillon bridge. It is housed in an octagonal Ø 42.5mm platinum case with tantalum bezel displaying the hours. The white-gold open dial is set with 22 baguette-cut black sapphires (1 carat) and 14 baguette-cut rubies (0.51 carat). This daring model is presented on a black folded alligator strap with grained folding clasp stamped with the brand symbol and is water resistant to 10atm.

GERALD GENTA

OCTO TOURBILLON INCONTRO - REF. OTL.Y.76.940.CN.BD

The Octo Tourbillon Incontro features the daring and exclusive combination of an in-house manufactured, automatic in-line lever tourbillon movement, offering a 64-hour power reserve on one side and a digital movement on the other. The tourbillon face presents a red, black and ivory ceramic dial on a white-gold base featuring retrograde hours, central minutes hand and a transparent sapphire tourbillon bridge; the openwork caseback displays the digital functions, 24-hour time indication, date, day (in three languages), second time-zone indication, chronograph and alarm. The Ø 42.5mm, octagonal platinum case with tantalum bezel, finely engraved on its back and side, is enhanced by two cabochon-set pearl-beaded crowns. This model is water resistant to 10atm.

GERALD GENTA

OCTO TOURBILLON RETROGRADE HOURS - REF. OTR.Y.50.930.CN.BD

The Octo Tourbillon Retrograde hours offers an exclusive Gérald Genta in-house tourbillon movement, entirely hand-decorated, featuring retrograde hours, central minutes hand and a transparent sapphire tourbillon bridge. It is housed in an octagonal Ø 42.5mm 5N red-gold case, enhanced by a 5N red-gold guilloché and cloisonné, black and red ceramic dial. This model offers a 64-hour power reserve and is water resistant to 10atm. It is also available in a platinum case with tantalum bezel and a white-gold guilloché black and red ceramic dial.

GREUBEL FORSEY

FIRST INVENTION: DOUBLE TOURBILLON 30°

The first Tourbillon system specifically invented for a wrist-worn watch, the Double Tourbillon 30° is composed of a large outer cage performing its rotation in four minutes, with a second cage inside inclined at a 30° angle and turning in 60 seconds. Proving itself more effective in the extreme positions adopted by a wristwatch, the Double Tourbillon 30° provides complete visibility of its mechanism in operation. While the movement comprises 301 parts, the set of two tourbillon cages is made of up 128 components weighing a total 1.17 grams. Twin series-coupled barrels endow the Double Tourbillon 30° with a 72-hour power reserve. This model comes in a choice of five versions: 18K white or red gold, as well as in platinum.

GREUBEL FORSEY

THIRD INVENTION: TOURBILLON 24 SECONDES INCLINÉ

Developed for the wristwatch, the Tourbillon 24 Secondes Incliné offers an original means of compensating for the effects of gravity: the use of new materials and a revolutionary system construction enable the single inclined cage to rotate at the impressive speed of one full turn every 24 seconds. A side opening in the case enables one to admire the asymmetrical mechanism and to appreciate the high velocity of the Tourbillon. The movement is made up of 280 components, while the high-speed tourbillon itself comprises 88 parts weighing 0.39 grams in all. The 72-hour power reserve is guaranteed by twin series-coupled barrels. This watch is available in 18K white or red gold.

GREUBEL FORSEY

INVENTION PIECE 1

The new model introduced this year, named the Invention Piece 1, is intended as a tribute to the first fundamental invention by Greubel Forsey: the Double Tourbillon 30°. The original architecture of the movement, distinguished by its off-centered double cage, is further enhanced by an original hour indication composed of triangular indicators arranged around the circumference of the Tourbillon system. The absence of dial reveals the upper bridges in grained nickel silver, a Greubel Forsey signature feature. Crafted in a once-only edition comprising three series of 11 watches in 18K white gold, red gold and platinum respectively, each Invention Piece 1 features a caseback engraved with a message from the two Inventor Watchmakers, Robert Greubel and Stephen Forsey. 388 parts contribute to the smooth running of the movement powering the Invention Piece 1, including 128 for the double cage weighing 1.17 grams.

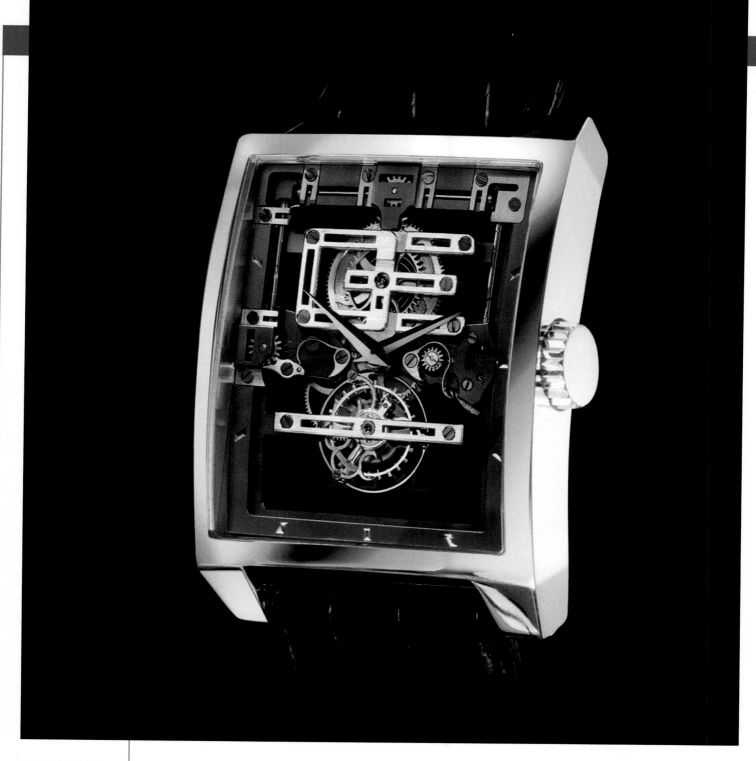

GUY ELLIA

TOURBILLON MAGISTERE

Designer Guy Ellia loves challenges. For this reason, he has designed a skeletonized mysterious winding tourbillon. The Time Square Tourbillon Magistere's movement was created by Swiss manufacturer Christophe Claret. It is the caliber GE-R97 with 110 hours of power reserve, mysterious winding, one-minute tourbillon, skeleton barrel and ratchet-wheel. The movement beats at 21,600 vibrations per hour. The tourbillon cage is entirely hand chamfered and features bridges in 18K gold. Tourbilon Magistere is available in 18K pink gold, white gold (also available with diamonds), or in platinum.

GUY ELLIA

TOURBILLON MAGISTERE PLATINUM

Guy Ellia's skeletonized mysterious winding tourbillon is shown here in its platinum version. The Time Square Tourbillon Magistere's movement was created by Swiss manufacturer Christophe Claret. It is the caliber GE-R97 with 110 hours of power reserve, mysterious winding, one-minute tourbillon, skeleton barrel and ratchet-wheel. The movement beats at 21,600 vibrations per hour. The tourbillon cage is entirely hand chamfered and features bridges in 18K gold.

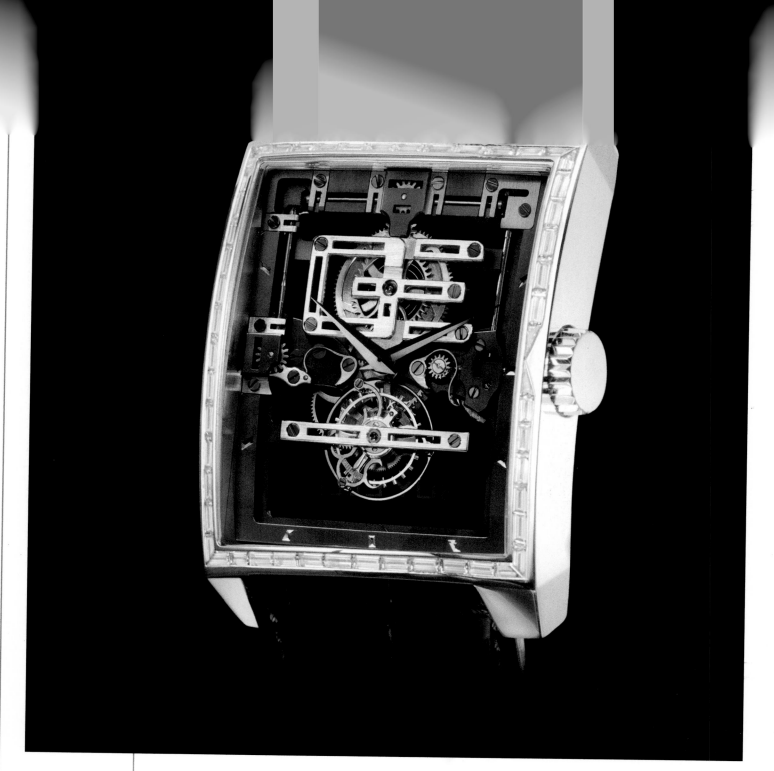

GUY ELLIA

TOURBILLON MAGISTERE

Baguettes frame this 18K white-gold version of Guy Ellia's skeletonized mysterious winding tourbillon. The Time Square Tourbillon Magistere's movement was created by Swiss manufacturer Christophe Claret. It is the caliber GE-R97 with 110 hours of power reserve, mysterious winding, one-minute tourbillon, skeleton barrel and ratchet-wheel. The movement beats at 21,600 vibrations per hour and the tourbillon cage is entirely hand chamfered and features bridges in 18K gold.

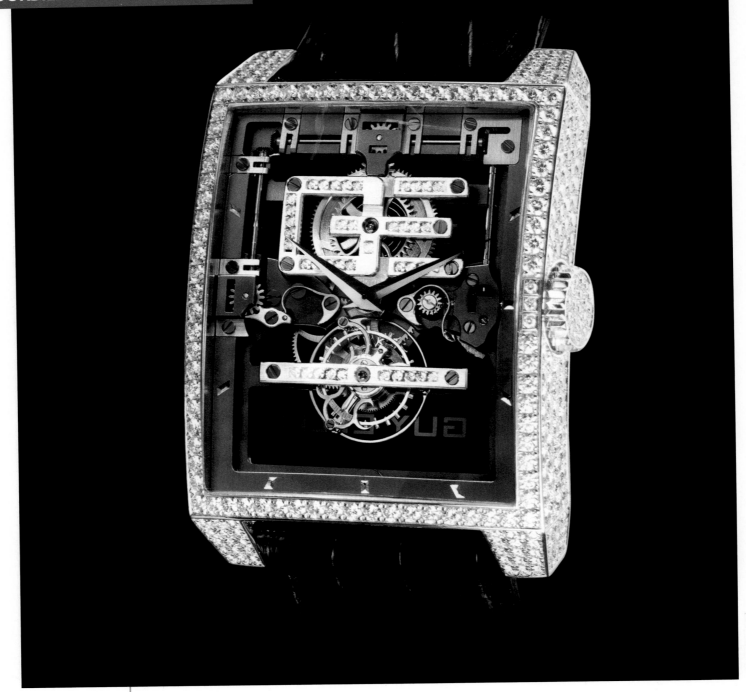

GUY ELLIA

TOURBILLON MAGISTERE

The Time Square Tourbillon Magistere's movement was created by Swiss manufacturer Christophe Claret. Caliber GE-R97 features 110 hours of power reserve, mysterious winding, one-minute tourbillon, skeleton barrel and ratchet-wheel. The movement beats at 21,600 vibrations per hour. Its tourbillon cage is entirely hand chamfered and features bridges in 18K gold. This full-set white-gold version bears 535 brilliants weighing 8.25 carats on its case. The tourbillon is also set with 52 emerald-cut diamonds.

HUBLOT

ONE MILLION DOLLAR BIG BANG

A one-of-a-kind timepiece, the spectacular One Million Dollar Big Bang's 18K white-gold case is "invisibly" set with 322 baguette diamonds (24.64 carats), its crown with 12 baguette diamonds (0.8 carat). The 18K white-gold and 150 palladium dial was designed with two types of settings for its 129 baguette diamonds (6.4 carats): traditional setting around the tourbillon cage; invisible for the upper dial. The mechanical manual-winding HUB Solo T with 60-second flying tourbillon and 120-hour power reserve was specially executed for this piece and is visible through the caseback. It's adjustable, smooth natural rubber strap is secured with an 18K white-gold deployant buckle is set with 30 baguette diamonds (3.33 carats).

HUBLOT

BAT BANG TOURBILLON ALL BLACK - REF. 305.CM.002.RX

Bat Bang Tourbillon All Black is powered by the manual-winding HUB 1000 SB, housed in a Ø 44.5mm satin-finished black ceramic Big Bang case with black composite resin bezel lug and lateral inserts. The movement has a 120-hour power reserve and a flying tourbillon raised 2.8mm above the base of the bottom plate for maximum visibility. The caseback is crafted of satin-finished titanium and fitted with a sapphire crystal and the dial reveals the black carbon-fiber bridge in the shape of a two-wheel gear train. Water resistant to 10atm and fitted on an adjustable, smooth natural rubber strap, this watch is limited to 50 individually numbered pieces.

HUBLOT

BIG BANG PLATINUM MAT BIG DATE - REF. 302.TI.450.RX

This watch is powered by the manual-winding HUB1050GD caliber with flying tourbillon in a Ø 13mm cage without ball bearings raised by 2.8mm over the base of the bottom plate, a 120-hour power reserve, and beating at 21,600 vph. The Ø 44.5mm Big Bang case is made of micro-blasted platinum and colorless PVD; the lugs and lateral inserts are crafted in black composite resin; the dial has a matte gray micro-blasted platinum effect on two levels, black nickel satin-finish numerals and appliqué index. Limited to 50 individually numbered pieces, this version carries a suggested price of $136,000.

HUBLOT

BIG BANG GOLD MAT BIG DATE - REF. 302.PI.500.RX

Crafted in red gold, this Ø 44.5mm watch is powered by the manual-winding HUB1050GD caliber with flying tourbillon in a Ø 13mm cage without ball bearings raised by 2.8mm over the base of the bottom plate, a 120-hour power reserve, and Gyromax regulating inertia-block balance. Water resistant to 10atm, this Big Bang is fitted on an adjustable, smooth natural black rubber with Hublot logo.

IWC

PORTUGUESE TOURBILLON MYSTERE - REF. IW504207

Housed in the Portuguese case, the Tourbillon Mystere is powered by the IWC 50900 caliber with 7-day power reserve. The watch features an elevated tourbillon that makes it appear to move freely and entirely independent of any other drive-elements. This watch is a limited edition of 250 watches in 18K white gold. It offers a minute tourbillon, Pellaton automatic-winding mechanism, power-reserve display and small seconds at 9:00.

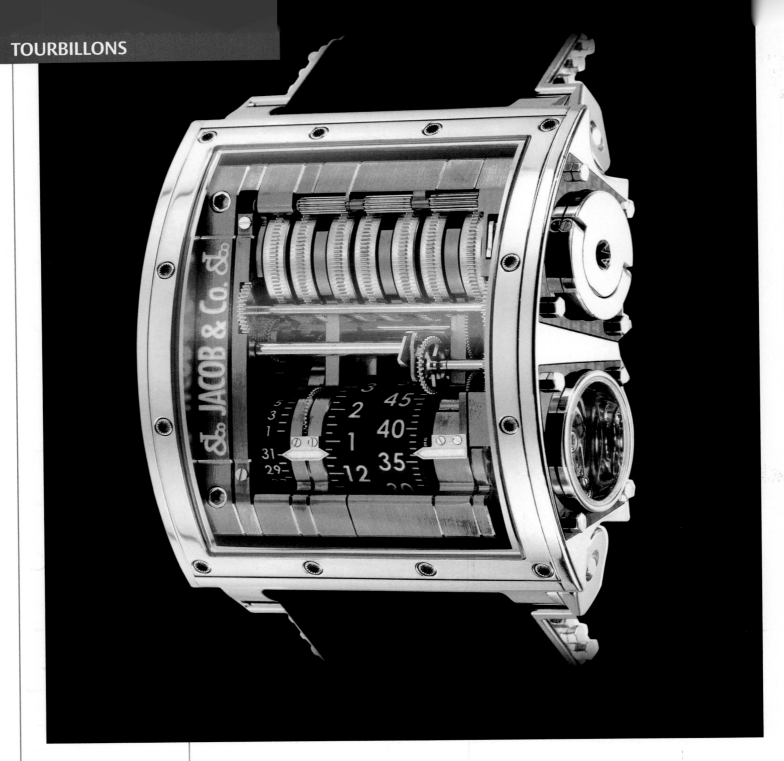

JACOB & CO.

QUENTTIN

This tourbillon is powered by a vertical mechanical movement and manual-winding escapement with 31-day power reserve. Seven barrels house multiple mainsprings that interact to drive the chain, generating constant power and torque to achieve such a high power reserve. Hours, minutes and power reserve are indicated via vertical disks assembled coaxially. The Quenttin is released in limited editions: 18K white gold (99 pieces) and rose gold (18 pieces; shown); red, black or blue magnesium (18 pieces); and platinum on request.

JAEGER-LECOULTRE

MASTER GRANDE TOURBILLON

Encased in Ø 43mm of 950 platinum, the Master Grand Tourbillon's mechanical automatic-winding Jaeger-LeCoultre Caliber 978 beats at 28,800 vph and holds 48 hours of power reserve. The watch features a 24-hour second time-zone indicator and an innovative date indicator, which jumps between15 and 16 so as not to spoil the view of the impressive technical feat that is the main highlight of the dial: the tourbillon. For the feather-like tourbillon (0.28 grams), Jaeger-LeCoultre's engineers designed a carriage from an ultra-light, precision-enhancing titanium alloy prized for its exceptional hardness. The cambered escapement bridge cleverly follows the curve of the carriage and the single-piece oscillating weight in 22K pink gold is embellished with a stamped medallion motif with relief engravings. The seconds display appears within the circular tourbillon opening with a three-arm hand including an arrow-tipped spoke that indicates the passing seconds in step with the revolving tourbillon carriage.

JEAN DUNAND *PIÉCES UNIQUE*

TOURBILLON ORBITAL

The patented Tourbillon Orbital is the first wristwatch of its kind to feature a one-minute flying tourbillon that orbits the dial once an hour on a revolving movement. The watch houses the IO 200 movement designed by Christophe Claret incorporating a series of wheels within wheels. The barrel and the flying tourbillon, set opposite each other, orbit the center between two plates held apart by pillars rotating on ball bearings. The top plate consists of the revolving dial (with an aperture revealing the raised tourbillon). The barrel unwinds against a central fixed pinion, driving itself and the tourbillon around. The tourbillon cage rotates once a minute against the fixed circumference wheel through a train of wheels and regulates the speed of rotation. The wheel train reduces the necessary number of jewels in the movement to 14, thereby also reducing friction.

JEAN DUNAND *PIÉCES UNIQUE*

TOURBILLON ORBITAL

It took Christophe Claret two full years to work out the mechanical solution to winding and setting a rotating movement with a mainspring barrel that never stays in one place. The solution is vertical winding and setting conducted through a folding key that is set into the caseback. Lifting the key ring engages a central wheel that turns the ratchet wheel to wind the barrel spring. Puling out the key connects the motion work of the hours and minutes hands to set them. The watch features the power-reserve gauge on the case side rather than on the dial—another world's first for which Jean Dunand has been granted a patent.

PARMIGIANI FLEURIER

KALPA XL TOURBILLON CHIAROSCURO 30TH ANNIVERSARY MODEL

In 2006, Michel Parmigiani celebrated his 30th year in watchmaking with special creations like this Tourbillon 30 Seconds Chiaroscuro dedicated to Haute Horlogerie. Its manual-winding PF Caliber 501 with 30-second tourbillon, 7-day power reserve 9 (at 12:00) and 29 jewels is handmade entirely in-house and enhanced by a PVD-coloring technique; the pierced bottom plate and bridges form a mosaic of metallic colors, the result of complex laboratory research. The sapphire dial is crafted with the unique layer-by-layer electro-deposition technique. The 30-piece 950 platinum series is fitted with Hermès Havana alligator-leather straps.

PARMIGIANI FLEURIER

KALPA XL TOURBILLON - REF. PF013512.01

This limited edition Kalpa XL Tourbillon is created in 25 18K rose-gold and 25 platinum pieces. The unique tourbillon features a cage with a 30-second rotation, making two complete revolutions in one minute. The watch houses the manual-winding PF50002 caliber with 8 days of power reserve. Beating at 21,600 vibrations per hour, the 28-jeweled movement offers a power-reserve indicator and Cotes de Geneve decoration. This Kalpa XL is water resistant to 30 meters and features sapphire crystals with anti-reflection treatment.

PARMIGIANI FLEURIER

KALPA TONDA TOURBILLON - REF. PF600695.JPG

This limited edition Kalpa Tonda Tourbillon is created in 18K rose-gold (100 pieces) and platinum (100 pieces). This unique tourbillon features a cage with a 30-second rotation, making two complete revolutions in one minute. The watch houses the manual-winding PF510 movement with 8 days of power reserve and beats at 21,600 vibrations per hour. The 28-jeweled movement features the Côtes de Genève decoration and hand-chamfered bridges. The watch features a Côtes de Genève decorated dial. Each watch is individually numbered on the back. The watch is water resistant to 30 meters and features sapphire crystals with antireflection treatment on the back..

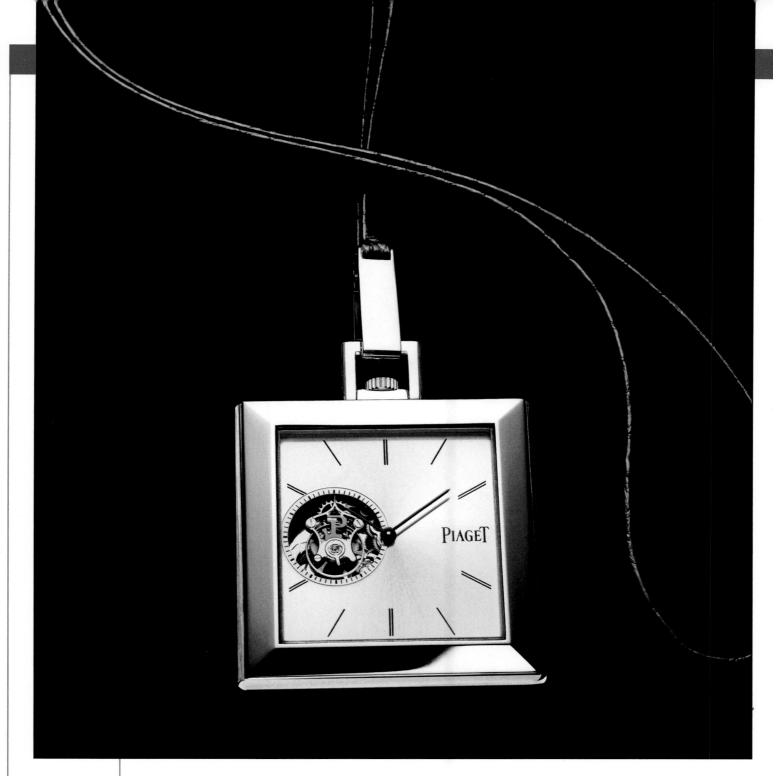

PIAGET

ALTIPLANO TOURBILLON GOUSSET

Piaget now revives the tourbillon pocket-watch, interpreted in a highly contemporary square form characteristic of the brand, that of the Altiplano collection. The 40mm white-gold case houses the Piaget mechanical hand-wound Calibre 600P, the world's thinnest tourbillon movement at just 3.5mm thick. Admirably reflecting the mastery inherent to the manufacture, the carriage of this tourbillon—visible through a dial opening at 9:00—is made up of 42 parts and weighs a mere 0.2 grams. Like all vintage Piaget models, the caseback is engraved with the brand's coat of arms. To provide a variety of manners of wearing it, this refined and elegant watch comes with a white-gold chain as well as a leather cordlet.

PIAGET

EMPERADOR MOONPHASE TOURBILLON XL - REF N°GOA31121

This Tourbillon maintains the sophisticated lines and finishings of the Emperador watches, but offers a more powerful and masculine size. It houses the Piaget mechanical hand-wound Calibre 640P, the world's thinnest tourbillon movement at just 3.5mm thick. Admirably reflecting the mastery inherent to the manufacture, the carriage of this tourbillon—visible through a dial opening at 9:00—consists of 42 parts and weighs a mere 0.2 grams. A moonphase display appears at 6:00 on the rounded base of a delicately guilloché-worked surface. The lapis lazuli moonphase disk is enhanced by a golden moon and a pyrite star-studded dial.

PIAGET

EMPERADOR TOURBILLON HAUTE JOAILLERIE - REF. GOA30018

Equipped with the mechanical manual-wind Piaget 600P shaped caliber, this high-jeweled Emperador Tourbillon is equipped with 24 jewels and 40 hours of power reserve. The three-piece case is crafted in 18-karat white gold and bedecked with 153 brilliant- and baguette-cut diamonds weighing 3.3 carats. Its dial is also ensconced in diamonds. The three bridges of the tourbillon are crafted in titanium and the movement is decorated with the Côtes de Genève pattern.

PIAGET

POLO TOURBILLON RELATIF - REF. G0A31123

Suspended from one end of the minute hand, the flying tourbillon carriage appears to be disconnected from the base movement driving it. The hours are read off on a central disk, while the tourbillon carriage is swept along in the rotation of the minute hand. Expressing the magic of perfect equilibrium, the Piaget Polo Tourbillon Relatif marks off time to the rhythm of the new proprietary Calibre 608P, a mechanical hand-wound flying tourbillon movement. Composed of 42 parts, the carriage—which spins on its axis once per minute, in addition to the hourly rotation around the dial—weighs a mere 0.2 grams! The new tourbillon movement, Piaget Calibre 608P, beats at a frequency of 21,600 vibrations per hour (3 Hz) and is endowed with a 70-hour power reserve.

PIAGET

POLO TOURBILLON - REF. GOA30111

A wonderful rendition of an iconic timepiece, this Polo Tourbillon is equipped with the 600P shaped caliber. The mechanical manual-wind movement consists of 24 jewels and offers 40 hours of power reserve. The bridges of the tourbillon are created in titanium. The case is crafted in 18-karat white gold and set with fancy-cut diamonds.

PIAGET

SET SKELETON TOURBILLON

The Emperador Set Skeleton Tourbillon symbolizes the alchemist's blend that Piaget achieves once again between haute horology and haute joaillerie. Piaget has developed the world's thinnest tourbillon, at a mere 3.5mm thick, and has chosen a flying version placed at 12:00 for aesthetic reasons. 159 round diamonds totaling approximately 0.2 carats and 7 sapphire cabochons (0.2 carats) adorn this exceptional caliber, whose lower side is graced with the extreme refinement of a sunray guilloché decorative motif comprising 60 divisions, which correspond to 60 seconds. This hand-wound movement has a power reserve of around 40 hours and beats at a cadence of 21,600 vibrations per hour.

RICHARD MILLE

002-V2

The RM 002-V2 Tourbillon–an evolution of the first Richard Mille timepiece–houses the hand-winding caliber 002-V2 built on a carbon nanofiber baseplate. It provides hours, minutes, indicators for power reserve and torque as well as a function indicator for Winding, Neutral and Hand-setting operations. The PVD-treated variable-inertia balance has an overcoil balance spring and ceramic endstone for the tourbillon cage to provide optimal chronometric results and long-term wear. Water resistant to 50 meters, the signature tripartite Richard Mille case with sapphire caseback is offered in titanium, 18K red or white gold and platinum.

RICHARD MILLE

RM 012

The RM 012 tourbillon represents yet another world premiere from Richard Mille Watches: the first tubular network construction created for a watch. Inspired by forms taken from architectural engineering, the RM 012's structure, made of Phynox tubes with titanium and steel parts, combines the function of baseplate and bridges into an integrated whole. Other features include a power reserve of 70 hours, a variable inertia balance with overcoil, a ceramic endstone for the tourbillon cage, fast rotating winding barrel with central involute profile, spline screws in grade 5 titanium and jewels set in white gold chaton. Limited to only 30 pieces worldwide, in 2007 the RM 012 was awarded first prize, the Aiguille d'or, by the jury of the Grand Prix de Genève.

RICHARD MILLE

RM 015 PERINI NAVI CUP

The RM 015 is a tourbillon with detailing inspired by nautical themes and the world of sailing. Many parts, such as the case design, crown and movement parts, have undergone an oceanic transformation. The timepiece uses the manual-winding marine caliber 015, built on a carbon nanofiber baseplate, providing hours, minutes, indicators for power reserve and torque, as well as a function indicator for Carica (winding), Neutrale (neutral) and Lancette (hand setting). The finely finished pushbutton, located at 9:00, advances the second time zone in one-hour increments by utilizing a rotating sapphire disk that displays the time zone near 10:30. Water resistant to 50 meters, the signature tripartite Richard Mille case with sapphire caseback is offered in titanium, 18K red or white gold, and platinum.

RICHARD MILLE

RM 018

Many new materials have found their way into wristwatches during the past years, but the RM018 represents a revolutionary application of well-known materials—precious stones. These are used for the wheels comprising the power reserve, barrel cover, hour, minute and second wheels, as well as the transparent, bipartite baseplate. The special techniques developed in order to create these parts make the RM 018 an ultimate synthesis of high-end elegance resulting from the application of the latest 21st-century technology. Other features include a power reserve of 70 hours with a new winding system, a variable inertia balance with overcoil, ceramic endstone for the tourbillon cage, and fast rotating winding barrel with central involute profile.

ROMAIN JEROME

FIVE BLACK I TOURBILLON

The DNA of Famous Legends collection was developed in tribute to the elegance and prestige of the Titanic. This ceramic limited-edition houses a tourbillon and features five black components: the deep black dial gets its color from coal recovered from the Titanic, the flank and crown are in blackened satin-finished steel, and the bezel and paws are crafted in black satin-finished ceramic with a special treatment that produces an unusual matte effect. Roman numerals and transversal crosses are elegantly designed visual references to the docks of the shipyard.

ROMAIN JEROME

RUSTED STEEL T-OXY III TOURBILLON

This limited-edition timepiece captures a piece of history in a tourbillon timepiece made with materials heretofore unused in horology. Its rusted steel bezel combines the authentic steel of the Titanic shipwreck and steel from the shipyards Harland & Wolff, where that luxurious ocean liner was built nearly a century ago. The hands of all the timepieces in the collection are inspired by the Titanic's anchor in another homage to the great ship, and coal recovered from the Titanic lends its deep black color to the dial.

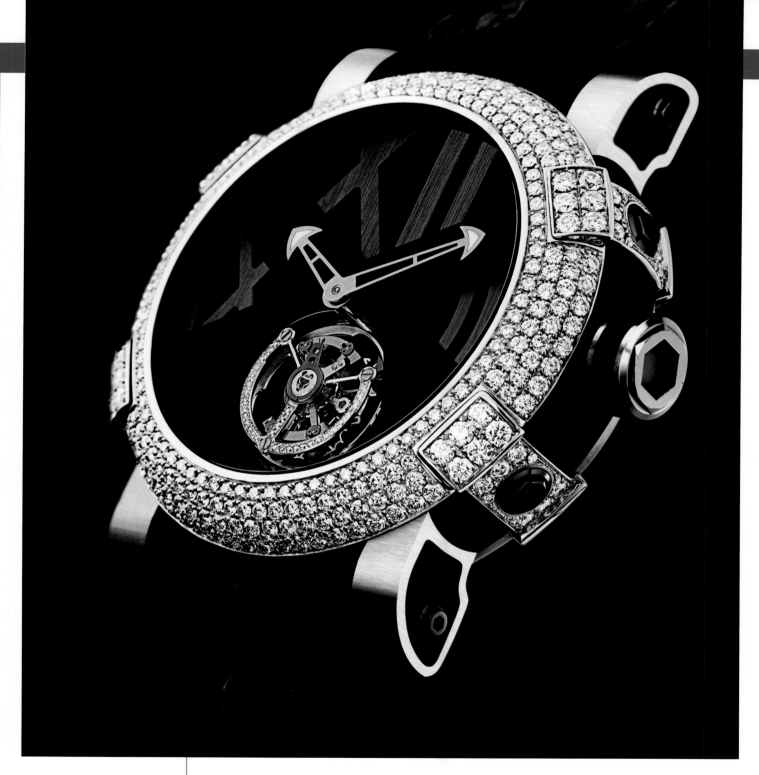

ROMAIN JEROME

THE WHITE STAR TOURBILLON

The carriage of this Romain Jerome tourbillon is an eloquent demonstration of horological mastery. For the first time in watchmaking history, the tourbillon carriage is set with white brilliant-cut diamonds. The manual setting of extremely small gemstones (measuring 0.4mm in diameter) leads to a certain dispersion of the component's center of gravity. As the tourbillon requires extremely precise adjustment, Romain Jerome's watchmakers had to further innovate and experiment in order to poise the tourbillon carriage after the miniature gems were set.

ULYSSE NARDIN

ROYAL BLUE TOURBILLON

The Royal Blue Tourbillon is crafted in platinum and houses Caliber UN-79 with flying tourbillon. The 41mm watch is equipped with a unique, circular rack "mystery" winding mechanism and sapphire bridges and main plates. The Royal Blue is also available is several configurations with and without diamonds.

ULYSSE NARDIN

FREAK 28'800 - REF. 020-88

The Freak bears Ulysse Nardin's patented dual Ulysse escapement and Carrousel-Tourbillon. Powered by the Caliber UN-200, this version of the 44.5mm Freak 28'800 is encased in 18K white gold. The Freak 28'800 is also available in 18K rose gold and in a Limited Edition in platinum.

VACHERON CONSTANTIN

MALTE TONNEAU TOURBILLON - REF. 30066

The sophisticated Malte Tonneau Tourbillon's 18K pink-gold case with curved sapphire crystal houses the mechanical manual-winding Caliber 1780 with one-minute tourbillon escapement, which has ruthenium-finished bridges. The 27-jeweled movement beats at 18,000 vibrations per hour and offers a minimum 55-hour power reserve (shown at 11:00).

VACHERON CONSTANTIN

OPENWORKED MALTE TOURBILLON

Housed in a stunning 18K pink-gold tonneau case, this Malte Tourbillon is powered by the hand-wound 1790 mechanical caliber with tourbillon regulator. It offers a 31-day analog date calendar, 55 hours of power reserve. and is completely openworked and beveled. The dial features baton hands and a crown signed with the embossed symbol of Vacheron Constantin.

WYLER GENEVE

WYLER GENEVE TOURBILLON

Flanked by a power-reserve indicator and Trust Index, a 24-hour GMT subdial joins the tourbillon to create a fluid balance of function in the new Wyler Genève Tourbillon. The tourbillon cage is equipped with unique spring-mounted aluminum bridges.

ZENITH

ACADEMY TOURBILLON EL PRIMERO HMS

Housed in an 18K rose-gold case that is water resistant up to 30 meters, this Academy Tourbillon has an El Primero 4041 automatic movement. Comprising 170 parts, it counts 36,000 vibrations per hour and has a 55-hour power reserve. The 18K rose-gold dial with a handmade "barley-corn" guilloché pattern has applique numerals of increasing size. The calfskin-lined alligator strap is hand stitched.

Equations of time

The equation of time indication, corresponding to the difference between true solar time and mean solar time, was formerly the exclusive preserve of ultra-complex clocks and watches. So-called "running" equation of time models, equipped with two minute-hands displaying both times simultaneously, were even more rare. Within this context, the recent appearance of the very first running equation-of-time wristwatches may well spell the renaissance of this highly exclusive complication, a blend of technical sophistication and poetry, which reminds us that the sun is our primary clock.

Celestial mechanism

There are two times: true solar time and mean solar time. True solar time (as shown on sundials) corresponds to the rhythms of nature. In orbiting around the sun, the Earth follows an elliptical trajectory, and its axis is inclined in relation to the plane of the equator. The result is that the time elapsing between two of the sun's passages, though its highest point in the sky (at noon) is not the same length throughout the year. It lasts exactly 12 hours only four times a year: on April 15th, June 14th, September 1st and December 24th. Otherwise, it is sometimes longer and sometimes shorter, following an inexorably repetitive curve. This difference, ranging from minus 15 minutes and 23 seconds on November 4th to plus 14 minutes and 22 seconds on February 11th, is called the "equation of time." Meanwhile, the mean solar displayed on our watches is merely a convention based on the mean length of all days in a year.

▶▶ 1 *Daniel Roth, Perpetual Calendar*
Equation of Time
In its Perpetual Calendar Equation
of Time, featuring an openworked dial
that shows off the movement, Daniel
Roth also included an indicator
between 10:00 and 11:00 to display
the number of minutes between mean
solar time and real time.

▶▶ 2 *Jaquet Droz, Equation of time*
The Equation of time by Jaquet Droz
features a "sun" hand sweeping across
an arc and two counters for the date
and the month.

Impressive constancy

The greatest watchmakers have vied with each other in developing ingenious systems capable of reproducing the variations in the equation of time. Since the variable lengths of true solar days occur at exactly the same dates each year, it is possible to "program" them using a cam performing one rotation per year. The display of the equation of time may be presented in various ways. Most watches are equipped with a hand moving from -16 to +14 across a graduated scale on a subdial or auxiliary sector; the user must mentally add or subtract this difference from the mean time in order to know the true time. Such is the case with the Breguet Equation of Time watch with perpetual calendar, or the Jaquet Droz Equation of Time model with its "sun" hand running over the arc of a circle and its two date and month counters. On its Perpetual Calendar Equation of Time model featuring an openworked structure revealing the movement, Daniel Roth also designed a sector positioned between 10:00 and 11:00 to indicate the number of minutes between mean and true solar times.

Instant readability

Easier to read but more complex in terms of their construction, running equation-of-time watches have two minute hands, one indicating mean time and the other true time. This system, formerly reserved for pocket watches, first appeared on wristwatches in 2004. Representing a major feat of miniaturization, the Le Brassus Equation Marchante watch by Blancpain is distinguished by its double equation of time display—featuring a central minute hand adorned with a gold sun, complemented by a subdial with retrograde hand at 2:00—along with an ultra-thin perpetual calendar. In 2005,

▶▶ 3 *Breguet, Equation of time*
Most equation of time watches are equipped with a subdial or supplementary zone swept across by a hand going from −16 to +14 minutes; the wearer must mentally add or subtract this difference from the mean time to know the real time. The model pictured is Breguet's Equation of time..

▶▶ 4 *Blancpain, "Villeret" Pure Running Equation*
The pure running equation "Villeret" houses an iteration of the mechanism contained in the running equation "Le Brassus."

▶▶ 5 *Blancpain, «Le Brassus» Running Equation*
The "Le Brassus" running equation is notable for its double display of equation of time, with a second central minute hand decorated by a golden sun, complemented by a subdial with retrograde hand at 2:00, all of which is combined with an ultra-thin perpetual calendar.

Blancpain introduced this innovative mechanism in a model from the Villeret collection named "Equation marchante pure," and then in 2006 in a special series of seven watches named Equation Marchante M.Y.S, in tribute to the brand's seventh partnership with the Monaco Yacht Show. As for the Jaeger-LeCoultre Gyrotourbillon 1, mostly acclaimed for its spherical tourbillon (see the chapter on Tourbillons), it also features a running equation-of-time display by means of an additional minute hand adorned with a small golden sun.

Taking account of longitude

Audemars Piguet took a further step in 2005 by offering the first system for reading off the equation of time adjusted to the exact degree of longitude—and no longer to an entire time zone. The dial with its dedicated flange enables one to directly determine the exact moment when the sun reaches its zenith (true noon) for the city whose name is engraved on the bezel. The Jules Audemars Equation of Time is also the first wristwatch to display sunrise and sunset times while taking three parameters into account: the date, the longitude, and the latitude. Again in 2005, the Arnold & Son brand, heir to the spirit of famous British horologer John Arnold, drew inspiration from its founder's research in creating an equation-of-time watch that also takes account of longitude, by means of a dial with two mobile rings. Moreover, this True North Perpetual features another original asset: when the 24-hour solar hand indicates true solar noon, one need only point it towards the sun for the mobile outer ring to indicate true geographical north.

▶▶ 1 Blancpain, Equation marchante M.Y.S.
In 2006, in a special series of pieces clad
in black and called "Equation marchante
M.Y.S.," Blancpain paid tribute to its seventh
year partnering with the Monaco Yacht Show.

▶▶ 2 Audemars Piguet, Equation of Time
Jules Audemars
The Jules Audemars Equation of Time is
the first watch to display sunrise and sunset
times while taking into account three
parameters: the date, the longitude and
the latitude.

▶▶ 3 Jaeger-LeCoultre, Gyrotourbillon I.
Although Jaeger-LeCoultre's Gyrotourbillon
1 is mostly known for its spherical tourbillon
(see Tourbillons chapter), it also features a
running equation with a minute hand
adorned with a small golden sun.

▶▶ 4 Arnold & Son, True North Perpetual
Arnold & Son's True North Perpetual has
an unusual distinctive feature: when
the 24-hour solar hand indicates exact solar
noon, the wearer can point it in the
direction of the sun, and the mobile exterior
dial points to true geographic North.

AUDEMARS PIGUET

JULES AUDEMARS - SELFWINDING EQUATION OF TIME

REF. 26003OR.OO.D002CR.01

This Jules Audemars Equation of Time is crafted in 18K pink gold and houses the self-winding Caliber 2120/2808. Visible through the sapphire crystal caseback, the 41-jeweled movement depicts conventional time and real solar time and offers hours and minutes, sunrise and sunset times, equation of time, perpetual calendar and astronomical moon. The solar culmination time is calibrated to the reference city chosen by the owner.

AUDEMARS PIGUET

JULES AUDEMARS - SELF-WINDING EQUATION OF TIME-WHITE HOUSE
REF. 26258PT.OO.D028CR.0157

Crafted in 950 Platinum, this Jules Audemars Equation of Time houses the self-winding Caliber 2120/2808. Visible through the sapphire crystal caseback featuring the inscription "William J. Clinton 42nd President of the United States," the 41-jeweled movement depicts conventional time and real solar time and offers hours, minutes, sunrise and sunset times, equation of time, perpetual calendar as well as astronomical moon. The solar culmination time is calibrated to the reference of the White House. This watch is also available in 18K pink gold (Ref. 2658OR) and white gold (Ref. 2658BC). Each version is limited to 42 pieces, as Clinton was the 42nd President of the United States.

AUDEMARS PIGUET

JULES AUDEMARS EQUATION OF TIME - REF. 26003BC.OO.D002CR.01

This Jules Audemars Equation of Time watch is created in 18K white gold and houses the self-winding Caliber 2120/2808. Visible through the sapphire crystal caseback, the 41-jeweled movement depicts conventional time and real solar time and offers hours and minutes, sunrise and sunset times, equation of time, perpetual calendar and astronomical moon. The solar culmination time is calibrated to the reference city chosen by the owner.

AUDEMARS PIGUET

JULES AUDEMARS EQUATION OF TIME - REF. 25963PT.00.D002CR.0100

This Jules Audemars Equation of Time watch is created in 18K white gold and houses the self-winding Caliber 2120/2808. Visible through the sapphire crystal caseback, the 41-jeweled movement depicts conventional time and real solar time and offers hours and minutes, sunrise and sunset times, equation of time, perpetual calendar and astronomical moon. The solar culmination time is calibrated to the reference city chosen by the owner. The dial reveals the elaborate hand-engraved work.

BLANCPAIN

VILLERET EQUATION MARCHANTE PURE

The Equation Marchante Pure, based on the Le Brassus model that was the first wristwatch capable of displaying the separate solar and civil times by two minute-hands, was launched in 2005 as part of the Villeret collection characterized by its pure lines and formal beauty. This limited edition of 50 pieces is crafted in platinum and houses the 364-part caliber 3863A, equipped with 72 hours of power reserve.

DANIEL ROTH

EQUATION OF TIME

Connoisseurs of grand complications will appreciate this watch as an exceptional watch, fitted with a self-winding movement with an 18K gold and platinum oscillating weight, hand decorated and benefiting from a power reserve of approximately 44 hours. An indicator segment at 10:00 shows the difference between the average solar time and the real solar time. It calculates the solar equation throughout the year with a difference, which culminates on February 11th (+ 14 minutes, approximately) and November 4th (-16 minutes, approximately).

Chronographs,
Chronograph Rattrapantes
and Flybacks

CEO of IWC

Georges Kern

Da Vinci Chronographe

"To really be a great brand," judges Georges Kern, CEO of IWC, "you must have a history, a design and technique." Based in Schaffhausen, the Manufacture he heads can pride itself on having all three.

"To really be a great brand, you must have a history, a design and technique"

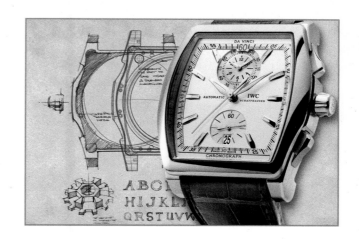

As it prepares to celebrate the 140th anniversary of the brand, founded in Switzerland by the American Florentine Ariosto Jones, under Kern's leadership IWC has experience impressive growth that shows not only in the company's ledger, but also in its fundamentals: a modern industrial facility, revealing the dynamism of the company, but also ever-increasing numbers of "proprietary" movements that power these timepieces so highly prized by collectors.

The latest of these is the impressive Caliber 89360, the first chronograph movement entirely conceived, developed and produced by the IWC manufacture. This movement sparked the launch of the new Da Vinci collection, which has been completely redesigned. "Da Vinci was a real classic of our manufacture," says Kern, "but we had to rejuvenate it. The name is magic, so we had to create a case worthy of the name. We've drawn upon the tonneau shape for the new lines of this collection, which has met with impressive success since its launch." This new version of the Da Vinci will shake the dust from the previous incarnation, popular almost exclusively in Germanic markets. "The new Da Vinci is meant not only for connoisseurs interested in the technical side," underscores Kern, "but also for the large number of people interested in design. And, of course, fans of manufacture-made movements. Considered in this light, our

FACING PAGE
Georges Kern.

THIS PAGE
TOP
New tonneau shapes for the Da Vinci collection.

BOTTOM
Exploded view of the chronograph mechanism in the proprietary Caliber 89360.

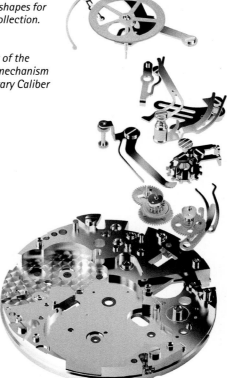

TOP
For those who love to fly first class, the rose-gold version of IWC's Pilot's Watch Chrono-Automatic is certainly a temptation.

BOTTOM
Three available versions of the Da Vinci chronograph.

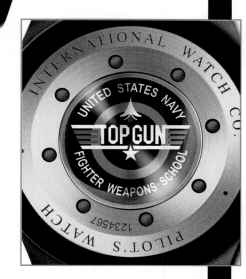

new chronograph has already proven its broad appeal!"

Proprietary caliber

Produced by Killian Eisenegger and his team of watchmakers, this new round-shaped automatic chronograph movement from IWC—which also has a flyback function and a 68-hour power reserve—shows a certain family resemblance with the manufacture's other calibers. One such similarity is the Pellaton winding system, already improved for the Caliber 80111 and further modified for this occasion. This innovation is the subject of a new patent: instead of the usual two pawls, there are two double pawls, four in total, which transmit the rotor's energy through the movements of pulling and pushing that work on the pawl wheel. The new position of the pawls improves efficiency by about 30%. The system that prevents backwards movement, with a Nivarox balance spring developed specially and exclusively for IWC, provides a superior oscillation for less energy consumption. Fine adjustment is made by means of precision screws placed around the outer rim (or felly) of the balance-wheel.

Another striking element of the new Caliber 89360 is its chronograph movement with flyback function, actuated via a classic column wheel, which permits the aggregate time recording of hours and minutes in the familiar form of an analog time display with two hands in a counter at 12:00. This system makes reading these times much easier than usual. It can also function at the same time as the watch's movement without losing any amplitude.

The production of this new chronograph Calibre 89360 will slowly increase at Schaffhausen, but obviously, no one should expect it to power all the brand's chronographs in the short term.

President of IWC North America

Benoit de Clerck

THIS PAGE
Benoit de Clerck.

THIS AND FACING PAGE
A bundle of energy for fans of
technical refinement with the
Spitfire Double Chronograph.

Globally, the luxury sector has been doing very well for several years in the United States, "and IWC is a euphoric brand right now," according to Benoit de Clerck, president of IWC North America. "We have had fabulous growth here, and everything indicates that this trend will continue in the years to come."

"IWC is a euphoric brand right now"

How are you handling distribution?

We have maintained a very selective distribution, with about 100 retail stores on American soil. But now we're working towards a geographical development of the brand. We're performing analyses aimed at the potential of certain cities or regions. That's also something that interests me about the United States: the immensity of it all. The stakes are enormous—there are cities within cities, villages of 300,000 inhabitants! This means that there is still an enormous potential in terms of distribution. We are also developing our presence in retail outlets by opening a lot of brand "corners" in stores. The results are impressive: as soon as we put a kiosk in place, we generally double sales. Through the dedicated "corners", the client begins to identify more with the brand; it's like we've brought a little of our Manufacture in Schaffhausen to the client.

Will you also be developing a network of your own retail stores?

IWC has an excellent reputation, but we still need to work on name recognition of the brand and reinforce its image. That's why we are planning to open several boutiques in America. After Las Vegas, we've planned openings in Los Angeles, Miami, New York and Dallas.

Americans are open, curious, always ready to discover something new. This mentality is all to the good of horology, which is certainly just in its infancy here. The potential is vast, as American culture, knowledge and interest in watchmaking are exploding right now. IWC has other arguments to make in our favor as well: the founder of the company was American, and you can see that in the brand's DNA. We are a brand whose image and whose products correspond perfectly to the demand of an American clientele that is young, educated, rich and passionately interested.

Are some products more suited than others to the American market?

Quite honestly, all of our collections have been successful in the United States. The advantage is that the target market is 300 million people. We've noticed very small differences among the regions; for example, we sell more Aquatimers on the coasts, but that makes sense.

What about the Pilot's Watch Double Chronograph Top Gun Edition?

We hadn't even received the first samples before they were all pre-sold. Black, imposing, with its high-tech ceramic 46mm case, and its commands in titanium, this piece corresponds perfectly to a certain American clientele that is looking for exclusive, technical and very distinctive watches. IWC is also the only Swiss brand to have an agreement with the US Navy. It's more than a symbol, it's the recognition of quality, reliability and resistance of IWC's pilot's watches, which include, you might recall, the Classic and Spitfire lines that carry the inscription "flight qualified." Given this context, you can understand why the Pilot's Double Chronograph Top Gun Edition, whose production is limited because of the complexity of producing the black ceramic case, is already a classic that is winning over watch lovers.

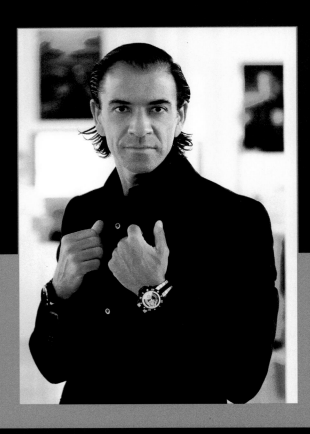

President and CEO of Zenith

Thierry Nataf

Defy Xtreme Open
El Primero Gold
and Titanium

At Zenith, the chronograph occupies a central place among the complications whose secrets the Manufacture knows inside and out. Introduced in 1969, the El Primero movement is at the foundation of this legend. Unequalled since its launch, it is the only horological motor to beat the speed record of 36,000 vibrations per hour. When the brand reintroduced it in 2001, Thierry Nataf, the current CEO, decided to reveal the under-exploited potential of this movement.

"The value of a chronograph stems from its power and its speed"

"There are a thousand faces to a chronograph," marvels Thierry Nataf, CEO of Zenith. "At first technical and virile, this adaptable complication is enjoying growing success. Women in particular are responding to it, and they are no longer concealing their interest in the chronograph. At Zenith, we've answered the call by creating 'His watch for her,' an entire collection that adapts the most technical pieces in our catalog to the feminine form."

For Nataf, who also heads Zenith's design department, the chronograph is first and foremost a concentration of power and energy. "The value of a chronograph stems from its power and its speed, two factors that ensure its precision. Our El Primero caliber beats at 36,000 vibrations per hour and can consequently measure times as short as one-tenth of a second. This super-fast cadence has allowed it to become a touchstone of the genre. Many competitors have tried to copy it, but its performance has never been equaled."

The idea of the Open

When he took the reins of Zenith in 2001, Nataf was intent on highlighting the caliber's rhythmic movement. He invented the Open concept, which involved a cutout in the dial to reveal the intricate motion of the escapement wheel.

FACING PAGE
Thierry Nataf,
President and CEO
of Zenith.

THIS PAGE
The Defy Xtreme Open
El Primero Gold and
Titanium is powered
by the next-
generation El Primero
movement 4021 SX,
which is mounted on
a rose-gold baseplate.

Grande Class Open
eller Multicity
ains a 24-hour
-zone system,
ding a day/night
ator.

Providing an unexpected peephole into the movement, this cutout was to enjoy a huge success among connoisseurs and was soon be applied to different collections. Certain pieces were released, such as the Grande Class Open Traveller Multicity, which features a 24 time-zone system, including a day/night indicator. Another groundbreaking creation, the ChronoMaster Open El Primero Retrograde, displays a power-reserve indicator and an instantaneous retrograde date in addition to its chronograph.

Although conscious of the fact that he is leading a brand with a rich and prestigious history, Nataf has no intention of fixating on the brand's legacy. "From 2001 to 2003," he says, "I introduced some very classic collections. In using the language of the past, I wanted to show that beauty never dies. Since then, I've integrated extremely modern elements into my work, while ensuring a continuity with everything that precedes it. This process is a delicate balance to achieve, but it allows Zenith to innovate and continue to contribute something to watchmaking history."

The Defy collection

Embodying this leap into the future, Zenithium® emerged from the brand's research and development laboratories in 2006. A mate-

rial developed by and exclusive to the manufacture, it combines titanium, aluminum and niobium for a resistance three times that of steel. Light and possessing a "shape memory," it completely the perfect choice for the demanding new Defy Classic and Defy Xtreme collections. Marrying sport-chic and mechanical revolution, these two lines now constitute must-haves in the Zenith range.

Public Prize

Last November, watch lovers rewarded Nataf for his strategic choices by awarding him the Public Prize for most popular watch at the Geneva Watchmaking Grand Prix. The model that won this accolade, the Defy Xtreme Open Stealth, perfectly illustrates this successful alliance between traditional savoir-faire and Nataf's futuristic technologies. "This watch has benefited from the accumulated experience of a manufacture that is over a century and a half old, as well as from the most modern technologies," states Nataf. "This blend of eras has made it a piece of science fiction." This prize also concluded a year, 2007, that Nataf described as "absolutely outstanding," adding that Zenith "is once again one of the world's top ten watch brands."

President and CEO of TAG Heuer

Jean-Christophe Babin

Calibre 360 & Grand Carrera

As can now be seen at the new "TAG Heuer 360 Museum" in La-Chaux-de-Fonds, the brand's rich history attests to its deep-felt attachment to the world of sports and the measurement of very short units of time. In fact, the chronograph is inscribed in TAG Heuer's very DNA, and the latest achievements by the company in this realm suggest that the future holds new surprises for all those who love speed and ways of measuring time.

"The chronograph is the very essence of time measurement"

A trip though the "TAG Heuer 360 Museum" leads the visitor to discover or rediscover the path of the Neuchâtel brand, dotted with countless milestone innovations. Opened in La Chaux-de-Fonds in January 2008, with Formula 1 star Lewis Hamilton in attendance, the museum offers visitors a fascinating audiovisual experience. An historic yet avant-garde gallery that pays tribute to the glory of the brand's heritage, featuring an unexpected architectural conception and circular panorama, the museum draws upon 150 years of an horological saga dedicated to mastering infinitely small lapses of time. Whether interested in sports timekeeping or wristwatches, visitors will find a stunning array of technical and esthetic innovations that have marked essential stages in the history of Swiss watchmaking.

In this same context, Jean-Christophe Babin, President and CEO of TAG Heuer, likes to recall that "the chronograph is one of the most difficult complications to produce, from a technical standpoint. When a movement is composed of 250 or 400 components, you can already see how difficult it can be. But the chronograph requires the simultaneous mastery of a certain number of extremely complex interactions. For example, in the case of the Calibre 360, one must be able to synchronize 1/100 of a second with the second, the minutes and the hours. That might appear

FACING PAGE
Jean-Christophe Babin.

THIS PAGE
The new Grand Carrera
chronograph beats to the rhythm
of the 17 RS caliber.

LEFT
Grand Carrera Chronographe: its evolution shows the esthetic that has made the Carrera collection a TAG Heuer icon.

RIGHT
The new "TAG Heuer 360 Museum," in La Chaux-de-Fonds.

BOTTOM
The F1 driver Lewis Hamilton came to the inauguration of the brand's new museum, and signed a mural that bore his likeness.

simple, but I can assure you that the designers of this type of movement have used all their knowledge and experience to perfect these marvels of miniaturization."

Faithful to its history, TAG Heuer scored another coup in 2005 when it introduced the prototype of the "Calibre 360 Concept Chronograph," the first mechanical chronograph wristwatch accurate to 1/100 of a second. This performance is made possible through the fusion of two independent movements, the second of which (powering the chronograph) beats at a frequency of 360,000 vibrations per hour! This cutting-edge movement was then offered in a rose-gold limited edition of the Carrera model, a legendary chronograph first introduced in 1964. "For TAG Heuer, this new milestone, this new historical advance in short-time measurement, was fundamental, as here we are getting to the very essence of horology, which is the measurement of time."

Trivialized at times, the chronograph is often underrated in the realm of complications. Jean-Christophe Babin deplores this, saying, "We speak too rarely about the chronograph in terms of complications, but it is in fact an extreme complication. And maybe, as the world leader in chronographs, TAG Heuer should emphasize this more."

The chronograph was still TAG Heuer's star attraction in 2007, and is this year as well, with the introduction of models in the new Grand Carrera collection. Innovative and contemporary, the collection stems from TAG Heuer's classic Carrera collection, launched in 1964 by Jack Heuer—now Honorary Chairman of the company—and continually reinvented ever since, to the point of becoming the brand icon. The new Grand Carrera embodies the ties woven between the brand and the world of automobile racing, as well as the watchmaker's passion for modern design and technologies. These new top-of-the-line models are unique for their displays, which include one or two windows with rotating disks that power the brand's exclusive developments. These original displays are powered by the 6 RS (Rotating System), 8 RS and 17 RS calibers. The rotating disks, the collection's signature, are underscored on their dial side by a metallic piece that is decorated with Côtes de Genève and facetted, an allusion to the interior mechanics of the piece. The Grand Carrera chronograph, in a steel Ø 43mm case, houses the 17 RS caliber with indication of hours, minutes, small seconds via a rotating disk at 3:00, chronograph seconds, date in a window at 6:00, and 60-minute chronograph counter via a rotating disk at 9:00. Jean-Christophe Babin, CEO of TAG Heuer, emphasized at the launch that, with regards to strategy, the Grand Carrera collec-tion does not mean the brand is becoming more upscale and exclusive; rather, it is an extension of what they have to offer. That means that the Formula 1, which has a quartz movement and an entry price point for the brand, will continue to have its role.

Innovation 2008, the Grand Carrera Calibre 17 RS2 chronograph, with its racecar-influenced design, presents a chassis in grade 2 titanium (Ti2), a pure, ultra-resistant, biocompatible metal that is half the weight of steel. The matte black strap in "soft touch" rubber-coated alligator leather and the curved lugs ensure maximum comfort on the wrist. This competition-worthy model has also been treated to a black titanium treatment, to avoid any scratches in case of shock. In esthetic terms, the use of red on the seconds hand, as well as on the crown, the stitching and the underside of the strap, provides some interesting visual touches. Driven, like the other models in the collection, by a COSC-certified chronometer movement, the Grand Carrera 17 RS2 is produced in a limited edition of 1,000 pieces. There won't be enough for everybody!

Chronographs

The chronograph is on a roll. There's never been such a bumper harvest of new models, new indications and new in-house calibers that set themselves apart from what came before—mostly from the same supplier. Despite this abundance, one shouldn't forget that the chronograph is a sophisticated mechanism, especially in its most noble version—the column-wheel chronograph. The many novelties in looks and technology of recent years show that this practical complication can still amaze enthusiasts of fine mechanisms.

The complication of our times

With the exception of multiple time zones, the chronograph is the youngest of the complications in the classical watchmaking repertory. Before watches could record elapsed times they had to reach a certain level of precision. Watchmakers also had to devise a way of stopping and starting the hand without affecting the rate of the movement. The breakthrough came in 1776 with the first watch with "independent dead seconds"— a mechanism recently revived in Audemars Piguet Millenary wristwatches, which are fitted with an unconventional oil-free escapement exclusive to the company. The first true chronograph appeared in 1822. The hand recorded the elapsed time to the fifth of a second by marking the dial with a spot of ink. This "time writer" thus got its name, chronograph, from the Greek words chronos—time—and graphos—write. Around the mid-century chronographs could zero their hands as well.

1 *Omega, Speedmaster*
The Speedmaster accompanied the astronauts of July 1969 on their first historic moon landing, hence its nickname of "moonwatch." Shown is the commemorative limited-edition model produced to mark the watch's 50th anniversary in 2007.

2 *Audemars Piguet, Millenary à seconde morte*
The Millenary Deadbeat Seconds features a brand-new escapement system, exclusive to Audemars Piguet, that functions without lubrication.

3 *Rolex, Cosmograph Daytona*
Zenith's famous El Primero movement used to beat in the mythic Cosmograph Daytona, before Rolex created its own chronograph movement at the dawn of the third millennium.

4 *Breitling, Navitimer*
Breitling's Navitimer (1952) has a circular slide rule that permits the wearer to perform all calculations related to aerial navigation.

5 *Zenith, Grande ChronoMaster Open El Primero*
Through an opening in the dial that reveals the beating heart of the watch, the Zenith manufacture has paid tribute to its finest creation in making the Grande ChronoMaster Open El Primero.

2

3

The first wrist-chronographs appeared around 1915. Like pocket-chronographs they had a single button for start, stop and zero. In 1934, Breitling gave the chronograph its current configuration by adding a second button for return to zero. In 1937, the Dubois-Dépraz workshops introduced a chronograph movement that was controlled by cams. It was cheaper and less difficult to manufacture than the traditional column-wheel mechanism. The chronograph embarked on a brilliant career which saw several celebrated models, including the 1952 Breitling Navitimer, with a circular slide rule for navigation, and the Omega Speedmaster, the so-called "moonwatch," which accompanied the American astronauts on their first lunar landing in July 1969.

1969 also saw the advent of the first two automatic chronograph movements. One, a cam-based modular mechanism developed by Breitling, Büren and Heuer-Leonidas working with Dubois-Dépraz, had a movement with an offset mini-rotor. Zenith's El Primero was the other—a column-wheel chronograph integrated with the movement, and a central rotor. With a balance frequency of 36,000 vph, it was also the first chronograph that could give a 1/10-second reading. In addition to equipping Zenith watches, the El Primero would also be fitted in some of the watches produced by other brands. It could be found in the legendary Cosmograph Daytona, for instance, before Rolex got around to developing its own chronograph movement at the end of the last millennium. The Zenith workshops have also paid tribute to their finest product in the Grande ChronoMaster Open El Primero, with an openwork dial revealing the fluttering heart of the watch.

The advent of the more precise quartz movements nearly killed the development of the mechanical chronograph, but it returned in style in the late 1980s with the revival of mechanical watchmaking. Let us remember, however that the brands or even manufacturers producing their own chronographs were few; the bulk of the mechanical chronographs under various signatures had been equipped with ETA's Valjoux 7750 movement in various guises and sold at prices that are sometimes hard to justify.

▶▶ *1   Maurice Lacroix, Masterpiece
       Le Chronograph ML 106*
       *Maurice Lacroix confirmed its high-end
       status by introducing the Masterpiece
       Le Chronograph ML106, which contains
       the brand's first "proprietary" movement.*

▶▶ *2   Patek Philippe, Annual Calendar
       Chronograph Ref. 5960P*
       *In 2006, Patek Philippe introduced its
       Annual Calendar Chronograph Ref. 5960P,
       with a disk engagement system that
       includes a central seconds hand and a large
       counter with the hour and minute totalizers.*

▶▶ *3   Chopard, L.U.C Chrono One Concept Watch*
       *Chopard launched its own chronograph
       movement, the automatic caliber L.U.C
       10 CF, with a column wheel, vertical
       coupling-clutch system, flyback function
       and 60-hour power reserve, presented
       in the L.U.C Chrono One Concept Watch*

In-house is the trend

Things are nevertheless changing. A better-informed public might be willing to pay the price demanded by a reputable brand, so long it has an exclusive movement or at least something original. The announcement by the head of the Swatch Group regarding restrictions on the deliveries of ETA movements also incited competition to find alternative solutions. The last few years have seen the increasing development of in-house chronograph movements featuring novel ideas. In 2006, Patek Philippe introduced its self-winding Annual Calendar Chronograph, Ref. 5960P, with a disk clutch, allowing the chronograph hand to be used permanently for the running seconds. Chopard has also come out with its own chronograph movement: the self-winding L.U.C 10 CF with column-wheel, vertical clutch, instant restart and 60-hour power reserve. The movement appears in the L.U.C Chrono One Concept Watch. Maurice Lacroix pursues its up-market course with its first in-house movement in the Masterpiece Le Chronographe ML106. In 2007, Piaget also produced its own chronograph movement,

4

3

2

1

5

▶▶ *1* *Eberhard & Co, Chrono4 Temerario*
Chrono4 Temerario, by Eberhard & Co., completely reinvents the
chronograph display, with four counters aligned horizontally or vertically.

▶▶ *2* *Vulcain, Vulcanographe*
Vulcain, master of the alarm, has reunited with the chronograph through
its Vulcanographe, which boasts a column-wheel automatic movement,
second time zone and large date.

the Piaget 880P caliber, with a second 24-hour time zone and
instant restart, appearing initially in the Polo model. Parmigiani
Fleurier entered the sportswatch arena with the Kalpagraph,
its in-house movement fitted into an original form case with
interesting curves. Vulcain by HD3, the master of the alarm, has
also awoken to the call of the chronograph, introducing the
column-wheel Vulcanographe with a self-winding movement,
second time zone and large date.

New looks, materials and indications

Chronographs have long kept their conventional look with
three small symmetrically arranged subdials. This traditional
configuration has now been topped by several models trying
to reinvent the indication of time. Eberhard & Co. set the pace
with the Chrono4 and its four vertically or horizontally aligned
subdials. The retrograde indication has become popular as in
Gérald Genta's Arena Chrono Quattro Retro. The chronograph
has also developed with the advent of new high-performance
materials, which are not only tougher and lighter but also
transform the styling possibilities. Examples include Zenith's
Defy Xtreme collection or the Tourbillon Chronographe MC12

▶▶ *3* *Piaget, Polo Chronographe*
In 2007, Piaget also created
a chronograph movement, the Caliber
880P. With a second 24-hour time zone
and flyback function, the movement
powers the famous Polo model.

▶▶ *4* *Parmigiani Fleurier, Kalpagraph*
Parmigiani Fleurier has entered into
the universe of sports watches,
introducing the Kalpagraph, with
a movement housed inside a case
featuring highly original elliptical shapes.

▶▶ *5* *Gérald Genta, Arena Chrono
Quattro Retro*
The Arena Chrono Quattro Retro was
created with a retrograde display.

1 *Audemars Piguet, Tourbillon Chronograph MC12*
Audemars Piguet's Tourbillon MC12 Chronograph marries high-tech materials to a daring design inspired by the automotive universe.

2 *Jaeger-LeCoultre, AMVOX2 Chronograph Concept*
In 2006, the AMVOX2 Chronograph Concept by Jaeger-LeCoultre sparked a revolution in the chronograph world by reinventing the way of activating the commands: the traditional pushbuttons have been replaced by a system in which the case middle pivots gracefully around the 9:00 to 3:00 axis.

3 *TAG Heuer, Carrera Calibre 360 Or Rose*
In 2005, TAG Heuer scored a coup in presenting the prototype of the Calibre 360 Concept Chronograph, the first chronograph wristwatch with precision to 1/100 of a second.

4 *F.P. Journe, Centigraphe Souverain*
In 2007, with its Centigraphe Souverain, F.P. Journe repeated its achievement of measuring extremely small units of time, but in a different way: a single balance beating at 21,600 vph.

1

2

by Audemars Piguet, which combines high-tech materials with a bold design inspired by automobile styling. In 2006, the AMVOX2 Chronograph Concept by Jaeger-LeCoultre caused a stir in the world of chronographs by reinventing the control mechanism in which the traditional buttons have been replaced by a caseband that rocks on a horizontal axis. The user presses the glass at 12:00 to start and stop the chronograph, and at 6:00 for a return to zero.

To the hundredth of a second
In 2005, TAG Heuer set high stakes when it unveiled the prototype of the Calibre 360 Concept Chronograph, the first mechanical wrist-chronograph with a 1/100-second readout. The exploit was achieved by combining two movements, one of which is dedicated to the chronograph and vibrates 360,000 times an hour. In 2007, François-Paul Journe matched the feat, but with a single 21,600 vph balance in his Centigraphe Souverain. The 1/100-second readout is on a flying-seconds subdial at 10:00; its tachometer scale allows speeds of up to 360,000km/h to be measured! The subdial at 2:00 records elapsed times of up to 20 seconds, and the subdial at 6:00 is a 10-minute recorder. F. P. Journe has also introduced a new start/stop control—a rocker at 2:00 that is said to be more ergonomic than the conventional buttons.

3

4

The era of the mono-counter

A number of watchmakers have followed Patek Philippe in abandoning the traditional small separate counters for the elapsed minutes and hours in favor of a mono-counter combining both indications. The idea is that the elapsed time is easier to grasp as if it is presented like the time of day. One example is the IWC Da Vinci Chronographe, featuring a new tonneau case and a new proprietary chronograph movement. In its Duomètre chronograph presented in 2007, Jaeger-LeCoultre brought out a novel movement construction with two autonomous gear trains, one for the time of day (gold hands) and the other for the chronograph (blue hands). They are synchronized by a single balance. The elapsed hours and minutes are shown on a single subdial at between 2:00 and 3:00, while a flying seconds hand at 6:00 stops on divisions of 1/6 second. Pierre DeRoche makes elapsed times even easier in its SplitRock, which has an exclusive Dubois-Dépraz caliber presenting coaxial chronograph hours, minutes and seconds hands.

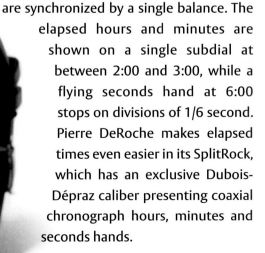

▶▶ 5-6 *Jaeger-LeCoultre, Duomètre à Chronographe*
With its new Duomètre à Chronographe, introduced in 2007, Jaeger-LeCoultre has invented a new concept of constructing a movement, with two independent mechanisms, one for the hours (with golden hands) and one for the chronograph (with blue hands), synchronized by the same regulating organ.

▶▶ 7 *IWC, Da Vinci Chronograph*
IWC's Da Vinci Chronograph features a new tonneau-shaped case and a new IWC-made chronograph movement.

▶▶ 8 *Pierre DeRoche, Splitrock*
Pierre DeRoche, with its SplitRock, goes even further in facilitating reading by offering a chronograph with three concentric hour/minute/seconds hands, boasting an exclusive Dubois Dépraz caliber.

1   *Maurice Lacroix, Mémoire1*
Maurice Lacroix prepares to introduce in 2008 its Mémoire1, the first mechanical watch with "memory," featuring two hands (minutes and seconds) as well as an hour-display disk.

2   *TAG Heuer, New Aquaracer Calibre S*
The three central hands of the New Aquaracer Calibre S display either the classic hours/minutes/seconds, the hours/minutes/seconds of chronometer time, or the minutes/seconds left in the "regatta" countdown.

3   *Porsche Design Indicator by Eterna*
On the Porsche Design Indicator chronograph by Eterna, the hours and minutes of chronometer time are displayed in a mechanical "digital" mode, with the help of rotating disks in a double window at 3:00.

4   *Ebel, 1911 BTR (Calibre 139)*
To enhance readability, the traditional small minute counter on the 1911 BTR by Ebel has been replaced by a 120° arc-shaped window with a three-arm red hand.

1

2

3

4

Two in one

Other pioneering brands have decided to use the same hands to indicate the time of day and the elapsed chrono times. One example is TAG Heuer's quartz-regulated New Aquaracer Calibre S. The three central hands show the conventional or the elapsed hours, minutes and seconds, or the minutes and seconds of countdown to the start of a sailing regatta. The three functions are selected by pushing the crown. Maurice Lacroix is getting ready to launch its Mémoire1 in 2008—the first mechanical watch with a "memory," with two hands for the minutes and seconds and a disk for the hours. Pressing a button in the crown switches from "time" mode to "chrono"; a third press brings the hands back to the exact time. You can change between functions even when the chronograph is running. Web surfers have been able to follow the development of the revolutionary caliber, containing 537 parts, including nine heart-pieces, on www.memoire1.ch.

Disk fever

To give dials a different look and to vary the readouts, watchmakers are resorting increasingly to disks. In Eterna's Porsche Design Indicator, the hours and minutes of elapsed time are in numerals on disks revolving beneath a double window at 3:00. The Grand Carrera Calibre 17RS by TAG Heuer—a highlight of the 2007 collection—features the Rotating System which has the running seconds and the elapsed minutes shown on disks. In a nod to tradition, these two sector apertures are bordered in Geneva stripes. Equally original are the indications in Ebel's 1911 BTR selfwinding chronograph, powered by the caliber 139, a movement exclusive to the firm. To the information easier to read, the traditional small minutes counter has been replaced by a 120° arc at 12:00, in which three red hands rotate on a hub. To indicate elapsed hours it employs an underdial disk showing 1 to 12 through a window at 6:00.

TAG Heuer, Grand Carrera Calibre 17RS
The Grand Carrera Calibre 17RS by TAG Heuer presents two disk displays,
one for small seconds, the other for the chronograph minute counter.

1

The single-button chrono

Among the specialties can be seen a resurgence of the single button chronograph—a sophisticated construction since the single button has to start, stop and return to zero in sequence. Among the protagonists is Blancpain, with its Chronographe Monopoussoir Villeret. The Chronographe Monopoussoir Hommage La Chaux-de-Fonds 1738 by Jaquet Droz is the first timepiece of this kind with an hour counter as well as off-center hours and minutes. In 2007, Officine Panerai introduced three exclusive movements, including the caliber P.2004 eight-day, hand-wound single-button chronograph with time zone. Montblanc affirms its high-grade ambitions by offering two expensive, single-button chronographs in its Collection Villeret 1858 line. The movements are signed by Minerva, a high-class manufacturer acquired by the Richemont Group in 2006 and put at the disposal of Montblanc. In a more daring style, the Tourbillon Chronographe FVa N° 4 by Franc Vila is remarkable for having the chronograph mechanism under the dial, revealing the operation of the direct clutch as well as the ballet of the timekeeping functions.

Time for women

Another strong trend of the early millennium has been the abundance of chronographs for women. They come in gentle colors, with crafted dials and even with diamonds, as if they were dress watches. In its Baby Doll Star Open Sea with an El Primero movement, Zenith blends mother-of-pearl, sharkskin and a decoration of stars. Girard-Perregaux also offers a fine combination of good looks and smart skills in its lady-sized, self-winding, column-wheel "Petite chronographe à roue à colonnes."

2

3

4

5

6

Split-seconds chronographs

Split-seconds chronographs have two elapsed seconds hands, one of which can be stopped independently to record an intermediary or reference time. A touch of a button makes the split hand catch up with the main chronograph hand and run concurrently with it. The highly sophisticated clutch work is one of watchmaking's most difficult complications, ranking with the minute repeater or tourbillon.

Girard-Perregaux, Chronographe à rattrapante Vintage 1945 XXL Foudroyante

Girard-Perregaux has given its Chronographe à rattrapante Vintage 1945 XXL Foudroyante a "jumping seconds" hand that circles the entire subdial in one second, enabling read-off of times as short as 1/8 of a second.

1 **A.Lange&Söhne, Tourbograph Pour Le Merite**
In its Tourbograph Pour le Mérite, A. Lange & Söhne adds to the split-seconds chronograph two of the most complex mechanisms ever conceived, designed to enhance the precision of the movement: a tourbillon and a fusée-chaîne transmission system that guarantees a regular transfer of energy.

2 **Patek Philippe, Chronographe à rattrapante Réf.5959**
In 2005, Patek Philippe presented the thinnest column-wheel split-seconds chronograph ever made (5.25mm) with a two-pushbutton system (instead of the usual three) and several patented characteristics.

3-4 **A.Lange&Söhne, Lange Double Split**
The German brand has also innovated in presenting the Lange Double Split, the first wristwatch chronograph with split seconds and split minutes.

5 **Blancpain, Chronographe monopoussoir à rattrapante «Villeret»**
Blancpain faced several challenges in creating a single-pusher split-seconds chronograph for the Villeret collection. It has two pushbuttons, one for the three chronograph functions, the other for the split seconds.

6 **IWC, Montre d'aviateur Double Chronographe**
In its Double Chronograph Pilot's Watch, IWC houses a movement in a high-tech scratch-resistant ceramic case, equipped with an interior cage in anti-magnetic pure iron.

7 **Dubey&Schaldenbrand, Spiral-Sixty**
The "mobile index" is a simplified form of the split seconds, limited to measuring times under a minute. Dubey & Schaldenbrand brought this original system back into the spotlight, notably in its new model,Spiral-Sixty.

Invented in 1838, the split-seconds chronograph is one of the great demonstrations of watchmaking skill. All the top brands thus have an interest in including a split chrono in their catalogs. In 2005, Patek Philippe produced the thinnest split-seconds columns-wheel chronograph (5.25mm high), operated by two, instead of the usual three, buttons and featuring a number of patented devices. In its Tourbograph Pour le Mérite, A. Lange & Söhne supports its split-seconds chronograph with two of the most complex precision devices, the tourbillon and the fusee and chain, which delivers regular torque to the escapement. The brand from Saxony, Germany, has also been inventive in producing the Lange Double Split, the first chronograph with two split hands, one with the minutes counter and the other with the chronograph seconds. Girard-Perregaux has fitted its Vintage 1945 XXL Foudroyante split-seconds chronograph with a flying seconds, which goes around its subdial in one second, stopping to the eighth of a second. Blancpain has compounded its difficulties to launch a single-button chronograph with a split-seconds hand controlled by a second button. For its Montre d'aviateur Double Chronographe, IWC has fitted the mechanisms within a high-tech scratchproof ceramic case equipped with an antimagnetic shield of mild steel inside.

6

Split seconds made simple

Introduced in 1946 by Georges Dubey, co-founder of the Dubey & Schaldenbrand brand, the index mobile is a simplified type of split seconds limited to elapsed times of less than a minute. The chronograph seconds and the split seconds hands are linked by a spiral spring, visible on the face of the watch. The split-seconds hand remains stopped as long as the button is held down; as soon as it is released, the spring makes it catch up with the chronograph seconds. Dubey & Schaldenbrand has returned this original mechanism to the limelight, notably in its Spiral-Sixty model.

SPIRAL RATTRAPANTE

7

1

2

3

4

5

Regatta chronographs

The run-up to the 32nd America's Cup, which took place in Spain in early summer 2007, saw an outpouring of "regatta" watches and chronographs. These are characterized by a countdown feature to the starting gun of the race. Omega, in tribute to its partner, Emirates Team New Zealand, launched the Seamaster NZL-32, with a two successive five-minute countdowns indicated by five hollow spheres and a counter at 3:00. On Louis Vuitton's Tambour LV Cup Régate, spinnaker-shaped apertures have replaced the round windows.

1 **TAG Heuer, Aquaracer Calibre S**
TAG Heuer interpreted its ingenious Aquaracer Calibre S (see "Chronographs" chapter) in a version called "Aquaracer Chronograph Calibre S China Team Limited Edition."

2 **Louis Vuitton, Tambour LV Cup Régate**
As official timekeeper of America's Cup, Louis Vuitton introduced the Tambour LV Cup Régate to mark the occasion.

3 **Omega, Seamaster NZL-32**
In tribute to its partner Emirates Team New Zealand, Omega launched its Seamaster NZL-32.

4 **Audemars Piguet, Royal Oak Offshore Alinghi Team chronograph**
Partnered with the Swiss champion, Audemars Piguet developed the Royal Oak Offshore Alinghi Team chronograph in forged carbon.

5 **Rolex, Oyster Perpetual Yacht-Master II**
In 2007, Rolex reaffirmed its unique standing in the sailing world by launching the Oyster Perpetual Yacht-Master II.

6 **Glashütte Original, PanoRetroGraph**
The PanoRetroGraph by Glashütte Original has the unusual quality of being able to measure time "in both directions."

7 **Girard-Perregaux, Laureato Regatta**
Match racing and haute horology make a perfect team at Girard-Perregaux—associated with BMW Oracle Racing—as is admirably illustrated by the Laureato Regatta single-pusher tourbillon chronograph.

6

Among the countdown chronographs, the German brand, Glashütte Original, was the first to introduce a chronograph that counts both up and down. Its PanoRetroGraph also has an instant restart function, which starts a new timing period with the press of the button at 4:00, eliminating the need to stop the chronograph and return it to zero.

Audemars Piguet, partner of the winning boat, presented the Royal Oak Offshore Alinghi Team chronograph with a minute-countdown window, central seconds and an instant-restart function that starts the chronograph again as soon as it is zeroed, allowing successive legs of a race to be timed. All this comes in a high-tech case of forged carbon. Girard-Perregaux, rooting for BMW Oracle Racing, created the Laureato Regatta, a single-button tourbillon chronograph, with a central hand for the minutes countdown. TAG Heuer has evolved its ingenious Aquaracer Calibre S into a version dubbed Aquaracer Chronograph Calibre S China Team Limited Edition, in support of its partner, the first challenger from China. Rolex asserted its rank in the sailing world with the launch of the Oyster Perpetual Yacht-Master II. Its clever combination of bezel, crown and button allows the user to track the countdown with a large hand tipped by a red triangle.

7

A. LANGE & SÖHNE

DATOGRAPH

A benchmark in the construction of superb mechanical chronographs, A. Lange & Söhne's Datograph houses the manually wound Caliber L951.1 chronograph movement with a frequency of 18,000 oscillations per hour and consisting of 90 meticulously hand-finished parts. The watch features a precise jumping minute counter with a stepped pinion, flyback mechanism, column-wheel chronograph and Lange outsized date with rapid date adjustment. The flyback mechanism allows the user to reset the chronograph hands to zero during an ongoing time measurement and to start a new measurement simply by releasing the pushpiece again, thereby eliminating the stop, reset and restart action.

A. LANGE & SÖHNE

THE LANGE DOUBLE SPLIT

This model features two rattrapante hands: one for the seconds and one for the minutes to be stopped. The chronograph and rattrapante hands are flyback hands. With the Lange Double Split, comparative lap measurements of up to 30 minutes are possible for the first time. A. Lange & Söhne has filed for a patent for the disengagement mechanism that allows the chronograph sweep seconds hand to continue revolving while the rattrapante sweep seconds hand is stopped. A true technological achievement, the watch is also equipped with a balance wheel (developed in-house) equipped with poising weights instead of inertia screws. The balance spring is not attached to a hairspring stud, but instead is secured by a balance-spring clamp for which a separate patent registration has been filed. The manually wound, 465-part Caliber L001.1 has 40 jewels.

A. LANGE & SÖHNE

THE LANGE DOUBLE SPLIT MOVEMENT

The A. Lange & Söhne Caliber L001.1 manually wound movement is precision adjusted in five positions and features plates and bridges made from untreated cross-laminated German silver. It houses 465 parts and 40 jewels, and is the world's first flyback chronograph with double rattrapante, controlled by classic column wheels. Other functions include jumping chronograph minute counter and rattrapante minute counter, flyback function, disengagement mechanism, hours, minutes, small seconds with stop seconds, power-reserve indicator, tachometer scale, and lap-time measurements between 1/6th of a second and 30 minutes.

AUDEMARS PIGUET

LADY ROYAL OAK OFFSHORE SELF-WINDING CHRONOGRAPH

REF. 26048SK.ZZ.D066CA.01

The stainless steel Lady Royal Oak Offshore Chronograph is topped with a bezel set with 32 brilliant-cut diamonds (1.25 carats) and clad in plum rubber on matching strap. The timepiece features hours, minutes, date and chronograph. The Royal Oak Offshore logo is engraved on the caseback and its plum dial features a Royal Oak Mega Tapisserie guilloché pattern with 8 polished cabochon hour markers. Supplied with gemstone certification.

AUDEMARS PIGUET

LADY ROYAL OAK OFFSHORE SELF-WINDING CHRONOGRAPH

REF. 26048OK.ZZ.D010CA.01

The pink-gold Lady Royal Oak Offshore Chronograph is topped with a bezel set with 32 brilliant-cut diamonds (1.25 carats) and clad in white rubber on matching strap. The timepiece features hours, minutes, date and chronograph. The Royal Oak Offshore logo is engraved on the case and its white dial features a Royal Oak Mega Tapisserie guilloché pattern with 8 polished cabochon hour markers. Supplied with gemstone certification.

AUDEMARS PIGUET

LADY ROYAL OAK OFFSHORE CHRONOGRAPH - REF. 26092OK.ZZ.D080CA.01

This 18K pink-gold Lady Royal Oak Offshore Chronograph in chocolate brown, with bezel, case and lugs set with brilliant-cut diamonds (5.9 carats), features hours, minutes, sweep seconds hand, 30-minute and 12-hour counters, date and chronograph. The Royal Oak Offshore logo is engraved on the caseback and its dial features a Royal Oak Mega Tapisserie guilloché pattern, with 8 diamond hour-markers. Supplied with gemstone certification.

AUDEMARS PIGUET

ROYAL OAK CHRONOGRAPH - REF. 25960OR.00.1185OR.01

This Royal Oak Chronograph houses the self-winding Caliber 2385 with rhodium-plated 18K gold rotor, Côtes de Genève decorative pattern and circular graining. Protected by a sapphire crystal, the dial is made with an exclusive, traditional, engine-turned Grande Tapisserie decorative pattern and displays the hours, minutes, date, and chronograph functions.

AUDEMARS PIGUET

ROYAL OAK CHRONOGRAPH - REF. 26068BA.ZZ.D088CR.01

Cased in diamond-pavé yellow gold, this Royal Oak Chronograph is set with a total of 449 brilliant-cut diamonds (4.04 carats). Its self-winding Caliber 2385 features a rhodium-plated 18K gold rotor, Côtes de Genève decorative pattern and circular graining. The diamond-pavé dial displays hours, minutes, date, cognac sapphire indexes, mother-of-pearl chronograph counters, and openworked gold hands under a sapphire crystal. Supplied with gemstone certification.

AUDEMARS PIGUET

ROYAL OAK OFFSHORE CHRONOGRAPH - REF. 26067BC.ZZ.D002CR.01

Bearing 341 brilliant-cut diamonds (5.86 carats), this white-gold Royal Oak Offshore Chronograph houses the self-winding Caliber 2840. The movement features a rhodium-plated 21K gold rotor, Côtes de Genève decorative pattern and circular graining. The diamond-pavé dial displays hours, minutes, date, satin-brushed chronograph counters and luminescent gold hands. The diamond-pavé case is fitted with a sapphire crystal. Supplied with gemstone certification.

AUDEMARS PIGUET

ROYAL OAK OFFSHORE ALINGHI TEAM - REF. 26062FS.OO.A002CA.01

The Royal Oak Offshore Alinghi Team features an exclusive and ultra-light material: forged carbon. The Royal Oak Offshore Alinghi team is equipped with a regatta "flyback" function and a countdown device specially designed for regatta starts. Limited series of 1,300.

AUDEMARS PIGUET

ROYAL OAK OFFSHORE CHRONOGRAPH - REF. 26170ST.OO.D305CR.01

Crafted in stainless steel, this Royal Oak Offshore displays hours, minutes, chronograph and date. The dial, with the exclusive Extra Grande Tapisserie pattern, bears luminescent hour-markers and hands. The Royal Oak Offshore Chronograph is mounted on a "Hornback" alligator strap with the AP folding clasp in steel. This watch is also available in brown (Ref. 2602ST.00.D091.CR.01).

BOVET

SPORT*STER* CHRONOGRAPH SAGUARO

The Sport*ster* 2007 Chronograph Saguaro has been entirely redeveloped with a new bezel, caseback and pushers. Now dressed in steel and red gold or blackened steel and red gold, it is one of the most innovative chronograph designs on the market. It is displayed in BOVET's classic Sport*ster* configuration of three subdials: hour and minute counters, and running seconds. The large date, the applied solid gold Art-Deco numerals, and the tachometer and pulsometer scales demonstrate that functionality need not compromise stylishness. The Saguaro is COSC certified and waterproof up to 1,000 feet underwater.

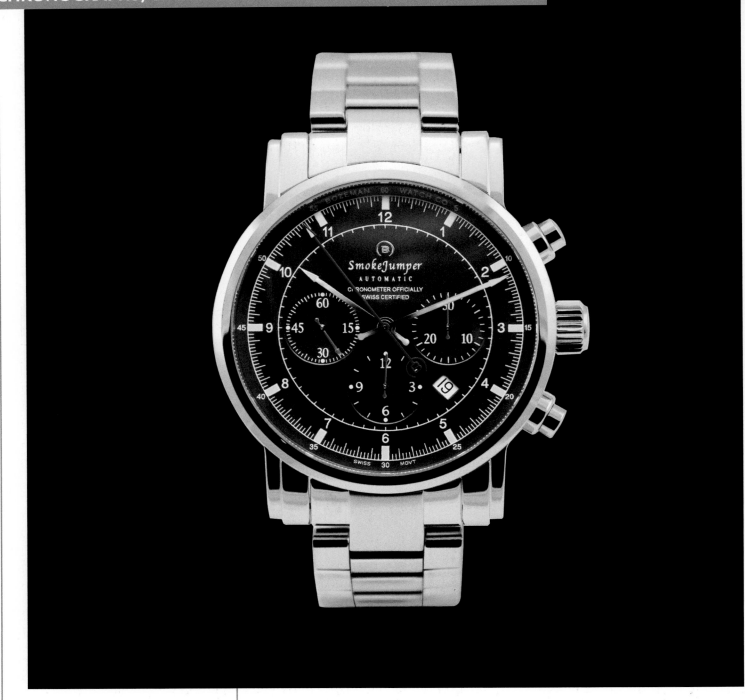

BOZEMAN WATCH CO.

SMOKEJUMPER - REF. 001

Smokejumper is the first model released by Bozeman Watch Co. Limited to 100 pieces, the chronograph features a mechanical automatic-winding ETA ValJoux caliber 7753 with 27 jewels and 28,800 vibrations per hour. Chronograph functions include: 30-minute counter at 3:00, 12-hour counter at 6:00 and automatic sweep second at 9:00. Also available on a tan or black leather strap, the Ø 45mm stainless steel Smokejumper is the official watch of the National SmokeJumper Association.

CLASSIQUE - REF. 5238BB/10/9V6 DD00

This Classique openworked chronograph is crafted in 18K white gold and houses a hand-wound movement with small seconds and 30-minute totalizer. The case features a bezel, lugs and caseband paved with 96 baguettes (approximately 13 carats).

BREGUET

CLASSIQUE - REF. 5947BA/12/9V6

This Classique split-seconds chronograph is crafted in 18K yellow or white gold and houses a manually wound movement with small seconds, compensating balance-spring with Breguet overcoil and 48-hour power reserve. Its gold dial, engine-turned and silvered, features a 30-minute elapsed-time counter at 3:00. Its case is enhanced with a sapphire caseback and is water resistant to 30 meters.

BREGUET

MARINE - REF. 5827BRZ25ZU

Encased in 18K rose gold and visible through a sapphire crystal caseback, a self-winding movement with 48-hour power reserve operates this Marine chronograph. Atop the black rhodium-plated dial in 18K gold—with a wave pattern hand-engraved on a rose engine—are: a chapter ring with Roman numerals; minutes expressed in Arabic numerals with 15-minute sector and luminous dots; center chronograph minutes and seconds; date-calendar aperture and 12-hour totalizer at 6:00; subseconds at 9:00. This Marine is water resistant to 100 meters and available in 18K yellow or white gold, on a leather strap or gold bracelet.

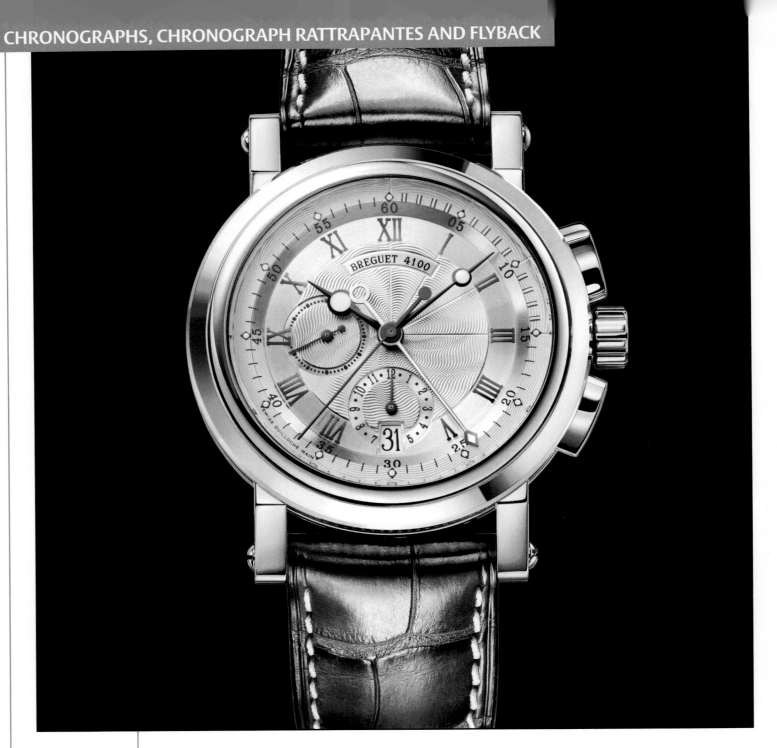

BREGUET

MARINE - REF. 5827BB/12/9Z8

This Marine chronograph is crafted in 18K white or yellow gold and houses a self-winding movement with date and small seconds. The silvered gold dial is hand-engraved on a rose-engine, has a 15-minute sector and features central chronograph minutes and seconds. The case features a sapphire caseback and a screw-locked crown, enabling water resistance to 100 meters. The model is available with bracelet as reference 5827BB/12/BZ0 or 5827BA/12/AZ0.

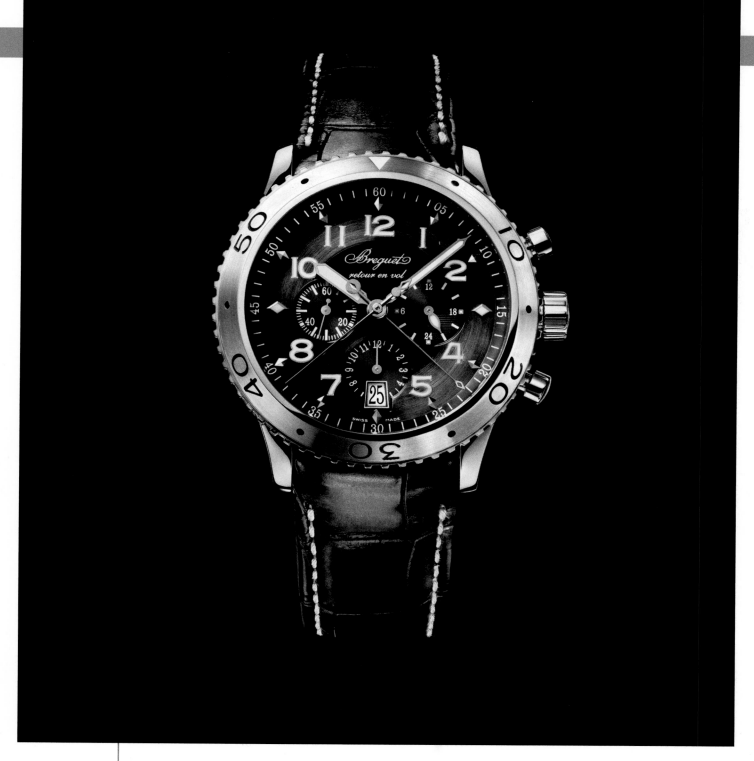

TYPE XXI - REF. 3810BR/92/9ZU

This Type XXI fly-back chronograph is crafted in 18K rose gold and its features include an elapsed-minutes register by a central hand, a self-winding movement with date and subdial for the seconds, a day/night indicator and 12-hour totalizer, while its dial is enhanced with luminous hands and hour-markers. Its case has a graduated turning bezel and screw-locked crown, enabling a water resistance to 100 meters.

BVLGARI

DIAGONO PROFESSIONAL SCUBA CHRONO - REF. SC40GVD

This large model 44mm COSC-certified chronometer has a mechanical automatic-winding movement with 42-hour power reserve, 49 jewels and 28,800 vph. Scuba Chrono displays date, central chronograph minute and second hands with fly-back function, and 24 hours indication. Shown in 18K yellow gold, the case has a counter-clockwise rotating bezel with graduated scale, screw-down crown and two pushbuttons; "Professional Diving" is engraved on its side. The dial is treated with a decorative pattern, 3 black azuré counters, hand-applied oversized indexes and numeral 12, rhodium-plated hour and minute hands coated with SuperLumiNova, a yellow central chronograph minute hand and a red central chronograph seconds hand with rhodium tip. The vulcanized rubber bracelet with 18K yellow-gold links is secured with an 18K yellow-gold déployante buckle. Water resistant to 300 meters.

DIAGONO PROFESSIONAL CHRONO RATTRAPPANTE - REF. CH40C6GLTARA

The Diagono Professional Chrono Rattrappante features an automatic-winding mechanical COSC-certified hand-decorated movement, with a 42-hour power reserve, 31 jewels and a vibration rate of 28,800 vph. Its functions include hours, minutes, small seconds, and split-second chronograph with hours, minutes and seconds. The 40mm brushed 18K yellow or white-gold case is fitted with an antireflective, scratch-resistant, sapphire crystal, a bezel with engraved tachometric scale, a security screw-down gold crown with case protection, gold pushbutton, a snap-on back, displaying the movement through a sapphire crystal, and is water resistant to 100 meters. The silver dial with vertical treatment displays 3 chronograph counters with gold-plated outline, hand-applied, gold-plated indexes with luminescent dots and luminescent, gold-plated hands, as well as a center second and split-second indication on the flange. The hand-sewn brown or black alligator straps are fitted with an 18K yellow- or white-gold triple-fold-over buckle.

CHOPARD

L.U.C CHRONO ONE CHRONOGRAPH - REF. 161916-1001

To mark the 10th anniversary of its creation, Chopard Manufacture wished to demonstrate its perfect mastery of haute horology by creating the L.U.C Chrono One chronograph. The result is a self-winding double-pusher chronograph, with two pushers handling chronograph start, stop and reset, as well as flyback function and small seconds reset on demand. The new L.U.C 10 CF caliber offers 60 hours of power reserve. This exceptional movement is housed in an 18K white-gold case and limited to a numbered series of 100.

CONCORD

CHRONOGRAPHE C1

The COSC-certified Concord C1 Chronograph marks the launch of a truly new construction born of an unusually sophisticated concept drawing on advanced technological research and innovation. This sinewy thoroughbred of a timepiece asserts its exceptional personality with an ambitious watch case 44mm in diameter and 16.7mm from front to back—a study in sturdiness at its best.

DANIEL ROTH

CHRONOGRAPH VINTAGE

In a limited edition of 40 pieces, this vintage edition is equipped with an El Primero column-wheel chronograph movement. It is an automatic chronograph with instantaneous date, hours, minutes and seconds counters, and 50 hours of power reserve. The watch is housed in white gold, and features a black laquered dial. It is water resistant to 10atm and rests on an alligator strap.

CHRONOGRAPH SÉQUENTIEL ACADEMIA - REF. AC.6005.28.M003

The Chronograph Séquentiel Academia is fitted with a DW 6005 mechanical self-winding movement, manufactured in the brand's workshops in Vandœuvres. This movement features 48 hours of power reserve and can be seen through a transparent sapphire caseback. It is housed in the Academia case with bezel and middle section engraved with the DeWitt Imperial Columns. This all-new version combines titanium with rose gold and black rubber. The black and gray engine-turned dial features a minute counter at 3:00 and the sequential seconds counter at 9:00; the seconds of the chronograph function are indicated by a central hand. This model is available on a black rubber strap stamped with the Imperial Columns motif. Water resistant to 30 meters, the watch is available in a limited series of 999 pieces.

GERALD GENTA

ARENA CHRONO QUATTRO RETRO - REF. ABC.Y.80.290.CN.BD

The Arena Chrono Quattro Retro features a self-winding manufactured chronograph movement offering a 45-hour power reserve and including a world premiere combination of a jumping-hour mechanism and four retrograde functions. The multi-layer perforated dial features a jumping hour, retrograde minutes and date, as well as two retrograde chronograph functions: hours and minutes. The movement is housed in a new titanium sport case with fluted caseband, screw-down beaded crown and two profiled chronograph pushpieces. This model is water resistant to 10atm.

GERALD GENTA

ARENA CHRONO QUATTRO RETRO GOLD - REF. ABC.Y.66.295.CN.BD

The Arena Chrono Quattro Retro Gold, features an exclusive self-winding chronograph movement entirely decorated by hand, with old-gold finish, It also offers a jumping hour, retrograde minutes and date, as well as a chronograph function with retrograde hour-counter at 9:00, retrograde minute-counter at 3:00 and large central seconds hand. It is housed in a polished white-gold case with fluted case middle, fluted gold pushbuttons and brushed-finish tantalum bezel, enhanced by a multi-level dial with satin-brushed counters, matte with holes for the central zone, and applied numerals. It is water resistant to 10atm.

GERALD GENTA

OCTO CHRONO QUATTRO RETRO GOLD - REF. OQC.Z.50.581.CN.BD

The Octo Chrono Quattro Retro features an exclusive self-winding GG7800 chronograph movement, entirely decorated by hand, old-gold finish. It offers a jumping hour, retrograde minutes and date; chronograph function with retrograde hour counter at 9:00, retrograde minute counter at 3:00 and large central chronograph seconds hand. It is housed in an octagonal satin-finished 5N red-gold or white-gold case, polished streamlined pushbuttons and round bezel with circular satin-brushed finish on its upper part and polished octagonal base. Multi-level dial with white-lacquered chronograph counters, black- and white-lacquered minute and date displays and vertical satin-brushed central zone. It is water resistant to 10atm.

JUMBO CHRONO

The first round men's watch created by GUY ELLIA, the Jumbo Chrono is based on an interesting technological approach demonstrating that it is possible to combine aesthetic balance with masculine detail and a fine mechanical movement. The Jumbo Chrono bares an exceptional Ø 50mm size that is rarely seen in the world of luxury watches. The Jumbo Chrono's slate-gray oscillating weight is unique and the impressive discovery dial reflects a strong graphic design: chronograph seconds hand is in center, hour and minute are at 12:00, date at 2:00, 30-minute counter at 3:00, seconds at 6:00, and 12-hour counter at 9:00. This model is created in white gold.

GUY ELLIA

JUMBO CHRONO

The first round men's watch created by GUY ELLIA, the Jumbo Chrono is based on an interesting technological approach demonstrating that it is possible to combine aesthetic balance with masculine detail and a fine mechanical movement. At Ø 50mm, the Jumbo Chrono bares an exceptional size that is rarely seen in the world of luxury watches. The Jumbo Chrono's slate-gray oscillating weight is unique and the impressive discovery dial reflects a strong graphic design: chronograph seconds hand is in center, hour and minute are at 12:00, date at 2:00, 30-minute counter at 3:00, seconds at 6:00, and 12-hour counter at 9:00. Shown in rose gold.

GUY ELLIA

JUMBO CHRONO

The first round men's watch created by Guy Ellia, this stunning version of the Jumbo Chrono is set with 301 diamonds totaling 7.24 carats and the buckle is set with 35 diamonds weighing 0.34 carat. Based on an interesting technological approach, Guy Ellia demonstrates that it is possible to combine aesthetic balance with masculine detail and a fine mechanical movement. At Ø 50mm, the Jumbo Chrono boasts an exceptional measurement that is rarely seen in the world of luxury watches. The Jumbo Chrono's slate-gray caliber has a unique oscillating weight. With its impressive discovery dial, this model reflects strong graphic design and is set with 301 diamonds totaling 7.24 carats. The buckle is set with 35 diamonds weighing 0.34 carats.

HUBLOT

"AYRTON SENNA" BIG BANG

Housed in the Big Bang Ø 44.5mm case of polished black ceramic with a satin-finished black ceramic bezel, the mechanical automatic-winding HUB44RT drives this flyback chronograph. The watch's titanium caseback is paired with a sapphire crystal. Its matte black dial is topped with shiny black appliqué indexes and numerals. The 42-hour power-reserve indicator is positioned between 6:00 and 7:00. The hands are faceted, diamond polished and shiny; the black chronograph hand has an H-shaped counterweight and the split-second hand is tipped with green and yellow. The adjustable, natural black rubber strap bears Ayrton Senna's name on the underside. Limited edition of 500 individually numbered pieces.

IWC

AQUATIMER AUTOMATIC CHRONOGRAPH "COUSTEAU DIVERS" - REF. IW378101

This Ø 44mm IWC divers' model is powered by the mechanical automatic-winding (Pellaton system) IWC 79320 caliber (integral chronograph), with a stop-seconds device, 44-hour power reserve, 25 jewels, and a balance oscillating at 28,800 vph. Displayed on the dark blue dial with glossy rhodium-plated chronograph subdials are the day, and date, and luminescent rhodium-plated hands and markers. The counterclockwise turning orange-blue ring has a luminescent minute track for measuring dive times. The polished and brushed stainless steel case is water resistant to 12atm and fitted on a dark blue rubber strap. Limited edition of 2,500 pieces.

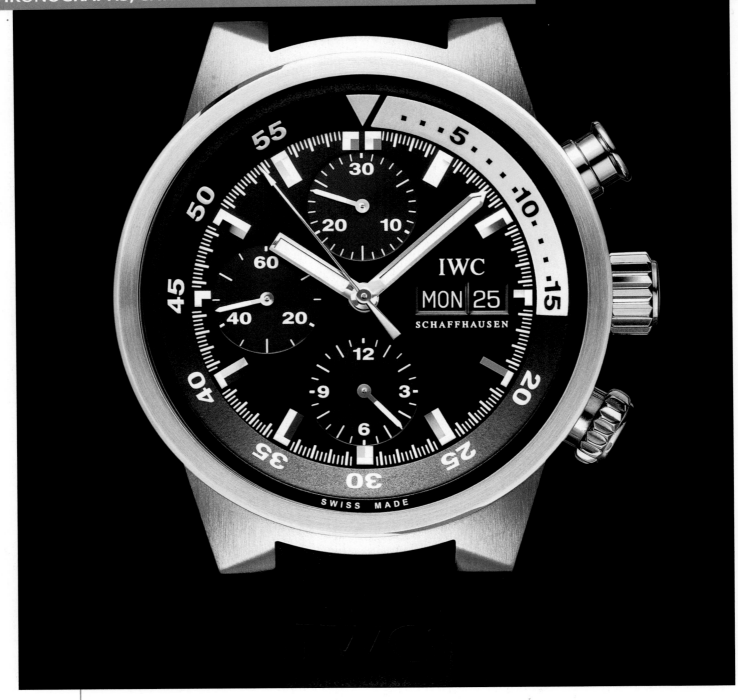

IWC

AQUATIMER CHRONO-AUTOMATIC - REF. IW371933

This watch features a mechanical chronograph movement and a mechanical rotating inner bezel. It houses an IWC 79320 caliber with 25 jewels and offers a day and date indicator and small seconds hand with stop function. By incorporating IWC's extensive experience in the technically demanding realm of pressure resistance, this watch is water resistant up to 120 meters.

IWC

DA VINCI CHRONOGRAPH

For the Da Vinci Chronograph, IWC developed its first proprietary chronograph movement and gave it a modern interpretation with an incomparable analog time display. The manufacture's Caliber 89360 boasts a 68-hour power reserve, an IWC double-pawl automatic-winding system, and is actuated via a classic column wheel. The Da Vinci Chronograph is available in platinum, rose gold or steel.

IWC

PILOT'S WATCH CHRONO-AUTOMATIC - REF. IW371701

The Pilot's Watch Chrono-Automatic features a robust mechanical chronograph with day and date indicator. It houses the IWC 79320 caliber with 25 jewels, 44 hours of power reserve and features a soft inner iron case to protect against magnetic fields. With its cockpit look, this watch has outstanding readability.

IWC

PILOT'S WATCH DOUBLE CHRONOGRAPH RATTRAPANTES EDITION TOP GUN
REF. IW3799

This limited edition features a mechanical chronograph movement and houses an IWC 79230 caliber with 29 jewels. It features a softer inner iron case to protect against magnetic fields. The black dial with recessed subdials has contrasting white numerals with stop-second hands in signal-red to enhance readability.

IWC

PORTUGUESE CHRONO-AUTOMATIC - REF. IW371431

This 18K white-gold Portuguese Chrono-Automatic features the classic pocket watch format on the wrist. It features a mechanical chronograph movement and a small seconds hand with stop function. This watch houses the IWC 79350 caliber with 31 jewels and 44 hours of power reserve.

SPITFIRE CHRONO-AUTOMATIC - REF. IW371702

Description: A tribute to the legendary Spitfire aircraft of the 1930s, this watch features a robust mechanical chronograph. It offers a day and date indicator and houses an IWC 79320 caliber with 25 jewels and a 44-hour power reserve. This watch also features a soft inner iron case to protect against magnetic fields and drop in air pressure.

JAEGER-LECOULTRE

AMVOX2 CHRONOGRAPH CONCEPT

One of Jaeger-LeCoultre's most dramatic innovations, the Amvox2 Chronograph Concept driver's watch features a patented technical breakthrough: the vertical-trigger chronograph. This mechanism makes it possible to start, stop and reset the chronograph simply by pressing on the sapphire crystal, eliminating the need for pushbuttons. Available in a limited series, the titanium and steel watch houses the recently developed chronograph Caliber 751B. Starting is achieved by pressing the crystal at 12:00, reset at 6:00. The watch consists of a ball-joint system that enables the case and bezel to pivot away from the shoulders of the watch, thereby activating a series of levers that transmit impulses to control the chronograph. There is also a three-position cursor that locks the column-wheel chronograph so it is not triggered by the wearer's normal arm motions. The 41-jeweled movement consists of 272 parts.

JAEGER-LECOULTRE

MASTER COMPRESSOR CHRONOGRAPH

The Master Compressor Chronograph houses the automatic Jaeger-LeCoultre Caliber 751 with 272 parts and 41 jewels. Beating at 28,800 vibrations per hour, it offers 72 hours of power reserve. The chronograph features an hour and minute counter and has a center second readout and offers date, and a tachometric scale on the inner bezel; the case features the 1000 Hours Control seal on the caseback.

JAEGER-LECOULTRE

MASTER COMPRESSOR DIVING CHRONOGRAPH LADY

Equipped with Caliber 751D with a 65-hour power reserve, this Ø 38mm Master Compressor Diving Chronograph Lady is fitted with a Jaeger-LeCoultre diving bezel set with diamonds and featuring characteristic touches of color. The hours and minutes as well as the chronograph seconds are indicated by central hands, whereas the other chronograph functions are displayed in two subdials on the opaline dial: an hour counter at 9:00 and a 30-minute counter at 3:00, complete with the two-tone wind rose, which is the signature feature of the Master Compressor Diving Line. The date appears through an aperture between 4:00 and 5:00 on a disk bearing turquoise transferred numerals against a white background. This ladies' chronograph is water resistant to 30atm and available on a white articulated rubber-molded metal-frame strap, triple-link steel bracelet, or white alligator leather strap.

JAEGER-LECOULTRE

MASTER COMPRESSOR EXTREME WORLD CHRONOGRAPH

This Master Compressor Extreme World Chronograph houses the mechanical automatic Jaeger-LeCoultre Caliber 752, which is crafted, assembled and decorated by hand. It beats at 28,800 vibrations per hour, offers 72 hours of power reserve and consists of 279 parts and 41 jewels. The chronograph indicates hours, minutes, date, running indication and simultaneous indication of the 24 time zone. The dial is black for the titanium-and-steel version, gray for the 200 titanium-and-platinum pieces. The crown, equipped with a compression key, starts the watch and adjusts the date. This Master Compressor is water resistant to 100 meters, equipped with a shock absorber and features the 1000 Hours Control seal on the caseback.

JAEGER-LECOULTRE

DUOMETRE A CHRONOGRAPHE

Positioned upon this prestigious Ø 42mm watch's finely grained dial are two large subdials: one on the left for the conventional hour and minute and the other for the chronograph hour and minute, in which a disk indicates the minute units 0 to 9—a new display for which a patent has been filed—and jumping seconds are positioned at 6:00. Duomètre's new case is distinguished by polished welded lugs and a satin-brushed caseband, and houses the Jaeger-LeCoultre 380 'Dual-Wing' with two independent barrels, which may be admired through a sapphire crystal. As the first model in this prestigious line, Duomètre à Chronographe will be issued in pink gold and 950 platinum, as well as a 300-piece limited edition in 18K yellow gold.

JAEGER-LECOULTRE

REVERSO SQUADRA WORLD CHRONOGRAPH

In this contemporary titanium version, the Reverso Squadra World Chronograph is powered by the new Jaeger-LeCoultre Caliber 753, which beats at 28,800 vibrations per hour and is endowed with a 65-hour power reserve. On the front, a guilloché black dial with white transferred numerals displays the hours and minutes, the chronograph functions with hour counter at 12:00 as well as small seconds at 6:00. The other side of the Reverso Squadra World Chronograph is distinguished by a central disk, enabling instant read-off of the time around the world on a 24-hour scale, with the time zones represented by city names appearing on the black dial. The Reverso Squadra World Chronograph is worn on an alligator leather strap with triple-blade folding clasp.

LEVIEV

CHRONOGRAPH DUAL TIME

This 18K white-gold version of the LEVIEV Chronograph Dual Time is adorned with 150 LEVIEV baguette-cut diamonds (6.15 carats in total), and produced in a limited edition. It comes equipped with a self-winding mechanical movement (LEVIEV Caliber LL 101, base A. Schild caliber 5008 with complications by La Joux-Perret). One of the few watches still made in the City of Geneva, it is engraved and decorated with Cotes de Geneve. A notable detail is the crown of the watch, set with a LEVIEV diamond (0.25 carat).

MAURICE LACROIX

MÉMOIRE 1 OF THE "ATELIER DE MAURICE LACROIX"

Maurice Lacroix presents the first memory function for a mechanical watch, which found its initial application in the strictly limited Mémoire 1 chronograph; this function is a completely new complication. The mechanism and the base movement of the ML 128 caliber, which is made of 537 parts and for which numerous patent applications were submitted, were completely designed and developed in the new "Atelier de Maurice Lacroix." A unique mechanism connects the time and chronograph indications—by pressing the button integrated into the crown, the minute and second hands as well as the hour disk change their positions from telling the current time to measuring time intervals without losing the information of the other function.

MAURICE LACROIX

MASTERPIECE LE CHRONOGRAPHE

Maurice Lacroix presented its first own manufacture movement—the ML 106 caliber in the Masterpiece Le Chronographe. This heralds the start of a new era for the Swiss brand. The chronograph movement is unique; its majestic proportions of Ø 36.6mm and the technology behind it are captivating. This technology is a marriage between traditional elements, including a quality column-wheel and an innovative, specially developed lever mechanism for stopping and zeroing, for which a patent is pending. The first 250-piece limited edition of the Masterpiece Le Chronographe is released in pink-gold case.

PARMIGIANI FLEURIER

KALPAGRAPH - REF. PF 003912.01

Shown in polished steel on a Hermès calfskin strap, the new 53.4x39.2mm Kalpagraph is powered by the automatic-winding PF Caliber 334.01 with 50-hour power reserve, 68 jewels, and beating at 28,800 vph. (The gold versions have a 22K gold oscillating weight.) The snailed chronograph counters are at 3:00 (small seconds), 6:00 (12-hour) and 9:00 (30-minute). The dial is decorated with "velouté" and "satin sun" finishes, applied indexes and luminescent delta-shaped hands. Each sapphire crystal caseback is individually numbered. Versions are available on rubber straps and in rose gold or 950 palladium.

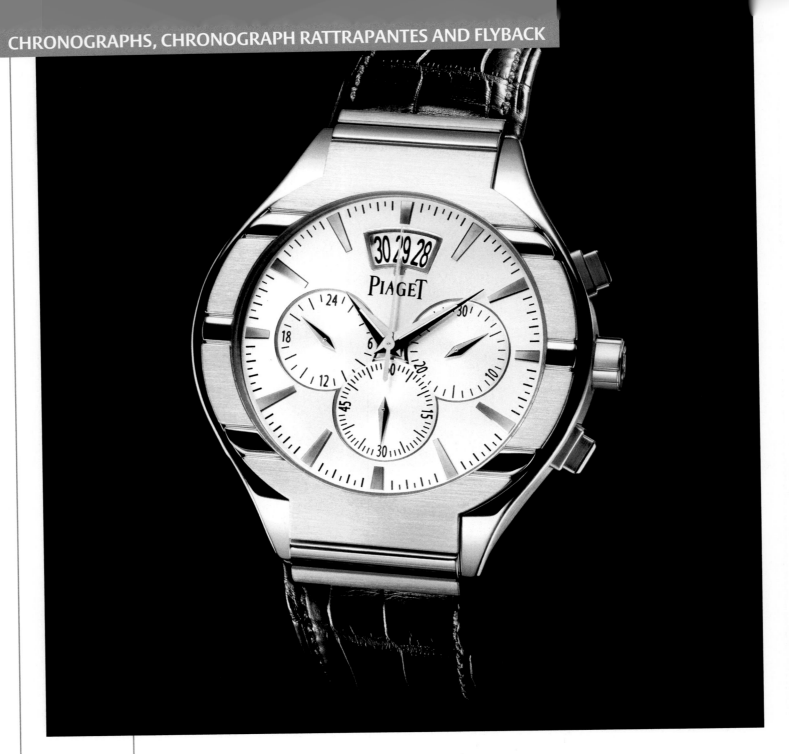

PIAGET

POLO CHRONOGRAPH - REF. G0A32039

The Piaget Polo Chronograph model houses the new Calibre 880P, the first mechanical chronograph movement entirely designed, developed and produced by the Manufacture de Haute Horlogerie Piaget. In addition to the chronograph and flyback functions, this proprietary movement drives the hours, minutes and small seconds at 6:00, as well as the date display at 12:00 and a second time-zone indication. Within the select circle of manufacture-made chronograph movements, Calibre 880P stands out for its 24-hour dual time-zone display positioned at 9:00, the place usually reserved for the standard chronograph hour counter. Featuring two barrels and a large balance with screws, this mechanical self-winding movement provides a 52-hour power reserve in activated chronograph mode. Equipped with a column-wheel mechanism and vertical coupling-clutch, the 5.6mm-thick Calibre 880P is endowed with all the attributes of an haute horology chronograph movement.

RICHARD MILLE

RM 011 FELIPE MASSA SKELETONIZED FLYBACK CHRONOGRAPH

This new Richard Mille creation offers a variety of functions, such as hours, minutes, 60-minute countdown, seconds, flyback function and oversized date at 12:00 with a month indicator (numbered 1-12) at 4:00, with an annual calendar requiring correction only for the month of February. Two unusually designed disks of cut-out metal digits are used for indicating the date. Using the skeletonized titanium, PVD-treated base caliber 005-S, the large case of 50x42x15.85mm has a central case ring in titanium with the choice of both front and back bezel in titanium, or in 18K white or red gold.

TAG HEUER

1911: THE TIME OF TRIP

This is the first dashboard chronograph, patented by Heuer in 1911, designed for aircraft and automobiles. With an 11cm diameter, it fits into all types of dashboards. The large hand at the center of the dial indicates the hour. The pair of small hands located at 12:00 gives the duration of the trip not exceeding 12 hours. The same pushpiece starts, stops and resets the watch to zero. A small window at 3:00 indicates whether the instrument is working correctly.
Private collection of Tag Heuer museum.a

1916: THE MICROGRAPH

The Micrograph, the world's first stopwatch accurate to 1/100th of a second, was patented in 1916. This model revolutionized timing, notably in Olympic sprint competitions and technical research.
Private collection of Tag Heuer museum.

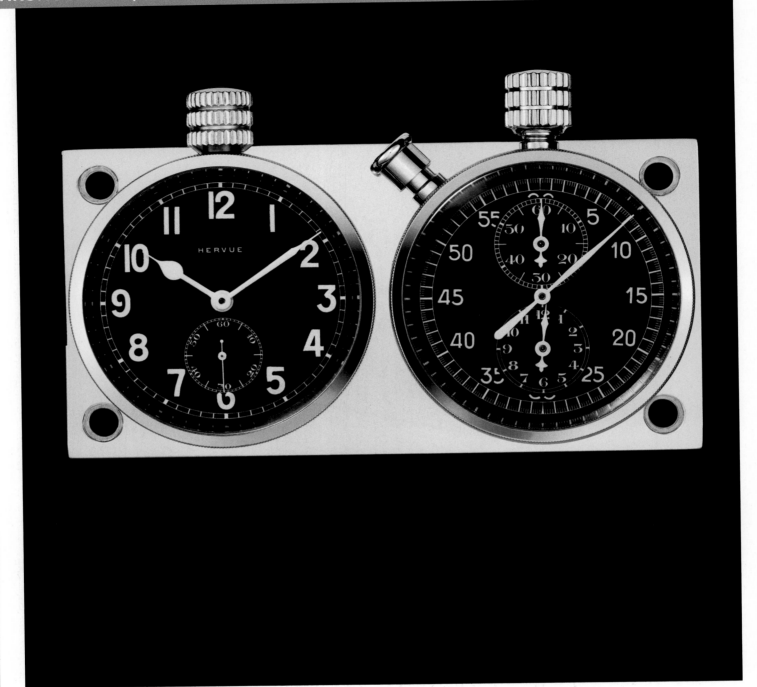

TAG HEUER

1933: HERVUE PAIR

In 1933 Heuer began offering the Time of Day Clock called the "Hervue" and Twelve-Hour Timer called the "Autavia" mounted together on a double back-plate. In the late 1950s, Heuer began to refer to the Master Time clock and Monte Carlo stopwatch as the "Rally-Master" pair.
Private collection of Tag Heuer museum.

1965: CARRERA DATE 45

After the launch of the Carrera series in 1964, Jack Heuer created the Carrera Dato 45 in 1965. It was one of the first chronograph models to feature a date disk (at 9:00). Previously, the date had been indicated by a hand.
Private collection of Tag Heuer museum.

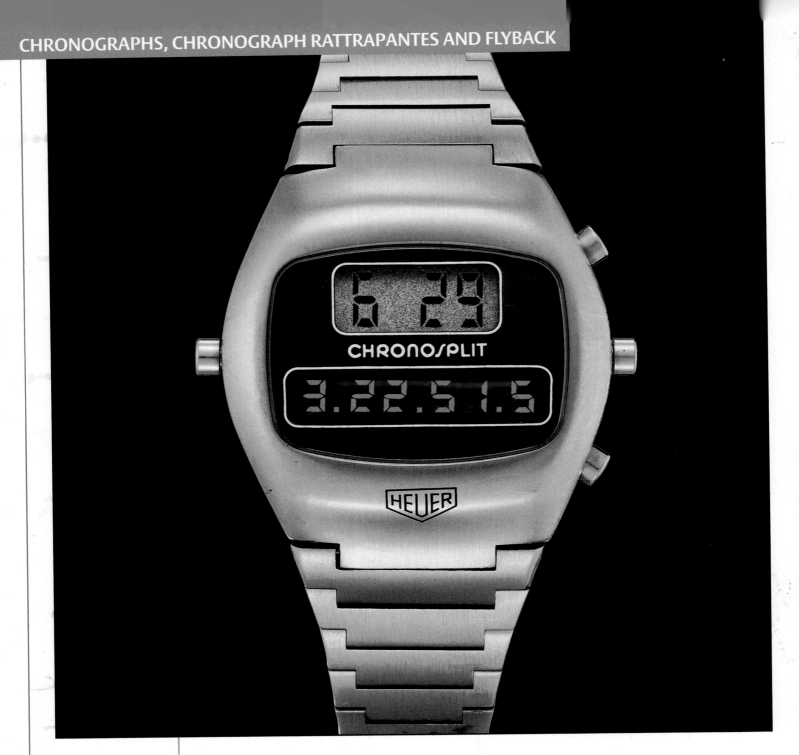

TAG HEUER

1975: THE CHRONOSPLIT

Chronosplit is the world's first quartz wrist-worn chronograph (with double digital display—LED and LCD; it is accurate to 1/100th of a second).
Private collection of Tag Heuer museum.

2005: THE CALIBRE 360

The Calibre 360 beats 10 times faster than the most precise mechanical wristwatch movements on the market today. It is like being endowed with two hearts—2 sets of escapement mechanisms are allowed to cruise at a regular speed (28,800 oscillations/hour) under normal conditions then accelerate to immense speed (360,000 oscillations/hour) in chronograph mode. For a movement to be this incredibly precise, it requires more than 230 components, a lightened and miniaturized hairspring and escapement mechanism (26% smaller in diameter than an ordinary balance wheel), and, finally, no fewer than 3 exclusive worldwide patents: 1. 1/100th-of-a-second display on a mechanical wrist-worn chronograph; 2. Bi-directional crown and rewind system: The single crown controls the automatic watch and the mechanical chronograph, as well as the watch's hour and date setting. When turned counter-clockwise, it rewinds the automatic watch; when turned clockwise, it rewinds the manual chronograph; 3. Transmission of the date from the base of the movement to the upper dial.

TAG HEUER

2006: THE CARRERA CALIBRE 360 ROSE GOLD LIMITED EDITION (500 PIECES)

At BaselWorld 2005, TAG Heuer presented the Calibre 360 Concept Chronograph, the first mechanical wrist-worn chronograph to measure and display time to 1/100th of a second. At BaselWorld 2006, privileged collectors looking for the most accurate mechanical timepiece ever made had their first glimpse of the Carrera Calibre 360 Rose Gold, in a special limited edition of only 500 pieces.
Private collection of Tag Heuer museum.

2006: MONACO CALIBRE 360 LS CONCEPT CHRONOGRAPH

At BaselWorld 2006, TAG Heuer introduced the next evolutionary phase of its 1/100th of a second chronograph technology: the Monaco Calibre 360 LS (Linear Second) Concept Chronograph, a daring new timepiece with an all-new architecture proudly exposing the unparalleled Calibre 360 LS precision technology within.
Private collection of Tag Heuer museum.

TAG HEUER

2007: THE GRAND CARRERA CALIBRE 17 RS CHRONOGRAPH

In 2007, TAG Heuer introduced a new premium collection of sophisticated timepieces inspired by the spirit of modern GT cars. Amongst its many premium features is the ingenious Rotating System, which makes it possible to replace conventional hands by a disk displaying functional information even more clearly on the dial and which enable the user to read small seconds and chronograph time effortlessly, intuitively and instantaneously. Launched worldwide in 2008.

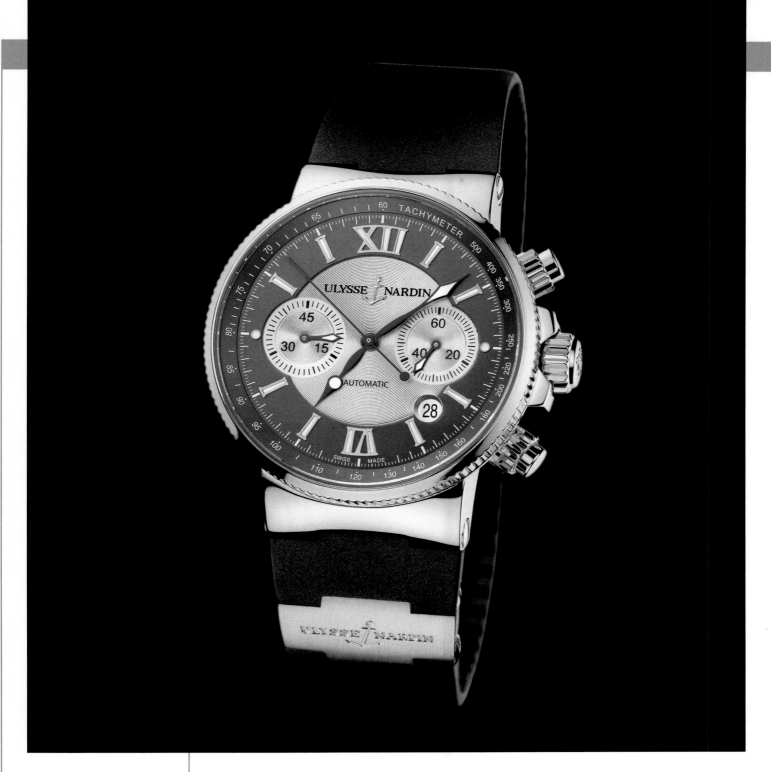

ULYSSE NARDIN

MAXI MARINE CHRONOGRAPH - REF. 356-66-3/319

Crafted in 18K rose gold or stainless steel, the Maxi Marine Chronograph's 41mm case houses the Caliber UN-35 equipped with an exclusive 45-minute register. The watch is also available on a bracelet or strap, and with various dial combinations.

ULYSSE NARDIN

MAXI MARINE CHRONOGRAPH - REF. 356-66/354

Also available in stainless steel, this Maxi Marine Chronograph's 41mm 18K rose-gold case houses the Caliber UN-35 equipped with an exclusive 45-minute register. The watch is also available on a bracelet or rubber-and-gold strap, and with various dial combinations.

ULYSSE NARDIN

MAXI MARINE CHRONOGRAPH - REF. 353-66/323

This Maxi Marine Chronograph's 41mm stainless steel case houses the Caliber UN-35 equipped with an exclusive 45-minute register. The watch is available on a bracelet or rubber/titanium strap and with various dial combinations. Offered in 18K rose gold. .

VACHERON CONSTANTIN

MALTE CHRONOGRAPH - REF. 47120

The timeless classic Malte Chronograph features a hand-wound mechanical movement, Caliber 1141, with column-wheel chronograph mechanism with telemetric tachymetric scale, 30-minute totalizer and subdial for the running seconds. Its dial is engine-turned by hand and graced with applied hour markers in 18K gold. Case diameter measures 41.5mm and features a see-through back with sapphire crystal. The timepiece is water resistance to 100 feet and available in 18K white or pink gold.

VACHERON CONSTANTIN

MALTE TONNEAU CHRONOGRAPH - REF. 49145

This 18K pink-gold Malte Tonneau Chronograph offers date indication via twin oversized apertures, in addition to the chronograph and time readouts. It is powered by the mechanical manual-winding Vacheron Constantin Caliber 1137 with 37 jewels and 40 hours of power reserve. The movement beats at 21,600 vibrations per hour. The chronograph offers a center seconds hand, 30-minute and 12-hour totalizers, and tracks to 1/6 of a second. On a hand-stitched alligator strap and pink-gold buckle.

VACHERON CONSTANTIN

OVERSEAS CHRONOGRAPH - REF. 49150/B01J

This 18K gold Overseas Chronograph houses the mechanical automatic-winding Vacheron Constantin Caliber 1137 with column-wheel chronograph. The movement beats at 21,600 vibrations per hour, is equipped with 37 jewels and offers 40 hours of power reserve. It is protected against magnetic fields by an inner iron case. Water resistant to 15atm, the watch offers hours, minutes, small seconds, large date and chronograph with three counters. In addition to a screw-down crown with case protector, the watch features a three-fold gasket and screw-down pushers. Its caseback is embossed with the Overseas sailboat and the hands and markers are luminescent.

ZENITH

CHRONOMASTER OPEN EL PRIMERO RETROGRADE

This ChronoMaster Open El Primero Retrograde houses the El Primero 4023 automatic chronograph movement with retrograde date indicator from the 30-minute counter axis. The 50-hour power-reserve indicator is at 6:00. The 39-jeweled movement consists of 299 components and beats at 36,000 vibrations per hour. The watch offers 30-minute counter at 3:00, a 3-branched small seconds hand at 9:00, central chronograph seconds hand, and measures short time intervals to 1/10 of a second. It is offered in 18K rose gold with opened Grain d'Orge guilloche-patterned guilloché-patterned dial at 10:00 to view the El Primero movement.

ZENITH

CLASS EL PRIMERO

The Zenith Class El Primero houses the El Primero 4002 automatic chronograph movement that is a COSC-certified chronometer. With 337 components and 31 jewels, the movement beats at 36,000 vibrations per hour. It offers a power reserve of 50 hours and measures short time intervals to 1/10 of a second. In addition to hours and minutes in the center, it offers small seconds at 9:00, date at 4:30, central seconds hand and 30-minute counter at 3:00. It is crafted in a 40mm steel case with a curved sapphire crystal with antireflective treatment on both sides. The caseback is transparent sapphire, as well, and the watch is water resistant to 50 meters.

ZENITH

CLASS OPEN EL PRIMERO

Housing the El Primero 4021H automatic chronograph movement, this Class Open El Primero watch offers hours, minutes, small seconds, 50 hours of power reserve at 6:00, chronograph timing to 1/10 of a second, 30-minute counter at 3:00 and 3-branch seconds hand at 9:00. The 248-part movement beats at 36,000 vibrations per hour and has 39 jewels. Water resistant to 50 meters, this Class Open El Primero is crafted in rose-gold and fitted with a sapphire crystal and transparent sapphire crystal caseback.

ZENITH

CHRONOMASTER GRANDE DATE

The ChronoMaster Grande Date houses the El Primero 4010 automatic chronograph movement with big date. The COSC-certified chronometer movement consists of 306 components, 31 jewels, beats at 36,000 vibrations per hour and holds 50 hours of power reserve. With bidirectional automatic winding, the watch is equipped with a central rotor on ball bearings and a 22K rose-gold oscillating weight. It measures to 1/10 of a second, has a 30-minute counter at 3:00, a 60-second counter at 9:00, and the big date at 6:00 features instantaneous double-jump function. A tachymetric scale rings the dial encased in 18K rose gold. The ChronoMaster Grande Date is water resistant to 50 meters.

CHRONOMASTER T

Housing the El Primero 410 automatic chronograph movement, this ChronoMaster T is a COSC-certified chronometer. The movement consists of 357 components and 31 jewels, beats at 36,000 vibrations per hour and retains up to 50 hours of power reserve. The chronograph measures to 1/10 of second. With bidirectional winding, the central rotor is on ball bearings and the oscillating weight features a grained pattern. In addition to the seconds and chronograph function with 30-minute and 12-hour counter, the watch offers day, date and month readout, moonphase at 6:00 and tachometric scale.

ZENITH

DEFY CLASSIC CHRONOGRAPH

Crafted in brushed stainless steel and water resistant to 300 meters, this Defy Classic Chronograph houses the El Primero 4000 SC automatic chronograph movement with 278 components. The balance bridge is crafted of shock-absorbing Zenithium Z⁺. The watch features an Incabloc anti-shock device and measures time to 1/10 of a second. The movement is built with a full Tungstentungsten oscillating weight with guilloché pattern, beats at 36,000 vibrations per hour and provides a power reserve of over 50 hours. Chronograph functions include 30-minute counter at 3:00, 12-hour counter at 6:00, and seconds at 9:00. This Defy Classic is equipped with a unidirectional rotating bezel and screw-in caseback.

ZENITH

DEFY CLASSIC OPEN

This Defy Classic Open houses the automatic El Primero 4021 SC chronograph movement with 248 parts, 39 jewels, 36,000 vph and 50-hour power reserve. Defy Classic Open offers 30-minute counter at 3:00, power-reserve indicator at 6:00, central chronograph seconds hand and a 3-branched seconds hand at 9:00. The rose-gold case measures 46.5mm and is equipped with a unidirectional rotating bezel. Complete with transparent sapphire caseback, the watch is water resistant to 300 meters and accented with SuperLumiNova-tipped hands.

ZENITH

DEFY XTREME CHRONOGRAPH

The El Primero 4000 SX automatic chronograph movement powers this black titanium Defy Xtreme Chronograph. This caliber consists of 248 parts, 31 jewels and a heavy metal oscillating weight with carbon-fiber inserts. The central rotor is on ball bearings, the balance, chronograph and pallet bridges are of shock-absorbing Zenithium Z⁺. The movement beats at 36,000 vibrations per hour and offers 50 hours of power reserve. The 46.5mm case is equipped with black titanium screw-in pushbuttons with carbon-fiber guilloché patterns, black titanium screw-in crown with special protective device, and a graduated unidirectional rotating black titanium bezel. The helium escape valve at 10:00 ensures water resistance to 1,000 meters. The dial is a multi-layered shock-resistant structure composed of silvered carbon fiber and displays a center chronograph hand, the 30-minute counter at 3:00, date at 4:00, 12-hour counter at 6:00, and small seconds at 9:00.

ZENITH

DEFY XTREME OPEN

Cased in 46.5mm of black titanium, this extraordinary Defy Xtreme Open is powered by the El Primero 4021 SX automatic chronograph movement with harmonic plate. The 13-lignes caliber consists of 248 parts and 39 jewels. The balance, chronograph and pallet bridges are built ofshock- shock-absorbing Zenithium Z+ and Defy Xtreme Open is equipped with a heavy metal oscillating weight with carbon fibercarbon-fiber inserts. It has a 30-minute counter at 3:00, small seconds at 9:00, power-reserve indicator from the hour axis, and central seconds hand. Water resistant to 1,000 meters, the high-tech case features a helium escape valve at 10:00 and black titanium screw-in pushbuttons with carbon-fiber guilloché patterns and protective crown device. The carbon-fiber dial is a multi-layered construction with Hesalite shock-resistant glass. The steel bracelet with Kevlar® inserts has links of carbon fiber and composite alloys for ultra resistance to extreme temperatures and pressure.

ZENITH

DEFY XTREME POWER RESERVE

Housing the Elite 685 SX extra-thin automatic movement, this Defy Xtreme Power Reserve watch offers power reserve readout at 1:00. Cased in a 43mm black titanium case, the movement is a 179-part caliber with 38 jewels beating at 28,800 vibrations per hour. The balance, automatic train and train wheel bridges are crafted in shock-absorbing Zenithium Z+. The watch features an Incabloc anti-shock device. It offers 50 hours of power reserve. The sapphire crystal is 3.8mm thick with antireflective coating on both sides to enable water resistance to 1,000 meters. There is a helium escape valve at 10:00. The high-temperature-resistant bracelet is crafted in brushed steel with Kevlar® inserts and carbon fiber and composite alloys for the central links.

GRANDE CHRONOMASTER OPEN EL PRIMERO

This Grande ChronoMaster Open houses the El Primero 4021 automatic chronograph movement with 249 parts. Beating at 36,000 vibrations per hour, the 39-jeweled movement measures short time intervals to 1/10 of a second. The watch has bidirectional automatic winding and holds more than 50 hours of power reserve, displayed from the center hour axis. A 3-branched small seconds hand is positioned at 9:00 and the 30-minute counter is at 3:00. Shown in stainless steel but also available in 18K rose gold, the 45mm case is water resistant to 30 meters and features a curved sapphire crystal with antireflective treatment on both sides and an exhibition sapphire crystal caseback. Available on alligator / Alzavel calfskin or rubber strap or stainless steel bracelet with triple-folding clasp; the dial is available in cobalt or white.

ZENITH

GRAND PORT ROYAL EL PRIMERO

Cased in brushed stainless steel with a sapphire caseback and crystal, this Grand Port Royal El Primero is a stunning bidirectional winding automatic chronograph that houses the El Primero 4021 B movement with 248 parts and 39 jewels. The movement beats at 36,000 vibrations per hour and offers 50 hours of power reserve. It measures short time intervals to 1/10 of a second. Functions include 30-minute counter at 3:00, power-reserve display at 6:00, and 3-branched seconds hand at 9:00. The 36x51mm case is fitted with a silver or black guilloché dial and water resistant to 50 meters. Shown on a rubber strap, the watch is also available on a black alligator leather strap lined with silky Alzavel calfskin.

ZENITH

PORT ROYAL OPEN EL PRIMERO CONCEPT

Crafted of black titanium with black titanium pushers and crown, this 34x48mm Port Royal Open Concept houses the El Primero 4021 FN automatic chronograph movement consisting of 248 parts, 39 jewels, 50-hour power reserve and beating at 36,000 vibrations per hour; its heavy metal oscillating weight features a Damier guilloché pattern. The rectangular auxiliary plate is new and indications include 30-minute counter at 3:00, power-reserve display at 6:00, and 3-branched seconds hand at 9:00. On a carbon-fiber strap integrated with rubber and calfskin, the Port Royal is water resistant to 50 meters.

Divers' watches

Although they are not generally considered complication timepieces, divers' watches form a world based on extreme feats and high performance. To accompany adventurers and professionals to the depths of the oceans, they must display peerless resistance and reliability, combined with a number of often sophisticated functions. The field even features certain iconic watches, of which some have been reissued recently.

All clammed up

Along with lubrication, water resistance has always been a major concern for watchmakers. Not that all customers are potential Cousteau followers, but water resistance provides welcomed protection, even on dry land, against two of a movement's worst enemies: dampness and dust. The first watertight case, the famous Oyster by Rolex, was launched in 1927. In 1953, the brand with the crown logo created a watch to accompany Professor Piccard's famous bathyscaph to a depth of 3,150 meters; in 1960, the Deep Sea Special even descended to 10,916 in the Mariana trench. In addition to serving explorers and scientists, many of the first divers' watches soon became part of standard equipment for the armed forces. Such was in particular the case for Officine Panerai watches designed for the Italian navy in the 1930s and 40s; their dials featured luminescent indications and their famous crown system guaranteed water resistance to 200 meters. In the 1950s, with the boom of water sports, the first series–produced divers' watches made their appearance.

Rolex set the tone in 1953 with its famous Submariner, initially water-resistant to 100 meters (now 300 meters). That same year, Blancpain launched its Fifty Fathoms, created in cooperation with two officers of the French naval combat divers. This watch, initially water resistant (as its name indicates) to a depth of fifty fathoms (91.45 meters), is distinguished by it black dial, bezel and strap. Blancpain revisited this piece in 2007 and created a collection comprising a "simple" model equipped with a new proprietary movement, a prestigious version with a flying tourbillon, as well as a flyback chronograph with pushbuttons that are perfectly water resistant and functional to depths of 300 meters. In 1957, Breitling launched its SuperOcean, a diver's watch with a single-piece case and "armored" glass that is water resistant to 200 meters. In 2007, the brand celebrated a half century of this ultra-sporty model by introducing the SuperOcean Heritage, with a rubber strap or woven steel bracelet lending a subtle vintage touch.

Wrist instruments

To deserve the title of "divers' watch," a timepiece must not only boast above-average water resistance (to at least 100 meters and generally guaranteed by a screw-lock crown and caseback), it must also provide all the functions that are indispensable to amateur and professional divers, including a rotating bezel to keep track of dive times and equipped, if possible, with a unidirectional rotating system to avoid any accidental disturbance of the programmed time. The dial generally features large and extremely visible hands and numerals, generously coated with a luminescent substance. The wristband—in

4

5

▶▶ 1   *Blancpain, Fifty Fathoms*
Blancpain released its Fifthy Fathoms in 1950, a watch created in collaboration with two officers from the "combat divers" division of the French Army.

▶▶ 2   *Rolex, Submariner*
With the rise of aquatic sports in the 1950s came the first diving watches. Rolex set the tone in 1953 with its famous Submariner, water resistant to 100m (now 300m). The version shown is the commemorative model produced in 2003.

▶▶ 3   *Longines, HydroConquest*
The new HydroConquest collection by Longines, launched in 2007, combines water resistance to 300m with reinforced crown protection.

▶▶ 4   *Breitling, SuperOcean Heritage*
In 2007, Breitling celebrated a half-century of the SuperOcean by releasing the SuperOcean Heritage, with a rubber strap or steel bracelet.

▶▶ 5   *IWC, Aquatimer "Cousteau Divers"*
IWC pays homage to its collaboration with the divers from Cousteau's team in its limited edition "Cousteau Divers" Aquatimer, a chronograph that is water resistant to 120m with a beautiful contrast between its luminescent orange and deep blue.

metal or rubber—is often equipped with an extension system to facilitate its fitting over a diving suit. Brands currently offer a broad range of divers' watches, from sporty chic models mainly intended for poolside conversations, to professional instruments equipped to face great depths. IWC pays tribute to its cooperation with the Cousteau team of divers in its Aquatimer Cousteau Divers limited-edition chronograph, water resistant to 120 meters and featuring a striking contrast of luminescent orange and deep blue colors. The internal rotating bezel is adjusted by means of the same pushbutton/crown as the chronograph reset function. The new HydroConquest line by Longines, launched in 2007, combines water resistance to 300 meters with reinforced protection of the crown. Graham, the British brand based in La Chaux-de-Fonds, presents a new version of its Chronofighter model, initially created for the World War II bomber pilots who wore gloves and thus found it easier to operate a pushbutton and crown placed on the side of the case. The Chronofighter Oversize Diver chronograph, water resistant to 300 meters, is equipped with a helium valve to vent excess pressure during deep dives. The Oris Mesitertaucher model in titanium, which is water resistant to 1,000 meters, features a regular-type dial that highlights the most important indication for divers, the minutes, by centering it. It is also fitted with a 4.7mm-thick sapphire crystal and a helium decompression valve. With its Chrono Avenger M1, Breitling offers the only chronograph to be water resistant and operational at a depth of 100 meters, a feat rendered possible by a patented magnetic pushbutton device serving to activate the controls even with no direct contact between the pushbutton and the movement.

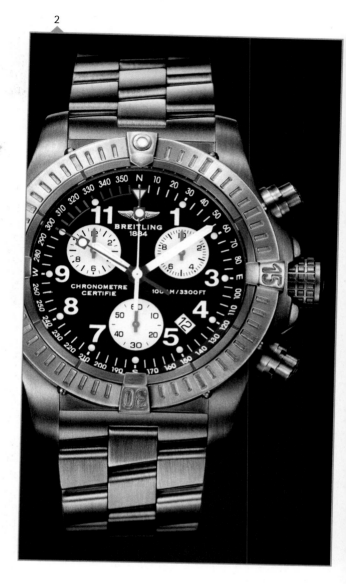

▶▶ 1   *Graham, Chronofighter Oversize Diver*
The diving chronograph Chronofighter Oversize Diver, water resistant to 300m, has a helium valve to avoid excessive pressure during deep dives.

▶▶ 2   *Breitling, Chrono Avenger M1*
With the Chrono Avenger M1, Breitling introduces the only chronograph that is water resistant and functional at 1000m deep, an achievement rendered possible by a patented magnetic pushbutton that allows commands be carried out even without direct to contact between pushbutton and movement.

▶▶ 3   *Oris, Der Meistertaucher*
The Oris Meistertaucher in titanium, water resistant to 1000 meters, uses a regulator-type dial to highlight the most important indication for divers, the minute, right in the cetre.

1

2

Depth fever

A few rare watches also boast another function that is not specific to watches, but is very useful for divers—the depth gauge—and offers another alternative to the electronic wrist computers currently flooding the market. Jaeger-LeCoultre has chosen to equip its Master Compressor Diving Pro Geographic with a mechanical depth gauge, placed on the left side of the case and fitted with a membrane that dilates and contracts according to water pressure. The movements of this membrane act on the large blue depth gauge hand by means of a clever transmission system partially visible on the dial. The depths measured range from 0 to -80 meters. This watch is water-resistant to 300 meters and also displays another time zone with city selection at 6 o'clock and a second 24-hour time-zone display at 9 o'clock. For the most important indications, including the power reserve and the depth gauge, blue has been chosen because it is the only shade visible from a certain depth. Meanwhile, Officine Panerai prefers the electronic option. The Luminor 1950 Submersible Depth Gauge, issued in a limited edition of 600 in titanium and steel and all chronometer-certified, combines an automatic movement featuring a membrane and chip system activating a large central yellow hand on the dial. To guarantee maximum security, the brand has had the calibration of each of its depth gauges tested by the Swiss Federal Measurement Office. The lever-controlled crown-protection system ensures water resistance to 120 meters.

▶▶ *1-3* *Jaeger-LeCoultre, Master Compressor Diving Pro Geographic*
Jaeger-LeCoultre has equipped its Master Compressor Diving Pro Geographic with a mechanical depth gauge placed on the left side of the case and fitted with a membrane that expands or contracts according to the water pressure.

▶▶ *2* *Officine Panerai, Luminor 1950 Submersible Depth Gauge*
The Luminor 1950 Submersible Depth Gauge, issued in titanium/steel limited edition of 600, all chronometer-certified, links an automatic movement with a membrane and computer chip system that activates a large yellow central hand on the dial.

BREITLING

SUPEROCEAN HERITAGE 46MM – REF. A1732024/B868

The mechanical automatic-winding Breitling caliber 17 (ETA2824-2base) beats at 28,800 vph and is a COSC-certified chronometer. This polished stainless steel case bears curved, antireflective sapphire crystals on both sides, a clockwise-turning bezel with knurled rim and aluminum ring with markers at 5 minutes, and a black dial with a brushed sunray pattern, luminescent dots and rhodium-plated Sports hands, and date at 6:00. Shown on a rubber Ocean Racer strap with fold-over clasp mechanism with comfort-enhancing extension that is adjustable in seconds, this watch is available on bracelets or straps, in a Ø 38mm size, and is water resistant to 20atm.

BREITLING

SUPEROCEAN HERITAGE 38MM – REF. A3732016/C73

Powered by the Breitling caliber 37, this Superocean Heritage is presented in Ø 38mm of polished stainless steel with curved, antireflective sapphire crystals on both sides. Water resistant to 20atm, it is topped with a counterclockwise-turning bezel with knurled rim and blue ring with markers at 5 minutes. Its blue dial features a sunburst pattern and the small seconds subdial is decorated with circular beads. Luminescent dots and luminescent rhodium-plated Sports hands light up the dial. Shown here on an Ocean Classic bracelet with interlaced steel links and fold-over steel clasp with two safety pushers and lengthening system. Also available in Ø 46mm size with different dial color, strap and bracelet combinations.

HUBLOT

BIG BANG KING PORTO CERVO – REF. 322.PH.230.RW

This Ø 48mm diver's watch in ceramic and pink-gold is designed to appeal to women, even those with the daintiest of wrists. Its mechanical automatic-winding Hublot HUB21 caliber provides a 42-hour power reserve, a tungsten-carbide oscillating weight, barrel with reinforced spring, and a Glucydur balance spring escapement. The Big Bang case is topped with a unidirectional rotating bezel in white ceramic graced with pink-gold numerals and features white composite resin bezel lugs and lateral inserts, a pink-gold crown with natural white rubber insert. Water resistant to 30atm, the Big Bang King Porto Cervo's caseback is crafted of pink-gold and engraved with BIG BANG KING. This watch is fitted on an adjustable, smooth natural white rubber strap with Hublot logo and fold-over clasp.

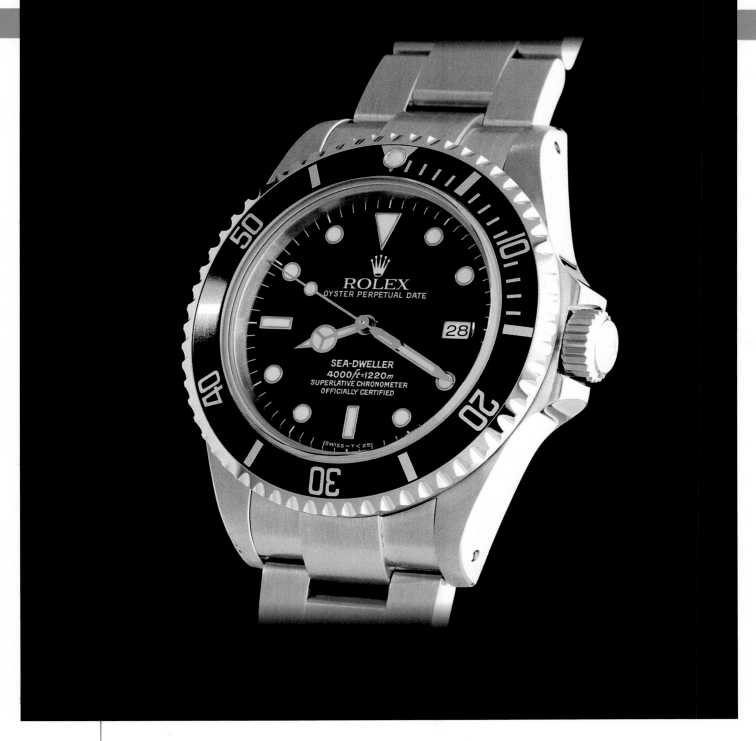

ROLEX

OYSTER PERPETUAL DATE SEA-DWELLER 4000 – REF. 16600

This Oyster Perpetual Date Sea-Dweller 4000 houses an automatic-winding Rolex 3185 caliber, which is COSC certified. Its polished and brushed Ø 40mm stainless steel case is fitted with a thick (3mm) sapphire crystal that resists high pressures, a counterclockwise-turning ring with graduated scale for the calculation of dive times, and a pressure-compensating valve for helium release. The piece is water resistant to 122atm and available on a brushed steel Oysterlock bracelet with fold-over clasp with Fliplock safety stop that comes with an additional link, an extension plate of the clasp, and a screwdriver to extend the bracelet to fit over a diver's suit.

Perpetual
Calendars

CEO of
Jean Dunand

Thierry Oulevay

The young watch brand Jean Dunand is run by two watch-industry veterans, Thierry Oulevay, former president of Bovet Fleurier, and the master movement-maker, Christophe Claret. Together, they have already set up the brand for a promising future. Since it was established in 2004, the company has released three models with technical features never before seen in watchmaking. The latest product, named Shabaka, is the first watch to display the full perpetual calendar on rotating cylinders.

"Watchmaking fit for pharaohs"

In the 1930s, an artist from Geneva named Jean Dunand first made a name for himself in Paris and then became widely admired for his talent in the decorative arts. Virtually unknown in his homeland, Dunand played a major role in the Art Deco movement. "Jean Dunand's career mirrored that of the Swiss architect, Le Corbusier—born in Switzerland but only successful abroad," Oulevay, the brand's CEO, points out. "We chose his name to pay tribute to his work and to underline the brand's visual identity: its Art Deco styling." As it's the kind of style that absorbs every artistic influence from Aztec Mexico to ancient Egypt, the name "Shabaka" fitted the new model like a glove.

Shabaka

Its name is not the only regal feature of the Shabaka. The ingenuity of its movement and its innovative devices qualify it as a watchmaking reference. It displays a full perpetual calendar, repeats the minutes on cathedral gongs, neatly interprets the indication of the leap year, the moonphases and the power reserve, and incorporates a number of patented devices, some inspired by automobile sport.

The most impressive novelty is the use of four cylinders to show the days, dates and months. Until now, watchmakers have displayed them

FACING PAGE
Thierry Oulevay, Jean Dunand's CEO.

THIS PAGE
Exploded movement of the Shabaka reference CLA88. The perpetual-calendar module is set on the minute-repeater plate, which has holes to accommodate the cylindrical indicators.

2:1

1:1

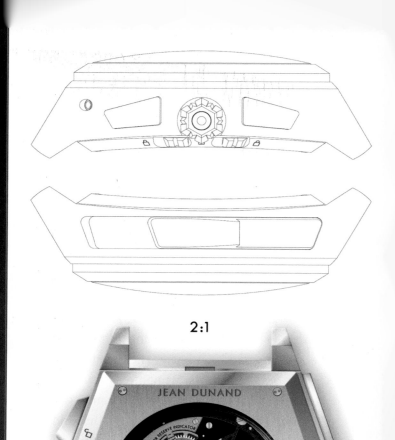

2:1

2:1

1:1

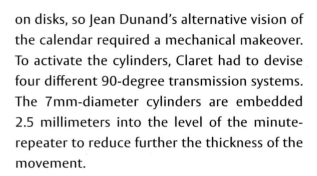

on disks, so Jean Dunand's alternative vision of the calendar required a mechanical makeover. To activate the cylinders, Claret had to devise four different 90-degree transmission systems. The 7mm-diameter cylinders are embedded 2.5 millimeters into the level of the minute-repeater to reduce further the thickness of the movement.

Added to the complexity of the perpetual calendar is the fact that it jumps instantaneously at midnight. To absorb the inertia of the cylinders turning in a fraction of a second and to reduce wear, the release spring is fitted with a gear train that ends in a spinning governor.
The unusual display is fitted into a four-level dial in an emphatic Art Deco style. A nickel-alloy frame delineates fields of blackened gold set with hour markers in red ceramic triangles and lapped pyramids of gold. The hard angles and rigid geometries of the dial are echoed in a case of gold or palladium.

The American market is the toughest of all

Thierry Oulevay is concentrating on the United States as the main market for his brand. "The American market is the toughest there is. You have to invest an enormous amount in advertising to be noticed and to create the indispensable brand magic. Relations with distributors and retailers can be difficult; they want to be assured that everything is being done to promote the product. Starting in this market meant that we had to be perfect in everything we do." Jean Dunand watches are currently available at Cellini in New York and at Wynn Jewelry in Las Vegas and Macao. These high-class shops correspond to the rank the brand aspires to. But a few other retailers have them in stock, notably in Singapore and Bangkok. While keeping North America as its major market, Oulevay intends to spread the brands wings in 2008 to outlets in Zurich, St. Moritz, London and Hong Kong.

Oulevay understands that his wealthy clients do not see borders as obstacles. "Our customers are entrepreneurs who have been successful in business and who run their own companies. Most are American, but some are based in Russia, the Ukraine or China where there is a strong culture of applied arts, despite a turbulent history. They are all looking for that unique blend in our watches of innovation and tradition, and they know how to wait long enough for delivery." Deliveries will total just 40 pieces in 2008. "Jean Dunand intends to be a reference brand for the elite; the price of the watches and their scarcity are the elements of that strategy."

Perpetu
Calenda

A grand classic among watch
perpetual calendar appears in
respecting Haute Horlogerie
manufacturers. While it has n
any major upheavals or innova
terms, the perpetual calendar'
demure and understated aesth
unexpected twists, with fascin
modes and transparency effec
witnessed the rise of annual c
requiring just one adjustment

Eternity—less one day

Calendar indications appeared on pocket watches at quite an early stage. By the 17th century, there were already astronomical watches displaying the time, the date, the day and the month, along with moonphases and Zodiac signs. Calendar watches subsequently proved very successful, mostly in the form of "simple" calendars requiring manual correction after each month with less than 31 days, meaning five times a year—just like most contemporary calendar wristwatches. It was not until the late 18th century that so-called "perpetual" calendars were developed, taking into account the leap-year cycle with 31, 30 or 28-day months and the quadrennial reoccurrence of February 29th. This sophisticated function calls for major feats of miniaturization—especially for a wristwatch—since the movement must be endowed with a mechanical memory of 1461 days (four years). Contrary to what people often believe—and what brands are careful not to contradict—perpetual calendars are not designed to function without correction "from here to eternity." They will all need to be advanced one day forward on March 1, 2100, since by virtue of the Gregorian calendar, three century years out of four are not leap years. There are a handful of "century" or "secular" calendars taking account of this specific characteristic.

▶▶ **1** *Breguet, montre «Classique» pour homme*
Playing with geometry, Breguet introduces a men's "Classique" watch with the displays for the day, month, leap year and date aligned on the same vertical axis.

▶▶ **2** *Jaeger-LeCoultre, Master Eight Days Perpetual*
In a beautiful example of revisiting a classic, Jaeger-LeCoultre's Master Eight Days Perpetual is the only manual-winding perpetual calendar with a power reserve of eight days.

▶▶ **3** *Blancpain, Tourbillon Semainier*
Blancpain's Tourbillon Semainier—even if its calendar is not a perpetual calendar—will appeal to all modern businessmen by its "week number" display, shown by a red-pointed hand on the perimeter of the dial.

1

2

3

New faces

Perpetual calendars are distinguished by their multiple displays—date, month, day, year, leap years—generally complemented by the moonphase indication (see the Moonphases chapter). These displays may be shown by means of hands or disks with an aperture system. Representing a fine example of classicism revisited, the Master Eight Days Perpetual by Jaeger-LeCoultre is also the only hand-wound perpetual calendar model to boast an eight-day power reserve. A pusher on the side of the case adjusts the entire set of indicators in one-day increments. Playing on geometrical effects, Breguet offers a men's model in its Classique collection indicating the day, month, leap year and date lined up along the same vertical axis. In tribute to its master-watchmaker Kurt Klaus, who in 1985 created the modular perpetual calendar movement destined to drive the famous Da Vinci model, IWC recently launched the Da Vinci Perpetual Calendar Special Edition Kurt Klaus. Housed in the new tonneau-shaped case now featured in the Da Vinci collection, this perpetual calendar is distinguished—like the original caliber—by its crown adjustment system and its four-digit year display. The Tourbillon Semainier by Blancpain—even though its calendar is not of the perpetual sort—will appeal to modern businessmen by its display of the week using a red-tipped hand gliding around the rim of the dial.

As a tribute to its master watchmaker Kurt Klaus, who created, in 1985, the modular perpetual calendar movement that would power the famous Da Vinci model, IWC recently presented the Da Vinci Perpetual Calendar Special Edition Kurt Klaus.

▶▶ 1
Patek Philippe, Calatrava Officier Quantième perpétuel Réf.5159
Renowned for its ultra-thin perpetual calendars that are highly prized among collectors, Patek Philippe also revived another brand tradition in 2007, introducing a slightly enlarged version of its Quantième Perpétuel with retrograde date and Officer's type case, protected by a hinged cover.

▶▶ 2
Blancpain, Quantième perpétuel avec correcteurs sous cornes
In its Perpetual Calendar with under-lug correctors, Blancpain marries classic design and technical innovation. Instead of placing the correctors underneath the case's flank, the brand developed a new system that allowed it to integrate them into the four lugs that connect the watch to the strap, on the side closer to the wrist.

2 ▲

3 ▲

Technical breakthroughs

In its Perpetual Calendar with under-lug correctors, Blancpain combines classic design and technical innovation. Instead of placing the correctors along the side of the case, the brand has developed an original system enabling to integrate them into the four bracelet lugs, on the wrist side. A press of the finger is enough to correct the date, day, month, leap-year cycle of moonphases. As for the Daniel Roth Instantaneous Perpetual Calendar, it has been equipped with a world-first original function involving instant jumping of the display hands daily at midnight. Its finely crafted self-winding mechanism is partially visible through the skeletonized dial.

Retrograding systems

The perpetual calendar is currently providing a scope for all manner of fancy touches in terms of display modes and designs. To vary the appearance of watch dials, more and more brands are using retrograde systems (see Retrogrades and Jump Hours chapter). Such is the case with the Toric Corrector Minute Repeater and Perpetual Calendar by Parmigiani Fleurier, equipped with a proprietary movement and a pusher serving to instantly correct all the calendar and moonphase functions. Jaquet Droz, known for the unusual geometry of its models, offers a Perpetual Calendar model with double retrograde display that takes up the entire upper part of the dial: days on the left, and date on the right. Famed for its ultra-thin perpetual calendars, which are highly sought after among collectors, Patek Philippe also revived another house tradition in 2007 by presenting a new slightly larger version of its Perpetual Calendar with retrograde date and officer-type case protected by a hinged cover. The retrograde hand moves over a 240° arc of a circle between 8:00 and 4:00. This Ref. 5159 is also one of the rare perpetual calendars fitted with a central seconds hand.

4

5

▶▶ 3   *Daniel Roth, Quantième perpétuel instantané*
Daniel Roth's Instantaneous Perpetual Calendar
boasts a world-first function: the instantaneous
displacement of the hand and counters every
night at midnight.

▶▶ 4   *Parmigiani Fleurier, Toric Corrector Répétition
minutes et Quantième perpétuel*
To vary their dials' aesthetic, many
watchmakers are using "retrograde" systems
(see "Retrograde Mechanisms and Jump Hours"
chapter). This is also the case with the Toric
Corrector Répétition Minutes et Quantième
Perpétuel by Parmigiani Fleurier.

▶▶ 5   *Jaquet Droz, Quantième perpétuel*
Jaquet Droz, whose every creation is remarkable
for unusual use of geometry, offers a Perpetual
Calendar with double retrograde display that
occupies the entire height of the dial—with the
days on the left and the date on the right.

1

2

The goal of transparency

Another definite trend is towards playing with transparency effects. Vacheron Constantin has equipped its Malte Perpetual Calendar in platinum with open-face retrograde date with a double sapphire crystal providing a plunging view into the heart of the mechanism. The retrograde date is displayed on a highly original checkered motif on the upper part of the dial. Small subdials indicate the date by means of tiny white panels, while the months and leap-year cycles are painted in black on one of the sapphire crystals. The Geneva-based manufacture also treated the perpetual calendar to a spectacular new setting with its Patrimony Traditionnelle Skeletonized Perpetual Calendar, featuring an entirely openworked movement and engraved décor inspired by Art Nouveau, particularly the motifs on the Eiffel Tower. Patek Philippe also played the magician by introducing the Grande Complication Ref. 5104 in 2006, fitted with a transparent dial enabling one to admire the mechanisms in action. In order to rise to this challenge, the manufacture has devised an original display system: the names of the days and months as well as the numeral corresponding to the leap-year cycle are printed directly on the sapphire dial; beneath these three circles are three tiny sapphire disks with a black rectangular circle; as they turn, these pallets reveals the contrasting white transferred markings. This platinum timepiece also features a minute repeater indication.

Vacheron Constantin, Calendrier perpétuel Malte en platine à date rétrogradante «Openface»
Vacheron Constantin has endowed its Malte "Open Face" Perpetual Calendar, crafted in platinum with a retrograde date, with a double sapphire crystal that offers a spectacular view into the very heart of the mechanism.

▶▶ **1** *de Grisogono, Instrumento Novantatre*
Housed in a rectangular case, this annual calendar watch designed by de GRISOGONO features a double large window for the date, as well as an arched opening for the number of the month. Its dial boasts oversized numerals for 9 and 3, inspiring its name: Instrumento Novantatre.

▶▶ **2** *Patek Philippe, Quantième Annuel*
Patek Philippe presented a new innovation in 1996 with its patented Annual Calendar, which conceals tremendous technical sophistication.

▶▶ **3** *Franc Vila, Chronographe Quantième annuel automatique calibre Fva12-A*
The automatic-winding Chronographe Quantième Annuel with its Fva12-9A movement combines two useful complications in a powerful, sporty and elegant design.

▶▶ **4** *Hermès, Dressage Quantième Annuel*
Hermès celebrated its 170th anniversary by presenting its Dressage Quantième Annuel, which beats to an exclusively movement crafted by Vaucher Manufacture Fleurier, a company of which Hermès recently acquired a 25 percent stake.

▶▶ **5** *A.Lange&Söhne, Datograph perpétuel*
The "large date" display is enjoying unprecedented popularity—as much for its readability as for its touch of originality. The German brand A. Lange & Söhne has even made it one of the company's trademarks, as on the dial of the Datograph perpétuel.

▶▶ **6** *Pierre DeRoche, GrandCliff Quantième annuel réserve de marche*
In 2007, the young company Pierre DeRoche, founded by the brother of the current directors of Dubois Dépraz, presented a Quantième Annuel Réserve de Marche model in its GrandCliff collection.

Time for annual calendars

Midway between the simple calendar and the perpetual calendar, the annual calendar recognizes the length of months of 30 and 31 days, but must be corrected once a year, at the end of February. The Dubois Dépraz manufacture was one of the first to offer this mechanism, as a module. In 1996, Patek Philippe also innovated by presenting its patented annual calendar. This ingenious system involves an extreme level of technical sophistication. Choosing to do mostly without lever-operated mechanisms, the engineers had to redesign the entire architecture of the movement that works mostly with the help of wheels and pinions. The result is an annual calendar with moonphases composed of 330 parts, while a traditional perpetual calendar with moonphases comprises 285. All the calendar displays are adjusted instantly by means of pushbuttons housed in the case middle. This mechanism has since been interpreted within several different exteriors and with various displays, and is asserting itself as one of the Patek Philippe's star products. In 2007, several other brands launched annual calendar models featuring original aesthetic touches. Fitted with a highly distinctive rectangular case, the annual calendar watch designed by de GRISOGONO features a large double date window as well for a month aperture shaped like the arc of a circle. The dial bearing oversized numerals 9 and 3 has inspired the name of this model: Instrumento Novantatre. The Chronographe Quantième Annuel Automatique Caliber Fva12-91 by Franck Vila combines two useful complications within a powerful, sporting and elegant design. Hermès celebrated its 170th anniversary by introducing the Dressage Annual Calendar with

a self-winding movement made exclusively for Hermès by Vaucher manufacture Fleurier, a firm in which the French brand recently acquired a 25% capital stake. This limited-edition watch stands out from the crowd thanks to its refined case and original dial featuring a retrograde 270° pointer-type date indication and visible day and month disks. In 2007, the youthful Pierre DeRoche brand, founded by the brother of one of the current leaders of Dubois Dépraz, presented the latest addition to its GrandCliff collection in the shape of an Annual Calendar Power Reserve model. This rectangular timepiece, equipped with an exclusive Dubois Dépraz movement, combines an annual calendar with a chronograph powering retrograde 60-minute and 6-hour counters, a flyback function and a large date display.

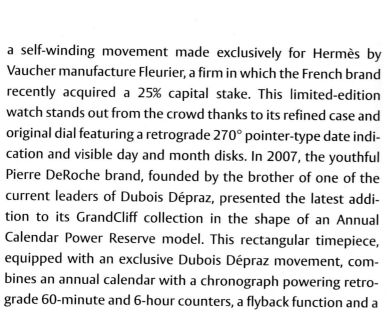

A. LANGE & SÖHNE

LANGEMATIK PERPETUAL

Powered by the self-winding Caliber L922.1 SAX-0-MAT, Langematik Perpetual is the world's first self-winding wristwatch with an outsize date and a perpetual calendar featuring separate pushpieces for individual corrections of the calendar indications (date, day of week, month, leap year, and moonphase displays), as well as a main pushpiece for collectively advancing all displays. Caliber L922.1 SAX-0-MAT has a power reserve of 46 hours, stop seconds with patented ZERO-RESET mechanism, plates and bridges made of untreated German silver, and a hand-engraved balance cock. Langematik Perpetual's three-piece, pink-gold case is fitted with antireflective sapphire crystals on the front and back, and a crown for winding the watch and setting the time. The dial is crafted of solid silver, argenté, with pink-gold, luminous hands. The watch's crocodile strap is secured via a solid gold buckle.

AUDEMARS PIGUET

MILLENARY CABINET #5 - REF. 26066PT.00.D028CR.01

Millenary Cabinet #5 is the fifth inductee into the Tradition d'Excellence collection that will include 8 models. This 950 platinum timepiece is limited to just 20 pieces and each houses the manual-winding Caliber 2899 and features a world-premiere high-performance direct-impulse escapement equipped with 2 balance springs that requires no lubrication, twin barrels with 7 days of power reserve, linear perpetual calendar with adjustment through pushpiece and correctors recessed in the middle case, deadbeat seconds. Off-center displays, exposed by openwork dial with indications on multiple planes make the technical achievement a visual awe.

AUDEMARS PIGUET

ROYAL OAK PERPETUAL CALENDAR - REF. 25820SP.00.0944SP.02

A combination of 950 platinum and steel, this Royal Oak Perpetual Calendar houses the self-winding Caliber 2120/2802 with 21K gold rotor. Water resistant to 20 meters, this complication calibrates the day of the week to the date, month, phase within the 4-year leap-year cycle, astronomical moon indication with no manual adjustment required until the year 2100. It is fitted with a sapphire caseback.

AUDEMARS PIGUET

ROYAL OAK SKELETON PERPETUAL CALENDAR - REF. 25829ST.00.0944ST.01

This complication features an openwork dial that exposes the function and integration of the perpetual calendar, which calibrates the day of the week to the date, month, phase within the 4-year leap-year cycle, astronomical moon indication with no manual adjustment required until the year 2100. Historic base movement is hollowed and engraved by hand. The case and bracelet are stainless steel; the case's assembly screws are 18K gold. Water resistant to 20 meters, the Royal Oak Skeleton Perpetual Calendar features a sapphire crystal and sapphire crystal caseback.

BLANCPAIN

VILLERET LADY'S ULTRA SLIM PERPETUAL CALENDAR

This limited volume nonetheless accommodates with unfailing precision no fewer than 248 components that enable caliber 5621 to give meticulous cadence to the hours and minutes, as well as the day of the week, date, month, leap years and moonphases. This caliber is housed within an 18K white-gold case with a diameter of 34mm. Water resistant to 30 meters, the case is fitted with a sapphire crystal, glare-proof on both sides, and with a glare-proof sapphire caseback.

SELF-WINDING PERPETUAL CALENDAR WITH RETROGRADE DATE AND MOONPHASE

This 18K white-gold BOVET Perpetual Calendar with Retrograde Date and 55-hour power reserve is a magnificent demonstration of how to display a full calendar and moonphases via letters, numerals and images. It is easy to advance the date-hand every 24 hours against a spring released by the perpetual calendar mechanism at the end of the month so that it flicks back to the beginning. The difficulty that underlies all such retrograde mechanisms is that the hand flies back through a 225° arc with such force that it bounces up again on the scale and catches on the second or third date. BOVET has solved this bounce-back problem by slowing the return of the date-hand with a train of wheels. (The dial is available in white or black lacquered enamel or mother of pearl.) .

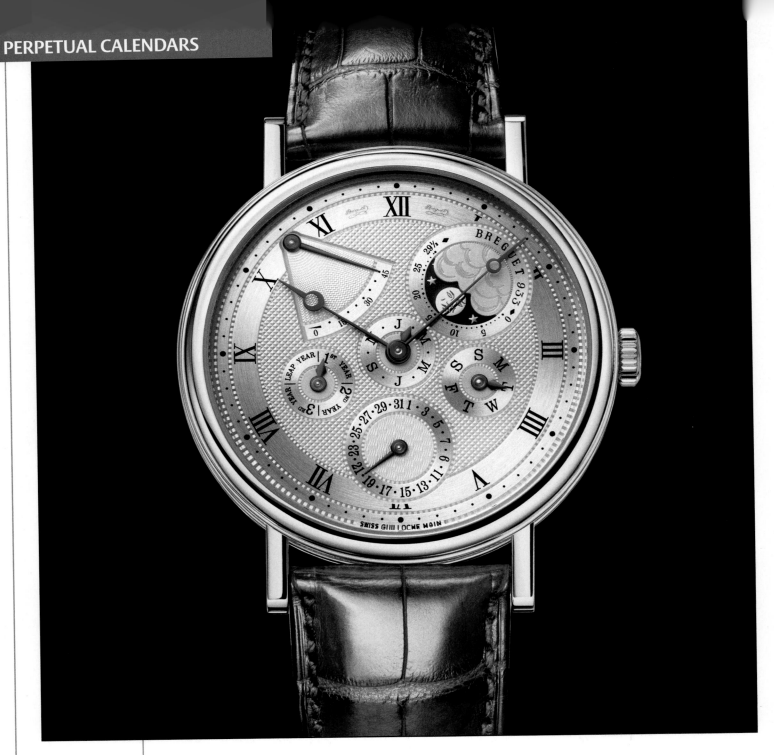

BREGUET

CLASSIQUE GRANDE COMPLICATION - REF. 5327BR/1E/9V6

This Classique Grande Complication wristwatch is crafted in 18K yellow, white or rose gold, and houses a thin, engraved automatic movement with perpetual calendar, precise moonphases, 46-hour power reserve and 3Hz balance frequency. Its engine-turned dial is in silvered 18K gold with a chapter ring displaying Roman numerals, central months indication, and showing dates, days and leap years on three subdials, power-reserve indicator at 10:30 and moonphases at 1:30. It also features a secret signature and power-reserve indicator. The engine-turned caseback is sapphire crystal and the case is water resistant to 30 meters.

BVLGARI

BVLGARI-BVLGARI - REF. BB38PLPC

The Bvlgari-Bvlgari Ref. BB38PLPC features a mechanical, automatic winding Caliber FP 5763, with 65-hour power reserve, 35 jewels and a vibration rate of 28,800 vph. This movement offers hours, minutes, perpetual calendar and bi-retrograde seconds and is finished and decorated by hand, with stippling and Côtes de Genève treatment. The 38mm, polished platinum case is fitted with an antireflective scratch-resistant sapphire crystal, snap-on back displaying the movement through a sapphire crystal, limited-edition number engraved on the case side and is water resistant to 30 meters. The pink dial with hand-applied indexes displays hours and minutes with seconds at 6:00, leap year and month at 12:00, date at 3:00, and day at 9:00. The hand-sewn brown alligator strap has a platinum triple-fold-over buckle. Limited edition of 99 pieces.

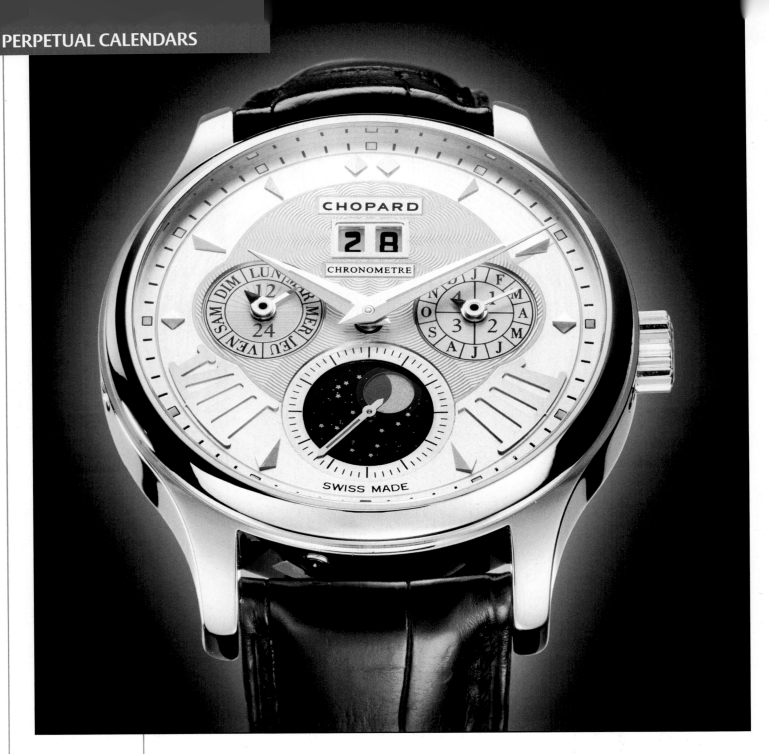

CHOPARD

L.U.C LUNAR ONE WITH ORBITAL MOONPHASE, REF. 161894-9001

Measuring ⌀ 11.4mm and 20mm thick, the L.U.C Lunar One is powered by the mechanical self-winding L.U.C 96 QP movement. The 354-part movement is a COSC-certified chronometer and bears the Poinçon de Genève quality hallmark. It has a power-reserve of approximately 65 hours and beats at 28,800 vibrations per hour. The L.U.C Lunar One features a perpetual calendar, date at 12:00, day of the week, leap year, 24-hour indication, power-reserve indicator and phases of the moon, which are presented in an extremely precise and original way. The moonphases rotate around the axis of the small seconds display, hence the term "orbital." This system's accuracy measures a mere 57.2-second difference per lunar cycle (or one day every 122 years). Water resistant to 30 meters, the watch is created in two limited editions: 250 pieces in pink gold (shown); 250 pieces in 950 platinum (Ref. 16/91894).

DANIEL ROTH

PERPETUAL CALENDAR MOON PHASE - REF. 118.X.60.154.CN.BD

The Perpetual Calendar Moon Phase features an automatic movement with perpetual calendar and indication of the moonphase, offering a 45-hour power reserve and presenting a hand guilloché solid gold and platinum rotor. The two-level white-gold dial, with white enamel base and black guilloché center, displays individual counters for the indication of the days of the week, months, dates and leap years. The moonphase appears on a special counter at 12:00 with a realistic black and white image of the moon in its starry sky, represented on a moving disk. This model is water resistant to 3atm.

DANIEL ROTH

INSTANTANEOUS PERPETUAL CALENDAR - REF. 119.X.60.896.CN.BA

The Instantaneous Perpetual Calendar features an entirely hand-decorated automatic perpetual calendar movement with central hour and minute hand and three subdials indicating the day of the week, month, date and leap years, all jumping instantaneously at midnight. This movement is housed in a white-gold double-ellipse case, enhanced by a gold openworked dial revealing the elaborate movement decoration, further unveiled through the caseback secured by four pentagonal screws. This model is presented on a hand-stitched alligator leather strap with pin buckle bearing the brand emblem and is water resistant to 3atm.

GERALD GENTA

ARENA PERPETUAL CALENDAR GMT - REF. AQG.Y.87.129.CM.BD

This Arena Perpetual Calendar GMT features an entirely hand-decorated automatic movement with perpetual calendar and second time zone on a 24-hour counter at 12:00, offering a 45-hour power reserve. It is housed in a Ø 45mm titanium case with fluted caseband and platinum bezel, enhanced by a blue and satin-finish metallic net-like dial. It is water resistant to 10atm.

GERALD GENTA

OCTO 48-MONTH PERPETUAL CALENDAR - REF. OQM.Y.60.515.CN.BD

This Octo 48-month Perpetual Calendar offers an exclusive Gérald Genta automatic movement, entirely decorated by hand, with old-gold finish and endowed with a 48-month perpetual calendar indicating the days of the week, the date, the months of the year over a 4-year cycle, and the leap years. It is housed in an octagonal case in 5N red gold or diamond-polished, white-gold and circular satin-brushed bezel with polished hour-markers, enhanced by an engraved, cloisonné and lacquered 18K gold dial, and a beaded crown with hawk's eye cabochon. This model is presented on a black hand-stitched alligator leather strap with a circular-grained folding clasp and enhanced with the brand logo and symbol. It is water resistant to 10atm.

DeWITT

QUANTIEME PERPETUEL SPORT - REF. AC.7004.31A.M623

The exclusive self-winding DeWitt caliber DW7004 with a 42-hour power reserve powers this model with automatic date correction (regardless of the number of days in a month or leap years). The black carbon-fiber dial is designed with see-through counters and retrograde hands for the days positioned at 9:00, the date at 3:00, the months/years indicator at 12:00 and the moonphase at 6:00. This exceptional perpetual calendar is stamped with the highly prized Geneva Seal (Poinçon de Genève), the ultimate recognition for a manufacture and an award that sets the highest standard in the quality of finish for a fine luxury watch movement. Limited edition of 99 pieces.

GUY ELLIA

TIME SQUARE Z1 - PERPETUAL CALENDAR

Virile and technical, the Guy Ellia style makes this watch immediately recognizable. The case is a full, simple, curved square that sits perfectly on the wrist. As for the face, it has stylized Roman numerals that create an extremely graphic universe. Overall, the watch offers strength and sobriety. On this Time Square Z1, the date, day of the week and month are indicated via hands, while the phases of the moon pass in an aperture at 6:00. The automatic Frédéric Piguet Calibre 5653 also offers leap-year indicator and three days of power reserve. It exists in white, yellow, pink and black gold and can be set with diamonds.

DA VINCI PERPETUAL CALENDAR EDITION KURT KLAUS

IWC's Da Vinci Perpetual Calendar Special Edition Kurt Klaus is the limited-edition tribute to the long-serving IWC chief designer. It was Klaus who made the Da Vinci famous with his inspired invention of the autonomous perpetual calendar 20 years ago. The Special Edition combines the original perpetual calendar chronograph with an automatic movement developed by Kraus within the new tonneau-shaped case.

IWC

PORTUGUESE PERPETUAL CALENDAR - REF. IW502218

This 18K white-gold Portuguese Perpetual Calendar watch is powered by the company's 5000 caliber and offers ingenious displays. It houses the Pellaton winding mechanism with an entirely new moonphase display, a world-first patent. The Portuguese Perpetual Calendar offers seven days of power reserve and all perpetual calendar readouts. The moonphase is represented in the sky's northern and southern hemispheres, as well as via a disk display with two opposing circular windows rotating above a yellow surface with two black circles. Both moons are constantly in motion.

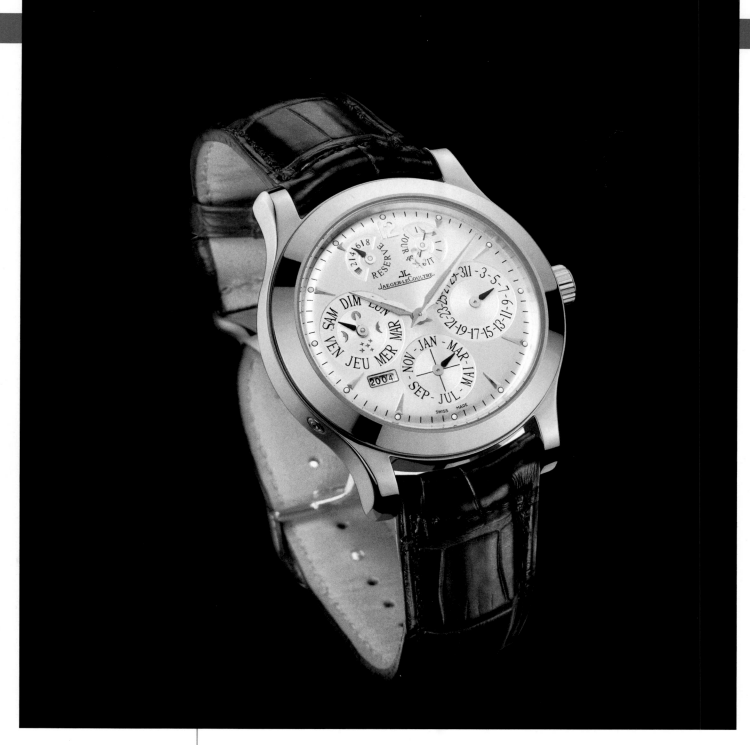

JAEGER-LECOULTRE

MASTER EIGHT DAYS PERPETUAL

Classically designed, this Master Eight Days Perpetual houses the mechanical manually wound Caliber 876 that is crafted, assembled and decorated by hand. It beats at 28,800 vibrations per hour and consists of 262 parts and 37 jewels. It offers hours, minutes, date, month, day of week, four-digit year display, moonphase, power reserve, and a day/night indicator with red safety zone for changing of the perpetual calendar. The watch is crafted in platinum or in 18-karat pink gold.

JAEGER-LECOULTRE

MASTER GRANDE REVEIL

The Ø 43mm Master Grande Reveil offers both an alarm function (with chime or vibration modes) and perpetual calendar. Available in stainless steel, pink gold or 950 platinum, it houses the mechanical automatic Caliber 909/1 with 363 parts and and 36 jewels. offers a 24-hour indicator and moonphase indicators for both hemispheres. The 1000 Hours Control seal is engraved on the pink-gold and platinum Master Grande Reveil casebacks.

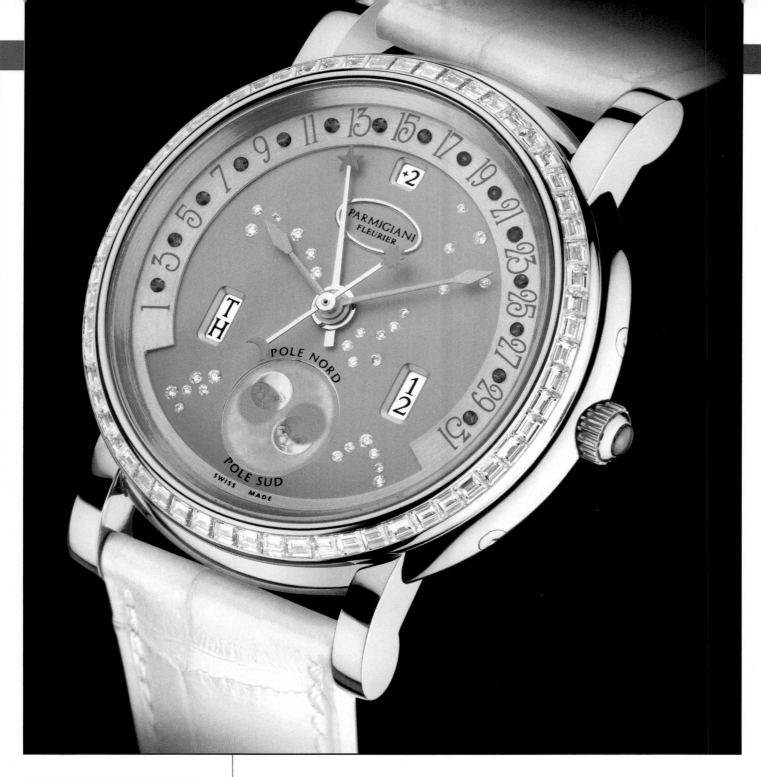

PARMIGIANI FLEURIER

TORIC RETROGRADE PERPETUAL CALENDAR LUNA BLU - REF. PF0011588-01

Luna Blu's perpetual calendar offers day, retrograde date, month, leap year, and high-precision moonphase in the northern and southern hemispheres. The proprietary mechanical self-winding PF Caliber 333 has 45-hour power reserve, 32 jewels, a 22K oscillating weight, hand-beveled bridges and beats at 28,800 vph. The 18K white-gold case is available with or without diamonds (1.6 carats of brilliant-cut, 3 carats of baguette-cut) and the blue lacquered 18K dial has a semi-matte circular satin-brushed rim for the date with blue transferred numerals separated by brilliant-cut sapphires. Brilliant-cut diamonds form Ursa Minor, Cetus, Lyra, and Corona Borealis. The watch comes on a Hermès crocodile leather strap.

PARMIGIANI FLEURIER

TORIC RETROGRADE PERPETUAL CALENDAR - REF. PF002614

This mechanical self-winding watch houses the PF333 caliber, created in house with a 22-karat gold oscillating weight and hand-beveled bridges. Beating at 28,800 vibrations per hour, the watch offers day, month, leap year, moonphase indicator and retrograde date. It is crafted in 18-karat rose gold with a slate-gray and rose-gold dial.

PATEK PHILIPPE

PERPETUAL CALENDAR - REF. 5140

Housed in a three-part 18K white-gold 37.2mm case, this Perpetual Calendar beats to the mechanical automatic-winding Patek Philippe 240 Q caliber. The movement, with 22K off-centered micro-rotor, features the Geneva Seal and is decorated with a Côtes de Genève pattern. The perpetual calendar offers 24-hour indication, day, date, month, year, and moonphase, plus hour and minute. Water resistant to 2.5atm, the watch features a silvered solid gold dial with applied gold markers and hands.

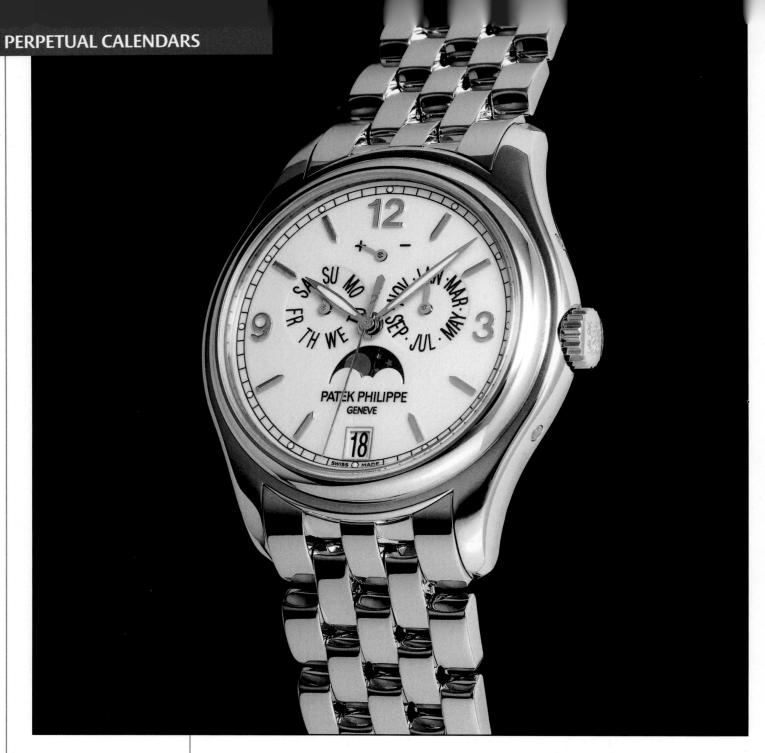

PATEK PHILIPPE

ANNUAL CALENDAR - REF. 5146/1

This superb Annual Calendar with date, day, month and moonphase takes the days of the every month except February into account. It is powered by the automatic-winding Patek Philippe 315 S IRM QA LU manufacture caliber, decorated with a Côtes de Genève pattern and beveled, bearing a 21K gold rotor and power reserve. The 18K white-gold three-piece case bears a curved sapphire crystal and the exquisite movement can be viewed through a sapphire caseback. The cream-colored dial is hand enameled and features applied gold numerals, markers and hands. The white-gold bracelet features a white-gold double-fold-over clasp.

PATEK PHILIPPE

ANNUAL CALENDAR - REF. 5146P

Crafted in 950 platinum, this Annual Calendar houses the proprietary mechanical automatic-winding Patek Philippe 315 S IRM QA LU manufacture caliber that is decorated with a Côtes de Genève pattern. It offers hour, minute, second, power reserve and annual calendar (date, day, month, moonphase). The calendar takes the days of a month into account over an entire year, except for February, which means it must be manually changed on March 1st. This Annual Calendar features a slate-gray dial and hand-stitched alligator strap.

PATEK PHILIPPE

CALATRAVA ANNUAL CALENDAR - REF. 5396R

Within its 18K pink-gold three-piece Calatrava case, this Annual Calendar is powered by the mechanical automatic-winding Patek Philippe 324-303 caliber. It is decorated with a Côtes de Genève pattern, features a 21K gold rotor, and is hallmarked with the Geneva Seal. The watch offers hour, minutes, seconds, day, date, month, and moonphase. It is water resistant to 2.5atm.

PATEK PHILIPPE

GONDOLO CALENDAR - REF. 5135P

Crafted in platinum and set with a single brilliant at 6:00, this Gondolo Calendar is powered by the automatic-winding Patek Philippe 324 S QA LU 24H caliber decorated with a Côtes de Genève pattern and beveled. The movement with its 21K gold rotor is visible through a sapphire caseback. The watch offers hour, minute and second, annual calendar and 24-hour indication. The month readout is at 2:00, moonphase with 24-hour is at 6:00, day of week is at 10:00, and date is at 12:00. The solid gold dial with slate-gray sun-patterned finish features white-gold markers and diamonds. Hallmarked with the Geneva Seal, this tonneau-shaped watch is also available in pink gold, white gold or yellow gold with different dial colors.

PATEK PHILIPPE

GONDOLO CALENDAR - REF. 5135R

This Gonodolo Calendar houses the mechanical automatic-winding Patek Philippe 324 S QA LU 24H manufacture caliber decorated with a Côtes de Genève pattern and featuring a 21K gold rotor. It offers hours, minute, seconds, 24 hours and annual calendar (date, day, month, moonphase, and takes the days of a month into account over a whole year, except for February). It is crafted in an 18K pink-gold two-piece tonneau-shaped case with curved sapphire crystal, pink-gold crown and screw-on caseback, displaying the movement through a sapphire crystal. It is water resistant to 2.5atm.

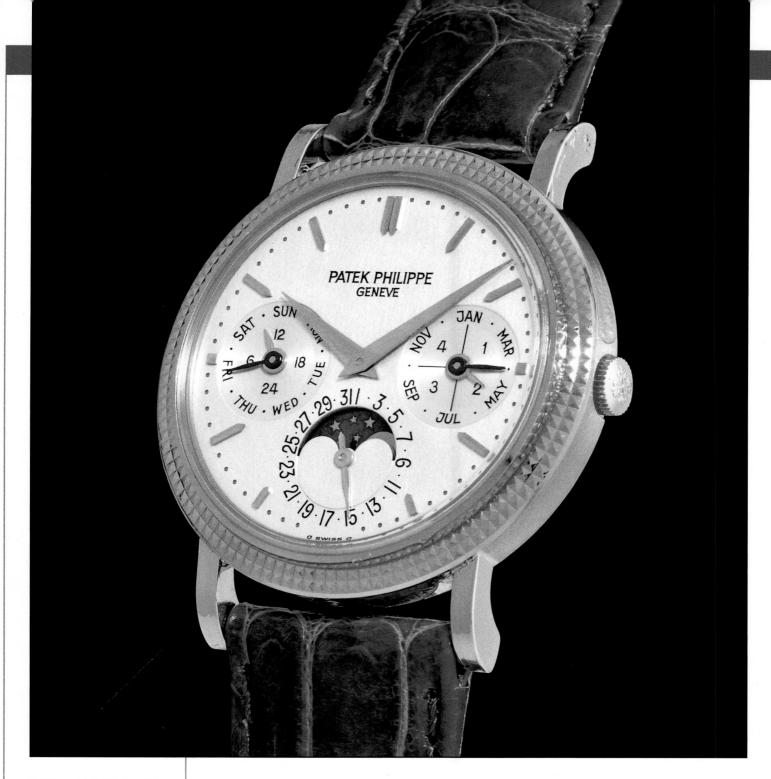

PATEK PHILIPPE

REF. 5039

The refined Clous de Paris pattern on the bezel characterizes this watch and is indicative of some models from the Calatrava collection. Its caliber 240Q with Geneva Seal is provided with a perpetual-calendar module and it is the most classic and recognizable movement among those produced by Patek Philippe. Caliber 240Q is displayed through the caseback and shows an off-center 21-karat gold micro-rotor and the exclusive Gyromax balance.

PIAGET

EMPERADOR PERPETUAL CALENDAR - REF. G0A33019

Mechanically programmed to cope with the irregularities of our Gregorian calendar up until the year 2100, the perpetual calendar is one of the major complications of the watchmaking art, as well as one of the most widely used. Measuring 5.6mm thick, the Manufacture Piaget Calibre 855P self-winding movement was designed, developed and produced entirely in-house. It displays the hours, minutes, small seconds at 4:00, month and leap years at 12:00, along with retrograde day of the week and date displays at 9:00 and 3:00 respectively. In addition to the latter retrograde indications, this Calibre 855P is stands out from most ordinary perpetual calendars by the addition of a double-hand dual time-zone display appearing in a subdial at 8:00. The self-winding Piaget Calibre 855P beats at a cadence of 21,600 vibrations per hour and is endowed with an approximately 72-hour power reserve.

ULYSSE NARDIN

GMT ± PERPETUAL - REF. 320-60/60

This GMT ± Perpetual houses within its 42mm, 18K white-gold case Caliber UN-32 with perpetual calendar, which is adjustable backwards and forwards from a single crown. The watch offers a second time zone on the main dial with the brand's patented quickset, and permanent home time is indicated by a third hand. Also available in 18K red gold, on a bracelet or strap and with various dial combinations.

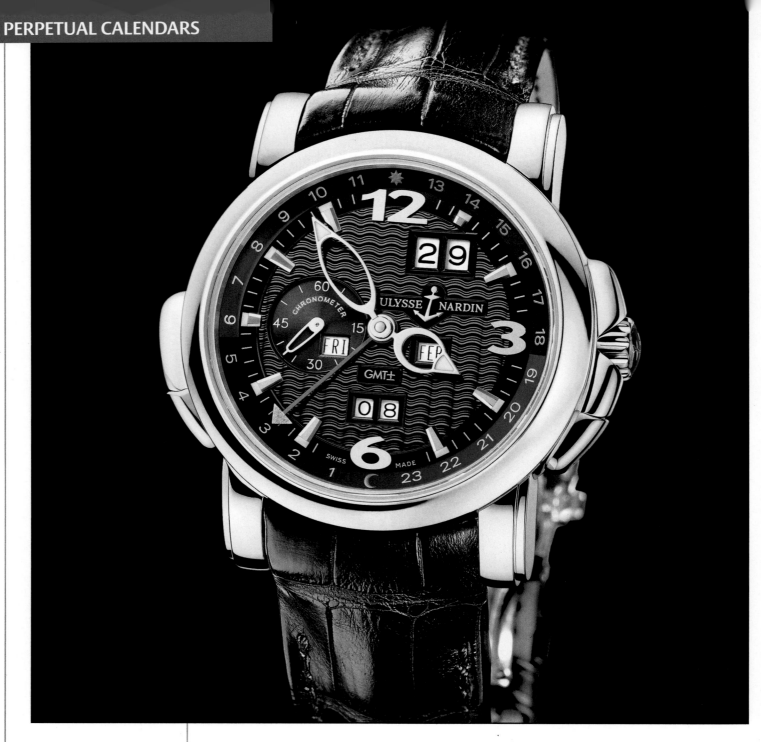

ULYSSE NARDIN

GMT ± PERPETUAL - REF. 320-60/62

This 42mm, 18K white-gold GMT ± Perpetual houses Caliber UN-32 with perpetual calendar, which is adjustable backwards and forwards from a single crown. The watch offers a second time zone on the main dial with the brand's patented quickset, and permanent home time is indicated by a third hand. Also available in 18K red gold, on a bracelet or strap and with various dial combinations.

ULYSSE NARDIN

QUADRATO PERPETUAL - REF. 326-90/91

This Quadrato Perpetual's 42x42mm, 18K red-gold case houses the Caliber UN 32 with perpetual calendar, which is adjustable backwards and forwards from a single crown. The watch offers a second time zone on the main dial with the brand's patented quickset, and permanent home time is indicated by a third hand. Quadrato Perpetual is also available in 18K white gold, with various dial combinations, and on a bracelet.

VACHERON CONSTANTIN

MALTE RETROGRADE PERPETUAL CALENDAR - REF. 47031

In this Malte model, Vacheron Constantin combines a perpetual calendar with a 31-day retrograde calendar. The Ø 39mm case, crafted in either platinum or 18K rose gold, houses the 1126 QPR automatic movement and offers hours, minutes, perpetual calendar, day and month indications via hands. Current year and leap year are displayed through a window. The retrograde crescent offers 31-day date and the movement beats at 28,800 vibrations per hour.

VACHERON CONSTANTIN

MALTE OPENFACE RETROGRADE PERPETUAL CALENDAR - REF. 47032

This platinum Malte Openface Retrograde Perpetual Calendar houses the mechanical automatic-winding Vacheron Constantin Caliber 1126 QPR. The 36-jeweled movement beats at 28,800 vibrations per hour, has 38 hours of power reserve, is hand-finished, and features a pink-gold mainplate. All of its parts have been hand-chiseled and etched away for exceptional viewing. The perpetual calendar offers date, day, month, digital year indication, and 4-year cycle. The dial consists of a sapphire crystal disk, luminescent peripheral date-ring, and white-gold hands. On an alligator strap with platinum clasp on an alligator strap with platinum clasp.

VACHERON CONSTANTIN

PATRIMONY TRADITIONNELLE SKELETON PERPETUAL CALENDAR - REF. 43172

The Patrimony Traditionnelle Skeleton Perpetual Calendar houses the 1120 QP SQ self-winding caliber, stamped with the prestigious Geneva hallmark. The movement is distinguished by the Art Nouveau motif of its beautifully finished engraving. Vacheron Constantin's master engravers were inspired by the motifs and elegant shapes of the Eiffel Tower. The dial was designed to provide an excellent view of the skeleton movement and perfect legibility of the perpetual calendar indications. Vacheron Constantin designed a transparent sapphire dial enhanced by a silvered ring with the hour markers and minute-track. The Perpetual Calendar indications sit on this transparent dial, consequently gaining in both size and legibility. It comes in platinum PT950 or in 18K rose gold, with 36 jewels, and 40-hour power reserve.

ZENITH

GRANDE CHRONOMASTER QUANTIÉME PERPETUAL EL PRIMERO BLACK TIE

Crafted in platinum, this Grande ChronoMaster Quantième Perpetual El Primero Black Tie is powered by the proprietary El Primero 4003 automatic chronograph movement with perpetual calendar. The COSC-certified chronometer caliber consists of 321 components, including 31 jewels. With 50 hours of power reserve, the watch indicates date, moonphases, day, month and leap year, chronograph functions, and tachymeter readout. The case's 60 baguette-cut Top Wesselton diamonds (5.4 carats) encircle a solid gold dial with genuine Polynesian mother-of-pearl and 11 diamond indexes. It is released in an exclusive limited and numbered edition on a handmade lambskin "Black Tie" leather strap with satin trim.

ZENITH

GRANDE CHRONOMASTER QUANTIEME PERPETUAL EL PRIMERO CONCEPT

This limited-edition 18K white-gold Grande ChronoMaster Quantième Perpetual El Primero Concept houses the automatic El Primero 4003 C (a COSC-certified chronometer with perpetual calendar that beats at 36,000 vph and carries 50 hours of power reserve), which is visible through the caseback. The movement with circular-grained mainplate is composed of 321 parts including a 22K gold oscillating weight with Côtes de Genève guilloché pattern. The perpetual calendar indicates date (in ring around 30-minute counter at 3:00), moonphase (inside 12-hour counter at 6:00), day at 9:00 and month and leap year at 12:00. The sapphire dial is ringed with a tachometric scale.

ZENITH

GRANDE CHRONOMASTER XXT QUANTIEME PERPETUAL EL PRIMERO

This Grande ChronoMaster XXT Quantième Perpetual El Primero is a COSC-certified chronometer that houses the El Primero 4003 automatic chronograph movement with perpetual calendar. It consists of 321 components and beats at 36,000 vibrations per hour. With a 22K white-gold oscillating weight, the 31-jeweled movement offers 50 hours of power reserve and measures to 1/10 of a second. The 45mm platinum 950 PT case is water resistant to 30 meters.

Moonphases

Formerly a mere component of perpetual calendar watches, the moonphase indication is currently asserting its independence. It is no longer afraid to give an almost solo performance on the center-stage of the dial, appearing in beautiful technical and aesthetic variations. But not all moonphase displays boast the same degree of precision, since they may show a one-day discrepancy every 2, 11 or 577 years, depending on the model.

Heavenly mathematics

Observing the lunar cycle—together with the recurring seasons and alternating pattern of days and nights—has always been one of the main foundations of our calendar systems. In particular, the lunar cycle has inspired our division of the year into months. In the West, the moonphase indication was an essential part of the first large medieval clocks. It also appeared on the first pocket-watches, alongside other astronomical and astrological displays. In the 20th century, although the moon had lost a good deal of the fascination it exercised on the human mind, watchmakers did their utmost to miniaturize this mechanism to wristwatch size, while maintaining a maximum of accuracy—which is no small feat. The length of a lunar cycle is in fact 29 days, 12 hours, 44 minutes and 2.8 seconds, meaning 29.53 days.

On ordinary moonphase displays, the disk carrying two moons is driven by a 59-tooth wheel (2 x 29.5). This system results in a one-day discrepancy in 2 years, 7 months and approximately 20 days. High-end watches are equipped with a far more complex and accurate device called an astronomical moon, boasting a wheel with 135 teeth. In such models, the difference between the mechanism and the real lunar cycle amounts to one day in 122 years. Such is the case, for example, on the new Cape Cod Moon Phases by Hermès, powered by a self-winding Vaucher Manufacturer Fleurier movement and retrograde date display. On its Portuguese Perpetual Calendar, IWC has further improved this astronomical precision. Thanks to an innovative system comprising three toothed wheels, the gap is reduced to one day in 577 years! This watch also uses the two moons depicted on the disc in an ingenious manner so as to simultaneously display the phases in both hemispheres. It is also endowed with a countdown device indicating the number of days until the next full moon.

A window on the stars

Revealing a little hint of heaven on the dial, the moonphase display imparts a touch of poetry and life to watches, while reminding us of the immemorial ties binding our time to that of the stars. In recent years, this complication has been enjoying renewed popularity, even occupying a place of honor on several new creations. Following on from its first "proprietary" calibers, Frédérique Constant recently launched the FC-935 Heart Beat Manufacture Moon Phases & Date model, issued in limited editions of 188 pink-gold and 1,888 steel pieces. The moon aperture, appearing in the center of a pointer-type date display, sits atop of the famous "open heart" window onto the dial. The new Nautilus Ref. 5712/1 by Patek Philippe, launched on the occasion of the collection's

Frédérique Constant, Heart Beat Manufacture Automatique Phases de lune & Date
Without breaking stride from its first brand-made calibers, Frédérique Constant recently launched the Heart Beat Manufacture Automatique Phases de Lune & Date in limited editions of 188 pieces in rose gold and 1888 pieces in steel.

1

30th anniversary, combines small seconds, a power-reserve indication, a pointer-type calendar as well as a moonphase display through a cintered aperture at the center of the circular date scale. Pierre Kunz, on its A014 HMRL, also offers an original dial layout. The retrograde hour and minute hands occupy two fan-shaped segments in the upper part, while the moonphase is displayed at the center of an oval cartouche speckled with stars, in a tiny aperture creating a beautiful depth effect.

New moons

2

The traditional aperture-type display is interpreted in various ways, including on the L.U.C Lunar One by Chopard. This perpetual calendar is distinguished by its orbital moonphase display: the window where the silvery moon waxes and wanes spins around the small seconds axis on a disk simulating the star-studded skies. The Grande Lange 1 Luna Mundi by A. Lange & Söhne comes as a twosome: a white-gold watch with the Northern hemisphere's Big Dipper on the dial for the moonphase; and a pink-gold watch with the Southern hemisphere's Southern Cross. The first "politically correct" moonphase! Moreover, instead of moving forward once or twice every 24 hours, this moonphase is coupled with the hour wheel and moves at a steady cadence. Meanwhile, some watchmakers prefer to give their imagination free reign to invent new ways of presenting the lunar cycle. De Bethune has equipped its Digitale with a patented spherical moonphase indication placed on the blue background on the caseback. On its Les Lunes watch with complete date/day/month calendar, Jaquet Droz offers a pointer-type display combined with a retrograde system: the hand follows the progress of the lunar cycle from one globe to another (new moon, first quarter, full moon, last

1   *Patek Philippe, Nautilus Réf.5712/1*
The new Nautilus Réf. 5712/1 by Patek Philippe,
launched on the occasion of the 30th anniversary
of the collection, marries small seconds,
power-reserve indicator and a calendar as well
as a moonphase display in an arched window
in the center of the circular date display.

2   *Pierre Kunz, A014 HMRL*
In its A014 HMRL, Pierre Kunz also offers
an original dial display.

3   *Chopard, L.U.C Lunar One*
The traditional window display can be
interpreted in various ways, such as on
Chopard's L.U.C Lunar One.

4   *A. Lange & Söhne, Grande Lange 1 "Luna Mundi"*
A. Lange & Söhne's Grande Lange 1
"Luna Mundi" is offered in a dyadic form:
a white-gold piece with Ursa Major on the dial
for the Northern Hemisphere moonphase
and a rose-gold watch with the Southern Cross
for the Southern Hemisphere.

5-6   *De Bethune, Digitale*
De Bethune has equipped its Digitale with
a patented "spherical" moonphase indication,
located on the caseback.

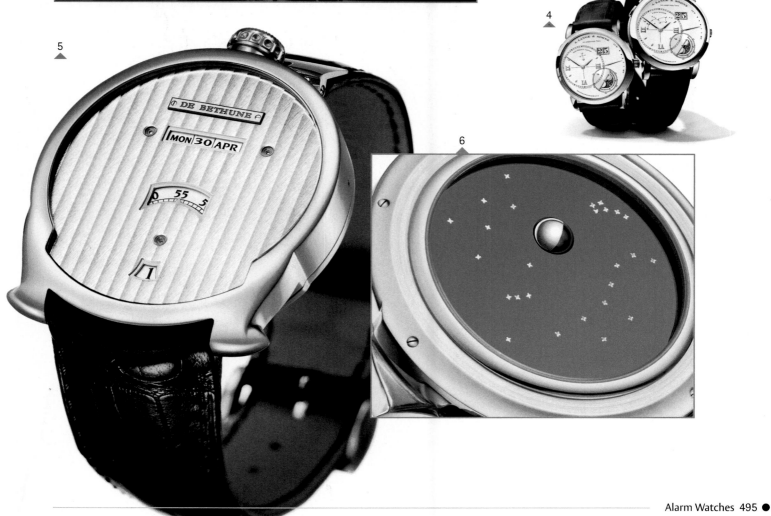

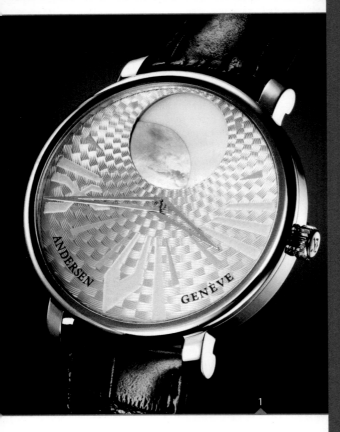

quarter, new moon), before jumping back instantly to its point of departure. In its Equation Marchante model (see the Equations of Time chapter), Blancpain also uses a retrograde hand display. The Kamar watch by Andersen Genève completely reinvents the traditional display mode with a round aperture equipped with a mother-of-pearl disk comprising a dark moon and a light moon, both of which stand out against a guilloché blue gold dial. This large-size display is particularly majestic.

Lady moon

As befits its romantic nature, the moonphase indication adorns an increasing number of refined models destined exclusively for women. Perrelet gives it star status in its Grande Phase de Lune centrale, featuring a pointer-type calendar driven by a self-winding movement; the lunar cycle stands out clearly against a white mother-of-pearl dial studded with diamond stars. Glamour is also the keynote for the Starmoon by Antoine Preziuso, presented as the largest moonphase model ever created: the black ceramic dial with luminescent numerals is framed by a case set with diamond and sapphire stars. Patek Philippe also had women in mind when creating its Ref. 4958 with small seconds and moonphases displayed through an unusually large aperture for a ladies' watch. On its Toric Quantième Perpétuel Rétrograde Luna Blu, Parmigiani Fleurier presents twin indications of the lunar cycles in both hemispheres. The blue-lacquered 18K gold dial is adorned with four diamond constellations: Ursa Minor, Cetus, Lyra, Corona Borealis. The Blancpain Women Complete Calendar Moonphase "Orchidée" model, featuring a central hand and day/month apertures, depicts a full moon with a face graced with exquisitely feminine features,

▶▶ 3 *Perrelet, Grande Phase de lune centrale*
Perrelet gives a starring role to the moonphase complication
in its Grande Phase de Lune centrale with automatic movement
and calendar hand; the cycle of the night stars shows up on
a white mother-of-pearl dial with a constellation of diamonds.

▶▶ 4 *Patek Philippe, Réf. 4958*
Patek Philippe was focused on women when it designed its
Ref. 4958, with small seconds and a moonphase display
in an unusually large window for a ladies' watch.

▶▶ 5 *Audemars Piguet, Millenary Ciel Etoilé*
One of the most noticed ladies' watches of 2007 was without
a doubt the haute jewelry Millenary Starlit Sky by Audemars Piguet,
with its oval case, its off-center dark blue dial sprinkled with
sparkling constellations, its moonphase window and crescent,
available in white mother-of-pearl or pavé with diamonds that
evoke the starry night sky.

▶▶ 6 *Antoine Preziuso, Starmoon*
Antoine Preziuso's Starmoon is the largest moonphase ever
created: the black ceramic dial with luminescent numerals
is framed by a case set with stars of diamond and sapphire.

▶▶ 7 *Parmigiani, Toric Quantième perpétuel rétrograde Luna Blu*
In its Toric Quantième Perpétuel Rétrograde Luna Blu,
Parmigiani Fleurier indicates the lunar months in both hemispheres.

▶▶ 8 *Blancpain, Blancpain Women Quantième complet Phases de lune*
The Blancpain Women Quantième Complet Phases de lune,
with a central-hand calendar and day/month, presents a full
moon with a woman's face, her features enhanced by a tiny
beauty mark in the shape of a star.

6

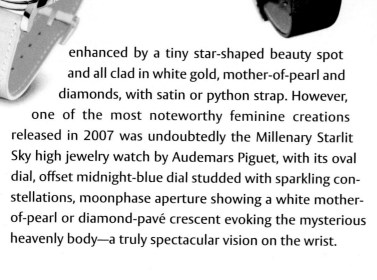

7

5

enhanced by a tiny star-shaped beauty spot
and all clad in white gold, mother-of-pearl and
diamonds, with satin or python strap. However,
one of the most noteworthy feminine creations
released in 2007 was undoubtedly the Millenary Starlit
Sky high jewelry watch by Audemars Piguet, with its oval
dial, offset midnight-blue dial studded with sparkling constellations, moonphase aperture showing a white mother-
of-pearl or diamond-pavé crescent evoking the mysterious
heavenly body—a truly spectacular vision on the wrist.

8

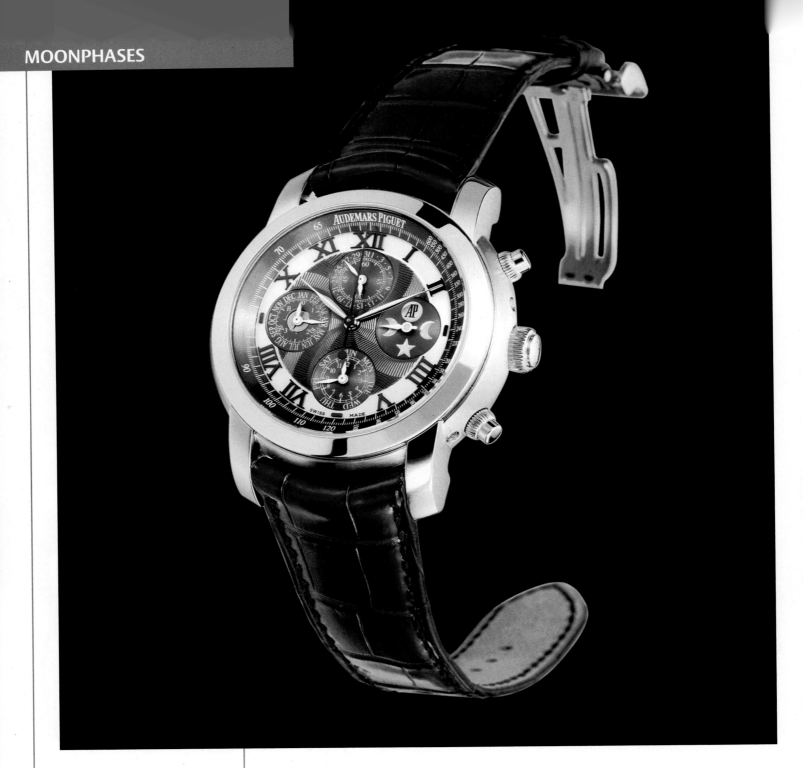

AUDEMARS PIGUET

JULES AUDEMARS PERPETUAL CALENDAR AND CHRONOGRAPH "ARNOLD ALL STARS"
REF. 26094BC.00.D095CR.01

Crafted in 18K white gold, this Jules Audemars "Arnold All Stars" houses the self-winding caliber 2326/2839 with 21K gold rotor. This limited edition of 100 pieces features the functions: hours, minutes, small seconds, date, day, month, 4-year leap-year cycle, astronomical moon indication (with no manual adjustments required until the year 2010) and chronograph. It offers a power reserve of 40 hours and beats at 28,800 vibrations per hour. The sapphire caseback is stamped with the "Arnold All Stars" Foundation logo.

BOVET

FLEURIER TRIPLE DATE

In the Fleurier 42mm dress watch, BOVET's designers show how attractive clarity and precision can be in indicating seven scales of time—from running seconds to lunar months—on the dial. Three disks under the dial show the day, month and phase of the moon. All the dates are clear around the edge of the dial. Each indication has its correcting pushpiece in the caseband and the self-winding movement—one of the finest in its category—delivers more than 70 hours of power reserve from twin barrels. In this watch, it's in a BOVET livery of rhodiumed Côtes de Genève, blued steel screws and a raised *fleurisanne* engraving on the 22K gold rotor.

JAEGER-LECOULTRE

REVERSO GRANDE SUN MOON

The generous proportions of this new addition to the Grande Reverso collection house the double barrels of its hand-wound mechanical movement, the Jaeger-LeCoultre Caliber 873, guaranteeing a power reserve of eight days. A turn of the legendary reversible case reveals a skillfully hand-decorated movement. Distinguished by its fine guilloché center, the dial also features the characteristically stylized figures and steel hands that are part of the Reverso's DNA. The day/night indicator at 2:00 swallows up the sun at the end of the day and serves up in its place a moon whose phase is recorded on a small round dial at 5:00, which is shared by the second hand. The power-reserve indicator occupies a delicate arc at 11:00. The Grande Sun Moon is available in steel or 18K pink gold on an alligator leather strap with folding clasp.

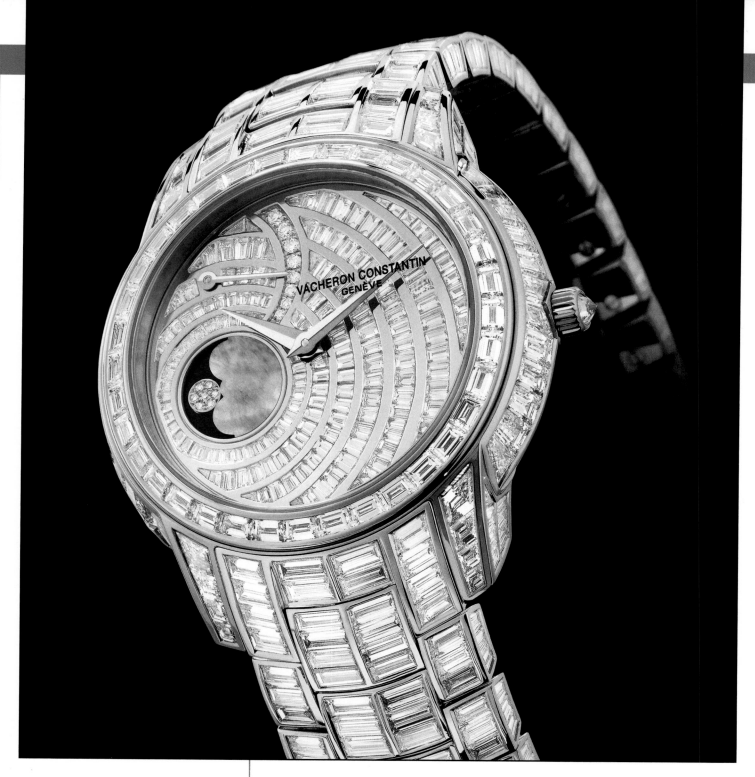

VACHERON CONSTANTIN

KALLA LUNE - REF. 83630

The newest addition to the Kalla collection is the KallaLune complication. Its hand-wound mechanical movement, caliber 1410, bears the prestigious Hallmark of Geneva. On the dial is the power reserve display and moonphase display set with 14 diamonds (0.03 carat). The case is set with 158 baguette-cut diamonds (13.60 carats), and its winding crown is set with a diamond (0.10 carat). The dial is set with 170 baguette-cut diamonds and 9 brilliant-cut diamonds (2.82 carats). Its 18K white-gold case measures 40.5mm in diameter, and its deployment clasp is set with 8 baguette-cut diamonds (0.38 carat).

VACHERON CONSTANTIN

MALTE MOONPHASE - REF. 83500

Available in either 18K white or yellow gold, this Malte Moonphase houses the Caliber 1410 manually wound movement with 40-hour power reserve, the Hallmark of Geneva, and beating at 28,800 vibrations per hour. The dial is engine-turned and 82 brilliant-cut diamonds weighing approximately 0.71 carat adorn this watch. Water resistant to 3atm.

VACHERON CONSTANTIN

TOLEDO 1952 - REF. 47300

This Patrimony Toledo 1952 is crafted in 18K pink gold and houses the mechanical manual-winding Vacheron Constantin Caliber 1125. Beating at 28,800 vibrations per hour, the complicated movement is equipped with 36 rubies and offers 40 hours of power reserve. In addition to small seconds, the watch offers a full calendar (date, day, month, moonphase). The three-piece square case is fitted with a curved sapphire crystal and is water resistant to 3atm. On a hand-stitched alligator strap with pink-gold clasp.

Retrogrades
and jump hours

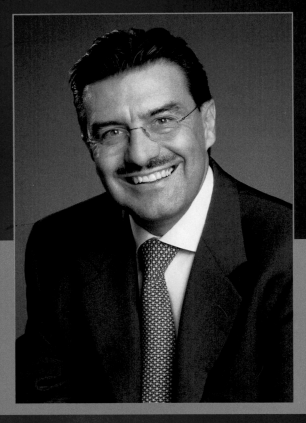

CEO of Vacheron Constantin

Juan-Carlos Torres

Contemporary Patrimony, day-date bi-retrograde

For world's oldest watch Manufacture, building on over 250 years of uninterrupted activity, a blend of heritage and prestige do not allow for idleness. In just a few years under the management of its CEO Juan Carlos Torres, Vacheron Constantin has made impressive strides towards the redefinition of its core know-how, with the launch of new collections that are perfectly contemporary, but steeped in the Swiss manufacture's DNA. The Contemporary Patrimony day-date bi-retrograde is the perfect example, and watch enthusiasts have already embraced it.

"This model is the essence of Vacheron Constantin's DNA"

As Juan-Carlos Torres remarks, the Manufacture has redefined its territory by reinforcing its Geneva roots, and particularly by increasing the number of watches meeting the exacting standards of the Hallmark of Geneva. Today, nearly 65% of Vacheron Constantin watches boast the Hallmark of Geneva label. At the same time, Vacheron Constantin has implemented a strategy of new in-house caliber development, from conception to production, and major surprises are in store for the coming months and years, says Juan Carlos Torres.

As a result of its success in the past few years, Vacheron Constantin has had to strengthen its teams. In 2007, the Plan-les-Ouates manufacture hired over 50 new people, and another few dozen will added in 2008. Vacheron Constantin is one of the very few Manufactures that have vertically integrated the craftsmanship that sets high watchmaking apart: enamelling, engraving, and the art of guilloche-work. Moreover, Vacheron Constantin has created a new division exclusively devoted to the production of bespoke watches. A rare endeavor in the watchmaking world of today, but one that has already prompted numerous watch aficionados and collectors to order unique timepieces. Because of the very nature of these timepieces, production is limited to less than 40 watches per year.

FACING PAGE
Juan Carlos Torres, CEO of Vacheron Constantin

THIS PAGE
Contemporary Patrimony day–date bi-retrograde: the essence of Vacheron Constantin's DNA

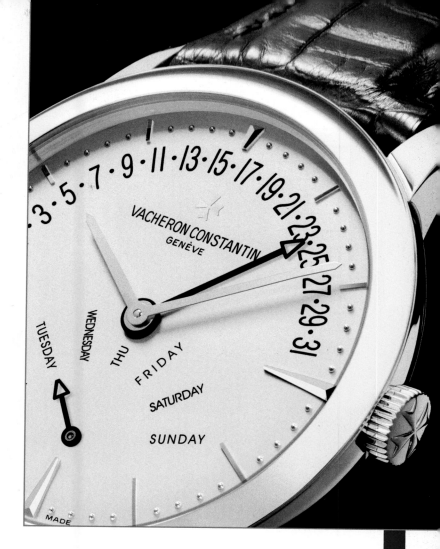

Vacheron Constantin's CEO is satisfied to see the new collections equally adopted and embraced in all regions of the world, ensuring the brand's stability in geographical sales.

Case in point, the new Contemporary Patrimony day-date bi-retrograde – which Juan-Carlos Torres views as, "the essence of Vacheron Constantin's DNA". Watch purists will appreciate the interior complexity of its mechanical movement, as well as the elegance and subtlety of its representation on the dial.

Subtlety for purists

The Contemporary Patrimony has enchanted collectors with dual complication revealed by two retrograde indications. Only an educated watch enthusiast could appreciate these creative displays that hide their complexity to better excite curiosity and desire. To complement the display of hours and minutes, the watchmaking engineers of Vacheron Constantin developed two of the most useful complications, with two retrograde indications: the day of the week and the date. A perfect example of technical prowess executed with aesthetical flair, the retrograde indications are as original as they are mechanically complex.

A considerable force for such a miniature mechanism is in play, so that the instant fly-back of the hands is executed in 1/10th of a second on a half circle of 180°. Immense energy is suddenly unleashed to permit the move of the hands in a fraction of a second, with infinite precision. Such is the feat that the two day of the week and date hands are made from a special alloy, characterized by its elasticity and weightlessness. At the heart of this timepiece, the 2460R31R7 caliber drives the of hours, minutes, date and day of the week functions, an automatic mechanical movement conceived, developed and produced by the Manufacture Vacheron Constantin. Bearing with the prestigious Hallmark of Geneva, this dual complication caliber is one of the new in-house 11_lines (25.6mm) automatic movements, produced as early as 2005 for the manufacture's 250th birthday.

President Vacheron Constantin North America

Julien Tornare

Vacheron Constantin is enjoying a strong dynamic today in the United States. Since his nomination at the head of Vacheron Constantin North America in the fall of 2004, Julien Tornare has devoted considerable effort to enhancing brand awareness. The young president has chosen to emphasize quality to achieve that goal. "To develop the brand's recognition," explains Julien Tornare, "we have worked on the fundamentals necessary for its development, namely service and training. Once those pillars were secured, we were able to redeploy and put forth quality on every level."

"The customer must enjoy a full Vacheron Constantin experience"

FACING PAGE
Julien Tornare, president of Vacheron Constantin North America.

THIS PAGE
As with the entire Contemporary Patrimony collection, the day-date bi-retrograde is elegant and refined.

As soon as he arrived, Julien Tornare worked on the organization of an extremely efficient after-sales service – a division often overlooked even in the luxury industry, but crucial in fulfilling the customer's exacting standards towards a trusted brand. At the same time, Julien Tornare emphasized all aspects of in-store training, Watch stores are the first ambassadors of a brand, and the sales personnel must have a comprehensive knowledge of its products.

For Julien Tornare, who never forgets luxury is also an emotion, "the customer must enjoy a full Vacheron Constantin experience". The US subsidiary has implemented a customer-loyalty program, with the possibility of signing up when purchasing a Vacheron Constantin watch, and benefiting from various privileged opportunities, invitations, and new product information.

When discussing the high luxury watch market today with Julien Tornare, one quickly understands that the president of Vacheron Constantin North America is entirely focused on customer satisfaction. The brand has been innovative in its approach, recently launching a "watch concierge service" that can answer a variety of questions, thus developing a trusted relationship with its customers. The endeavor has proved extremely successful, as confirmed by Vacheron Constantin North America's excellent results, as well as a substantial increase in brand awareness and media coverage. These efforts have also been complemented by rare limited-edition watches – exclusively made for the US – that Julien Tornare has been successful in obtaining from the Manufacture of in-les-Ouates.

Quality over quantity – Julien Tornare has also applied that principle to the Vacheron Constantin distribution. With some 50 doors today – 15 less than in 2004 – Vacheron Constantin is proud to be sold in the best points of sale in the United States. This emphasis on quality has not only increased the brand's exclusivity, but also its sales. Never before has Vacheron Constantin enjoyed such success in America, and every indicator shows the trend will strengthen.

Retrogrades and jump hours

Retrograde and jumping indications have long been among the favorite exercises of watchmakers seeking to vary the appearance of their dials and show off their technical skills. But today we are witnessing an outpouring of models that reinvent the indication of time in the least expected ways.

Back to the future

Watchmakers have long sought to develop alternatives to the clockwise turning hands as a way of telling the time. One solution they came up with is the "retrograde" indication, in which the hand travels along an arc to the end of its scale and then flies back to the beginning to resume its course. Retrograde indications are currently in fashion, since they enable more animated and original dials to be designed. One example is the Sectora II Automatic by Jean d'Eve, where the hour-scale is on an arc of 120°, which dictates the unusual shape of the case. In addition to the hours, retrograde mechanisms can also be applied to indicate other scales of time. The Double Rétrograde II by Maurice Lacroix has flyback indications for the dates and a 24-hour scale, as well as the conventional hours, minutes and seconds. In 2007, Vacheron Constantin introduced a bi-retrograde day-date model into its Patrimony collection. With retrograde indications for the dates at 12:00 and the days at 6:00, the watch has an unaffected design and a proprietary movement.

The big spectacle

A hand that flies back to its starting position is a spectacular sight, even more so if the dial has several indications of the sort—or if the watchmaker has other fancy ideas. Pierre Kunz, for example, offers an acrobatic display on its Seconde Virevoltante Rétrograde. The seconds hand dives and climbs in a 417-degree loop before flying back to its starting point in one-twentieth of a second and resuming its flight. The Merea Triretrograde Seconds Skeleton signed by Milus features retrograde seconds in three 20-second sections at 6:00, 10:00 and 2:00. Each sector travels its 20 seconds and flies back, passing the relay to the next.

Jumping hour

Mechanisms that cause the indication to jump from one unit of time to the next constitute another revolt against convention. The time is marked on a disk that moves in discrete steps. In its new Jules Audemars minute-repeater with jumping hours, Audemars Piguet combines two of the firm's specialties in a watch with conventionally modern lines. The hours appear in a shaped aperture at 12:00, while the central minutes have the dial to themselves. Jumping hours are often associated with retrograde minutes—Gérald Genta has, in fact, made this combination its trademark. The Gefica Safari, an updated version of one of the brand's classics, joins jumping hours, retrograde minutes, and dates in a bronze and titanium case styled in an African Art Deco look. FG One by de GRISOGONO is distinguished by its elongated case with two dials, one with retrograde minutes across a 230° arc, jumping hours and a continuous second time zone; the other with retrograde seconds and a day/night indicator syn-

▶▶ 1 *Vacheron Constantin, Patrimony contemporaine day-date bi-rétrograde*
In 2007, Vacheron Constantin added to its Patrimony Contemporaine collection a day-date bi-retrograde model, with retrograde displays of the date at 12:00 and the day at 6:00.

▶▶ 2 *Jean d'Eve, Sectora II Automatic*
Jean d'Eve's Sectora II Automatic displays the hours and minutes on a 120° arc—a geometric motif that allows for a uniquely shaped case.

▶▶ 3   *Maurice Lacroix, Double Rétrograde II*
The Double Rétrograde II by Maurice Lacroix presents
—in addition to the "traditional" hours, minutes and
seconds—a retrograde display of the date and hour
(on a 24-hour scale).

▶▶ 4   *Pierre Kunz, Seconde Virevoltante Rétrograde*
In its Seconde Virevoltante Rétrograde, Pierre Kunz
presents a "loopy" design, inspired by aerial acrobatics.

▶▶ 5   *Audemars Piguet, Jules Audemars Répétition*
minutes à heures sautantes
For its new Jules Audemars Minute Repeater Jumping
Hour model, Audemars Piguet combined two of the
Manufacture's specialties in a timepiece that is both
classic and contemporary.

▶▶ 6   *Gérald Genta, Gefica Safari*
The new version of Gérald Genta's Gefica Safari combines
a jump hour, retrograde minute and retrograde date in an
original bronze and titanium case that features both
African and Art Deco influences.

1 *De Bethune, Digitale*
De Bethune's Digitale presents a display driven entirely by disks, with a day/date/month window on top, a minute window in the middle and a jump-hour window on the bottom, all on a dial decorated with Côtes de Genève and rubies evoking the finest mechanical movements.

2 *de GRISOGONO, FG One*
de GRISOGONO's FG One stands out for its elongated case on which two dials are shown: one with retrograde minute on 230°, instantaneous jump hour and second time zone, the other with retrograde second complemented by a day/night window coordinated with the second time zone.

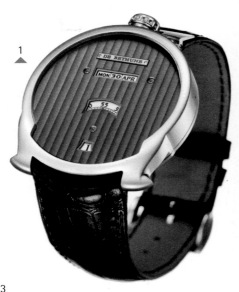

chronized with the time zone. For its part, the De Bethune Digitale displays the time exclusively via disks, with the days, dates and months in the upper window, the minutes in the middle and jumping hours at the bottom of a dial decorated in Geneva stripes and jewels, as befits the finest mechanical movements.

New faces of time

Digital indications are more popular than ever with watchmakers, since they open the way to a wide range of fantasies. HAUTLENCE, the relatively new brand from Neuchâtel, has developed a novel shaft-driven jumping hours and retrograde minutes indication; its HLS collection offers this original system in a new generation of square cases and easily readable dials in eight different versions, each limited to 88 watches. Vincent Calabrese demonstrates an equally original way of showing the time in his Baladin watches, which he poetically calls the "hobo hours." The hours jump in a round aperture, which itself marks the minutes by orbiting the dial, while a central hand sweeps the seconds. Vianney Halter conceived an entirely digital time display for Harry Winston's Opus 3. Jumping hours, minutes, seconds and dates appear in six separate portholes. Two movements totaling 250 parts drive the 10 revolving disks. Also for Harry Winston, but this time for its Opus 7, Andreas Strehler, the young watchmaker from German-speaking Switzerland, devised a system of multi-purpose disks. Pressing the crown guard brings the right hour on its disk against a marker at 10:00; a second push indicates the minutes, and a third, the power reserve. Strehler also re-engineered the conventional going train, displaying it in an

▶▶ 3   Hautlence, HL⁵06

Hautlence, the young brand from Neuchâtel, has come up with another innovation in its development of jump-hour and retrograde-minute displays with a system of pistons that guarantees the transmission of energy; the HLS collection offers this unique device in a new generation of square cases and dials.

▶▶ 4   Harry Winston, Opus 3

For Harry Winston's Opus 3, Vianney Halter designed a completely digital display, with hours, minutes, seconds and date appearing in six separate round windows.

▶▶ 5   Vincent Calabrese, Baladin

Under the appealing name of "vagabond hour", Vincent Calabrese offers a completely new way of reading time on the Baladin watch,. The jump-hour numeral is displayed in a small round window; the same window marks the minutes by turning around the dial, while a large central hand indicates the seconds.

▶▶ 6   HD3, Three Minds

HD3's Three Minds offers an original display with three rotating disks for the hours, minutes and seconds, all in a square case with a futuristic look.

▶▶ 7   Harry Winston, Opus 7

For the Opus 7, the young watchmaker Andreas Strehler created a system of "alternative display" disks.

4

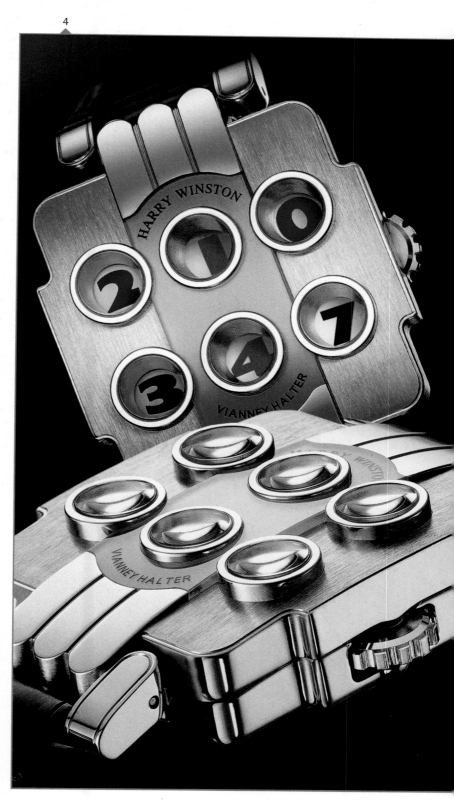

5

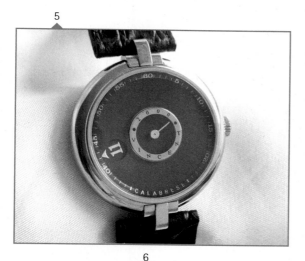

6

7

ethereal structure of Art Nouveau fluidity. The Three Minds watch by HD3 offers an interesting indication of three disks for the hours, minutes and seconds in a futuristic-looking square case. The Vulcania, also from HD3 is a watch that is regulated by a tourbillon on two axes and shows the hours on a vertical wheel at 9:00 and the minutes on a horizontal disk at 12:00. It offers a number of technical and styling features inspired by the underwater world presented by Jules Verne.

The third dimension

Among the latest innovations are three-dimensional indications. Daniel Roth set a theme with its Ellipsocurvex Papillon, which has two minute hands in a straight line. When it reaches 60, the first hand pivots 90° and disappears under the dial, while the same mechanism pivots the other hand to 0 on the scale. In 2006, the American brand Jacob & Co. launched the Quenttin, with seven mainspring barrels, which are visible under the glass and provide a running time of one month. The hours, minutes and power reserve are displayed on vertical cylinders lined up on the same axis. The watch even has a tourbillon that is visible through the side of the case. The same year, Vianney Halter and DMC launched a most original watch dubbed Cabestan (capstan), which is wound by a fixed crank. The hours, minutes, seconds and power reserve are shown on engraved rotating drums. The watch is regulated by a tourbillon and the power is transmitted through a fusée and chain. The star of the 2007 unveilings was undoubtedly the new 201 by Urwerk, a young brand specializing in futuristic timepieces on the "wandering hours" principle. The hours in this colossal wristwatch are displayed on the revolving extremities of a three-armed rotating star. Each of the four-sided extremities makes a quarter turn every three hours in sequence to display the

▶▶ 3 *Vianney Halter DMC, Cabestan*
Vianney Halter and DMC launched the very original Cabestan watch, which winds with the help of a movable crank, the source of its name (a French word meaning "capstan," a rotating machine).

▶▶ 4 *Jacob & Co, Quenttin*
In 2006, the American brand Jacob & Co. launched the Quenttin, with seven barrels—visible under the crystal—providing a month of power reserve.

▶▶ 5 *Urwerk, 201*
The star of 2007 was without a doubt the new 201 by Urwerk—a young brand already famous for its futuristic timepieces and their "satellite" system.

hour (1-4-7-10/2-5-8-11/3-6-9-12). Tiny telescopic rods extend in turn from the ends of the arms to follow the scale of minutes at the bottom of the dial, and then retract. A control board at the back of the watch, with racecar-style gauges, features three additional functions enabling the owner to monitor the performance of the watch.

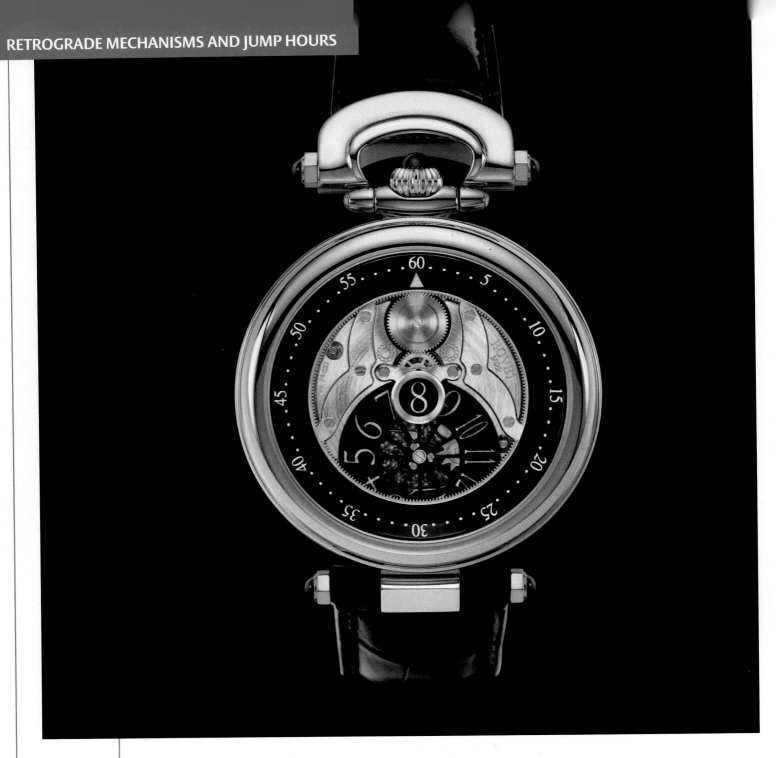

BOVET

FLEURIER JUMPING HOUR OPENWORK 42MM

BOVET's most unusual timepiece features a central jumping digital hour set in a rock crystal glass revealing the poetry of its original movement. The minutes are displayed on a blacked rotating ring with a white LumiNova triangle index. The 12 central hours are all on one blackened disk, offset so that its rim is leveled with the movement's rim. They jump instantaneously as the 60th minute reaches the dot at 12:00. A sapphire crystal caseback reveals the movement and its gold winding rotor, engraved in *fleurisanne* style. The jumping hour watches are also available in 18K red gold; with a 16-point Compass Rose painted in different colors on a mother-of-pearl or fired-enamel dial; or in a jewelry version upon which the Compass Rose is paved in diamonds and sapphires.

FLEURIER JUMPING HOUR WITH MINIATURE PAINTING

BOVET's Jumping Hour with mother-of-pearl dial is a perfect canvas for personalized miniature paintings. The rotating ring shows the minutes at 12:00. The 12 central hours hidden underneath are all on one disk, offset so that its rim is leveled with the movement's rim. They jump instantaneously as the 60th minute reaches 12:00. A sapphire crystal caseback reveals the movement and its gold winding rotor, engraved in *fleurisanne* style. On this model, the bezel, bow, lug and case side are fully set with baguette-cut diamonds.

BREGUET

CLASSIQUE - REF. 5207BB/12/9V6

This Classique watch is crafted in 18K white or yellow gold, housing a self-winding movement with a 65-hour power reserve. Its engine-turned and silvered gold dial features off-center hours and minutes, a power-reserve indicator at 12:00 and retrograde small seconds at 6:00. The movement is protected by a water-resistant case with sapphire crystal caseback.

BREGUET

TRADITION - REF. 7037BA/11/9V6

This Tradition wristwatch is crafted in 18K yellow or white gold and houses a self-winding movement. Its dial is in silvered 18K gold, hand-engraved on a rose-engine, off-centered at 12:00 and displays a chapter ring with Roman numerals. Retrograde small seconds are engraved on the movement. Its case is enhanced with a sapphire caseback.

BVLGARI

ASSIOMA - REF. AAP48GLHR

The Assioma features an in-house manufactured, mechanical, automatic-winding Caliber BVL 261. This movement, consisting of 261 pieces offers a 45-hour power reserve, 44 jewels and a vibration rate of 28,800 vph, is finished and decorated by hand, including a stippled anthracite back and a skeletonized rotor with engraved ring. Its functions include off-centered retrograde hour (240°), minutes, AM/PM indication and small seconds. The curved, 48mm, polished 18K pink-, yellow- or white-gold case, fitted with a curved, antireflective, scratch-resistant, sapphire crystal, an 18K pink-gold crown, and a snap-on back displaying the movement through a sapphire crystal, bears the limited-edition number engraved on its side and is water resistant to 30 meters. The in-house manufactured dial has hand-applied indexes, and opaline silver central and external decorations, circular satin-finished anthracite hour and minute areas and an opaline small second circle. Its display includes AM/PM Indication and small seconds at 6:00. The pre-curved, rolled-edge, brown alligator strap has an 18K matching gold triple-fold-over buckle. Limited edition 99 pieces.

DANIEL ROTH

ELLIPSOCURVEX PAPILLON - REF. 318.Y.70.351.CM.BD

Available in white gold, 5N red gold or platinum, this Ellipsocurvex Papillon features a unique system with two retractable hands that are positioned at 180-degree angles to one another and that always turn in the same direction on a single axis. The minute track is a U shape that runs from 00 to 60 between 3:00 and 9:00. On reaching the 60 position, one of the hands pivots 90 degrees on its own axis and disappears behind the hidden part of the dial, while the other hand appears at the same time on the dial at 00 minutes—activated by the same pivoting mechanism. This exclusive patented movement is hand-beveled with Côtes de Genève finishing.

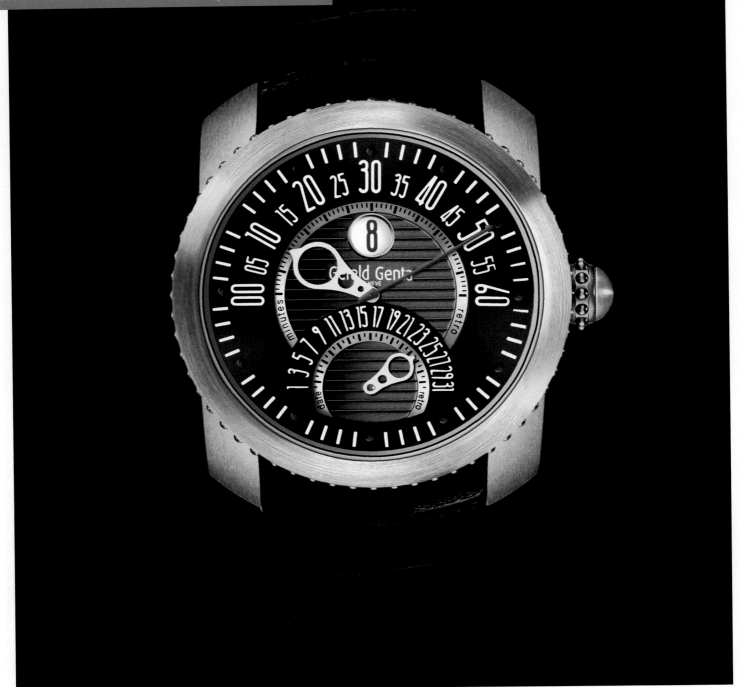

GERALD GENTA

GEFICA

The watch presented is made in bronze and titanium. Bronze is a copper and pewter alloy that acquires a distinctive patina over time, yet without ever deteriorating. Gefica is powered by the automatic GG 1004 movement with an 18K gold rotor with potter finishing. It is a jumping hours and retrograde minute, with curved seconds hand. The watch is shaped like a ship with a convex sapphire glass with antireflective treatment. The case size Y (46.5mm) with beaded tantanium ring fits all wrists. The watch is presented on an alligator strap with titanium triple-folding clasp, and is water resistant to 10atm.

GERALD GENTA

ARENA BIRETRO GOLD - REF. BSP.Y.66.269.CN.BD

The Arena Biretro Gold offers the exclusive Gérald Genta biretro self-winding movement, entirely hand-decorated, "Potter" finishing, equipped with jumping hours through an aperture at 12:00, a 210° retrograde minutes segment in the upper part of the dial between 8:00 and 4:00, and a 180° degree retrograde date segment on the lower part of the dial between 4:00 and 8:00. It is housed in a polished white-gold case with fluted middle, brushed white-gold crown guard and circular satin-brushed tantalum bezel. It is enhanced by a multi-layer tantalum colored metallic dial with circular satin-brushed finish, polished applied minute numerals, and retrograde date segment with a sunray guilloché motif. This model is water resistant to 10atm.

GERALD GENTA

ARENA SPICE

Sporty and outrageous by its complication, the spirit and the genius of the brand are expressed in the Arena Spice timepieces. The watch presented is powered by the automatic GG 7510 movement with jumping hours and retrograde minutes. The case is in steel, and the mother-of-pearl dial has raised SuperLumiNova dots, matte sapphires with multicolored hour disk. Arena Spice's rubber bezel is set with a row of diamonds and is shown on a rubber strap.

GERALD GENTA

OCTO BIRETRO - REF. OBR.Y.50.510.CN.BD

The Octo Biretro features the exclusive Gérald Genta biretro hand-decorated automatic movement with a jumping hour and retrograde minutes and date, offering a 45-hour power reserve. It is housed in a Ø 42.5mm or Ø 39mm (X size) octagonal 5N red-gold or white-gold case, enhanced by a black and red or ivory and black lacquered dial. This model is presented on a black alligator strap with folding clasp and is water resistant to 10atm.

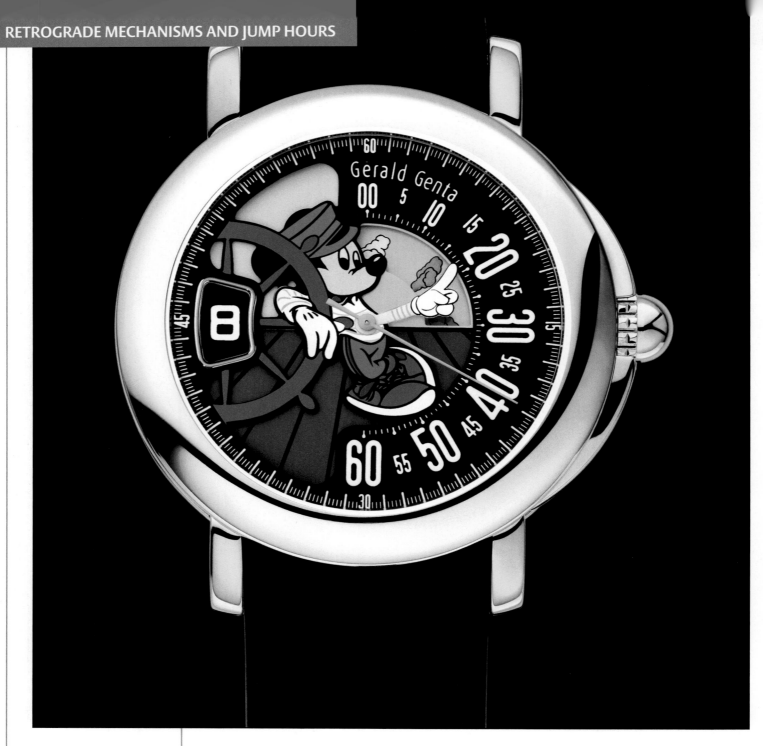

GERALD GENTA

FANTASY NAVIGATOR

These watches break away from conformity to give a vision of the provocative. The Fantasy Navigator is powered by the automatic GG 7510 movement. It is a jumping hours, with retrograde minutes hand, offering a fantastic power reserve about 42 hours and housed in a 41mm steel case. The originality of the pieces resides in its fantasy dial presenting a Mickey Mouse navigator motif with an articulated arm showing the retrograde minutes. The watch is water resistant to 3atm. The Mickey Mouse Fantasy Navigator is also available on a steel bracelet, rubber or leather straps with a folding clasp with Gérald Genta logo.

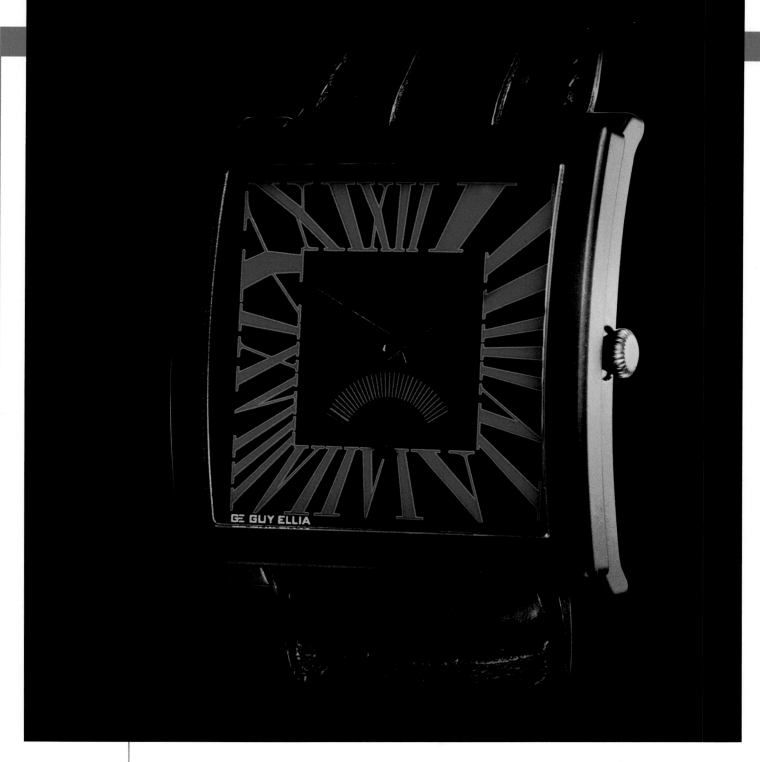

GUY ELLIA

TIME SQUARE Z1 – JUMPING SECOND

Masculine and technical, Guy Ellia's style makes this watch immediately recognizable. The case is a full, simple, curved square that sits perfectly on the wrist. It has stylized Roman numerals that create an extremely graphic universe offering strength and sobriety. Set in a semi-circular counter at 6:00, the jumping retro-second hand comes back around to its starting point every 30 seconds (automatic mechanism by Frédéric Piguet). With pure pleasure the wearer can contemplate the passage of time, from half-minute to half-minute. This watch is created in white, yellow, pink or black gold and can be set with diamonds.

GUY ELLIA

TIME SQUARE Z1 - JUMPING SECOND

Virile and technical, Guy Ellia's style makes the watch immediately recognizable with a full, simple, curved square case lying as flat as possible and sitting perfectly on the wrist. The dial has stylized Roman numerals that describe an extremely graphic universe and offers strength and sobriety. In the jumping retro second set in a semi-circular counter at 6:00, the second-hand comes back around to its starting point every thirty seconds (automatic mechanism by Frédéric Piguet). This elegant and discreet style exists in white, yellow, pink and black gold and is also available with diamonds.

PIAGET

RECTANGLE À L'ANCIENNE - REF. G0A32062

This powerful and extremely masculine watch, with its oversized white-gold case housing a mechanical self-winding 561P movement driving the retrograde seconds and power-reserve display, is intended for men with a taste for distinctive design and fine watchmaking. Issued in a limited, numbered edition of 100, this model is equipped with an ultra-thin (5.1mm) mechanical hand-wound movement endowed with superlative finishing including circular Côtes de Genève, a circular-grained mainplate, beveled and hand-drawn bridges, as well as blued screws. The Piaget manufacture thereby confirms its longstanding tradition and undeniable know-how in the field of exceptional Haute Horlogerie.

VACHERON CONSTANTIN

MALTE RETROGRADE PERPETUAL CALENDAR - REF. 47031

In this Malte model, Vacheron Constantin combines a perpetual calendar with a 31-day retrograde calendar. The Ø 39mm case, crafted in either platinum or 18K rose gold, houses the 1126 QPR automatic movement and offers hours, minutes, perpetual calendar, day and month indications via hands. Current year and leap year are displayed through a window. The retrograde crescent offers 31-day date and the movement beats at 28,800 vibrations per hour.

VACHERON CONSTANTIN

MALTE OPENFACE RETROGRADE PERPETUAL CALENDAR - REF. 47032

This platinum Malte Openface Retrograde Perpetual Calendar houses the mechanical automatic-winding Vacheron Constantin Caliber 1126 QPR. The 36-jeweled movement beats at 28,800 vibrations per hour, has 38 hours of power reserve, is hand-finished, and features a pink-gold mainplate. All of its parts have been hand-chiseled and etched away for exceptional viewing. The perpetual calendar offers date, day, month, digital year indication, and 4-year cycle. The dial consists of a sapphire crystal disk, luminescent peripheral date-ring, and white-gold hands. On an alligator strap with platinum clasp on an alligator strap with platinum clasp.

VACHERON CONSTANTIN

PATRIMONY BI-RETROGRADE - REF. 86020

Powered by the mechanical automatic-winding Vacheron Constantin Caliber 2460 R31 R7, this Patrimony Bi-Retrograde is hallmarked with the Geneva Seal. Beating at 28,800 vibrations per hour and offering 43 hours of power reserve, the 27-jeweled movement is equipped with a guilloche pink-gold rotor. Retrograde day is provided at 6:00 and retrograde date is shown at 12:00. The 18K pink-gold three-piece case is high-polished and water resistant to 3atm. The sapphire caseback reveals the exquisite movement.

ZENITH

CHRONOMASTER OPEN EL PRIMERO RETROGRADE

This ChronoMaster Open El Primero Retrograde houses the El Primero 4023 automatic chronograph movement with retrograde date indicator from the 30-minute counter axis. The 50-hour power-reserve indicator is at 6:00. The 39-jeweled movement consists of 299 components and beats at 36,000 vibrations per hour. The watch offers 30-minute counter at 3:00, a 3-branched small seconds hand at 9:00, central chronograph seconds hand, and measures short time intervals to 1/10 of a second. It is offered in 18K rose gold with opened Grain d'Orge guilloche-patterned guilloché-patterned dial at 10:00 to view the El Primero movement.

Multiple time zones and GMTs

CEO of de GRISOGONO

Fawaz Gruosi

Meccanico dG

Fawaz Gruosi founded de GRISOGONO 15 years ago. Despite its youth, the company has found its place amongst the most prestigious brands thanks to strong creations and a baroque style where the color black is dominant. To celebrate this birthday, the founder has just unveiled several watches with unique complications, and notably the Meccanico dG, a futurist timepiece with a dual mechanically operated analog–digital display.

"My only wish is for de GRISOGONO to retain the audacious and instinctive spirit of a 15-year-old"

"My only wish is for de GRISOGONO to retain the audacious and instinctive spirit of a 15-year-old", confides Fawaz Gruosi, CEO and founder. With his unique Italian panache, the Florentine believes a great part of his success is due to spontaneity, "which is an excellent guide, even in business. Finance is important, but without the creators, artisans and dreamers this industry could not exist. To sell dreams is not to sell air. To sell dreams is to sell a objet d'art infused with craftsmanship and emotion".

Fawaz Gruosi cornered the visual identity of de GRISOGONO with the use of black diamonds, a gem previously under-used in the watch and jewelry industry. He established the precious stone as his trademark, spiking the interest of his competitors who followed suit shortly thereafter, including the gem in their collections.

Exclusively devoted to jewelry in its beginnings, de GRISOGONO ventured into watchmaking in 2000. Never inconsequential, always carrying the strong imprint of their creator, the de GRISOGONO watches explore an uncharted artistic territory. Watch complications soon made their appearance. As early as 2002, the Instrumento Doppio boasted a chronograph and a dual time zone. The race to master techniques reached a first milestone in 2005, with the Occhio Minute Repeater, a minute repeater with a cathe-

FACING PAGE
Fawaz Gruosi, founder and CEO of de GRISOGONO.

THIS PAGE
Launched in 2002, the Instrumento Doppio was de GRISOGONO's first foray in complications, with chronograph and dual time zone functions.

dral gong, whose dial opens up like the reflex diaphragm of a camera when the watch rings.

"For the past 15 years, de GRISOGONO has sought to produce creative jewelry and timepieces", comments Fawaz Gruosi. "We have endeavored to develop a signature style reflecting our ideas and desires, unlike the style of any of our competitors or friends. And our strength is probably that we have always been anti-commercial. De GRISOGONO is a niche, elitist brand, and we are convinced there is a path worth treading well off the beaten track."

Meccanico dG

A single number is sufficient to measure the scope of the Meccanico dG feat: 651 components, a number that defines it as one of the most complex watch movements today.

It is the first watch to offer 2 time zones with a double display, one analog and the other digital, both mechanically operated.

This patented de GRISOGONO world premiere hides an extremely complex technical construction underneath its ultra-modern design. Even if it took a high degree of audacity and folly to launch this extraordinary project, Fawaz Gruosi never doubted he could pull it off, as that was the direction he wanted to give de GRISOGONO.

For the first time in watchmaking history, a watch associates the technique of digital display with the energy of mechanical movement. Digital display first appeared with the use of quartz movements, and was confined to electrical watches, a world apart from traditional watchmaking. Thirty years later, the fusion between two opposite worlds is finally accomplished. In that sense, the Meccanico dG send a masterful signal to watchmaking history by opening up a wholly new dimension.

Embodying a concentrated blend of micro-systems, the Meccanico dG is an assembly of delicate mechanisms and sophisticated gears that enable the rotation of the digital display.

The 23 articulated numbers are operated by a mechanism that drives and synchronizes the hour display. The 9 mm vertical segments are coupled with 2.9 mm horizontal segments, with a combined weight of only 10 milligrams. Each segment has 2 colored visible sides and 2 invisible sides. The passage to the following hour operates with a 90° rotation of one or several segments. The jump is instantaneous, and between 1 to 12 segments come into play to go from one hour to the next. The Meccanico dG is a "Back to the future" watch, offered in a limited series of 177 timepieces in rose gold, in titanium, and in titanium coupled with either rubber, rose gold, or platinum.

Multiple time zones and GMTs

In the age of the global village, watches that can tell
you the time simultaneously in two, three, four or
even 24 time zones have become really useful.
Riding the wave of this popularity, watchmakers
have come out with a wide range of travelers'
watches featuring practicality and ease of use, or
with original designs and indications.

Around the world in 24 hours

Until the end of the 19th century, each region had its own local time more or less based on its longitude. But with the advent of long-distance travel and especially the development of the railroads, the need for standard times became urgent. At the international meridian conference in 1884, governments agreed to divide the planet into 24 time zones taking the Greenwich meridian as the reference point at 0° longitude. The first watches to show the times in two zones had two, though not entirely synchronized movements showing the times on separate dials. Then came time-zone watches with a single movement and a clutch device for a second hour hand. Today watchmakers compete with ever more ingenious mechanisms for the times in several parts of the globe.

Analog systems

The most common way of indicating another time is to have a second hour hand distinguished by its shape or color. This is the solution chosen by Ebel for its 1911 BTR GMT, with a second time zone on a 24-hour dial to determine whether it's day or night, and a pushpiece to set the time-zone hand in increments of an hour. This basic indication by hands can however be translated into endless technical and stylistic variations. Pierre Kunz has provided his Second Time Zone model with a retrograde hand for the second time zone, and a sun or a moon in an aperture to show day or night. Vacheron Constantin's Malte Régulateur Dual Time has the minutes in the center, the hours in a subdial at 12:00 and the 24-hour second time zone in a subdial at 9:00. The Longitudes watch by Jaquet Droz also adopts a regulator style face with two subdials, one having Roman numerals for the local time, and the other with Arabic numerals for the other time zone. Chopard has thought up an original way of knowing distant time in its L.U.C Pro One GMT. To see the time in another part of the world, the user turns the bezel with the big luminous orange numerals to bring the second zone against the triangular hand. Franck Muller has taken into account the needs of countries like India, which is 5.5 hours ahead of Greenwich. The face of its Master Banker II displays three synchronized time zones, one of which can be set to half-hour increments.

▶▶ 1 *Ebel, 1911 BTR GMT*
The most common solution to indicate a second time zone is to add another hand, a colored one, for the hours. This is what Ebel has done with its 1911 BTR GMT, which has a 24-hour second time zone display and a corrector pushbutton.

▶▶ 2 *Jaquet Droz, Les Longitudes*
Les Longitudes by Jaquet Droz is inspired by regulating dials with two subdials, one in Roman numerals for the first time zone, the other in Arabic numerals for the second, 24-hour time zone.

▶▶ 3 *Pierre Kunz, Second Time Zone*
Pierre Kunz gave its Second Time Zone model a retrograde hand for the second time zone; the appearance of the sun or the moon in a window serves as a day/night indicator.

▶▶ 4   Chopard, L.U.C Pro One GMT
For its L.U.C Pro One GMT, Chopard designed a brand-new way of reading time. When the wearer wants to display the time anywhere else on the globe, he need only turn the bezel, which bears large orange luminescent numerals, to position the second time zone with respect to the triangular hand.

5   Franck Muller, Master Banker II
Franck Muller was inspired by countries like India, which is five and a half hours ahead of Greenwich Mean Time, when the brand included three coordinated time zones on its Master Banker II, one of which can be set to the half-hour.

6   Vacheron Constantin, Malte Régulateur Dual Time
In Vacheron Constantin's Malte Dual Time Regulator, the minute is in the center, the main hour is in a subdial at 12:00 and the 24-hour second time zone is in a subdial at 9:00.

5 ▲

6 ▲

1

2

Double whammy

Even though the minutes are usually the same across time zones, some watchmakers prefer to display the different times fully, with hour and minute hands. One example is the Oris Worldtimer with a double analog hours and minutes display, and dates that can be set forwards or backwards. The Pontos Décentrique GMT by Maurice Lacroix shows two complete times on two offset subdials and the sun or moon in a window for the day and night indication. Piaget's Altiplano Double Jeu recreates the "secret" watches with two superimposed hinged cases housing the ultra-thin mechanical movements that are a specialty of the brand.

▶▶ 1 *Oris, Artelier Worldtimer*
Using its Worldtimer caliber, which has a double analog hour/minute display and an automatic date correction in either direction, Oris has chosen to display two complete time zones on its Artelier model.

▶▶ 2 *Piaget, Altiplano Double Jeu*
Piaget's Altiplano Double Jeu reinvents "secret" watches with one case atop another, linked by a hinge and featuring the ultra-thin mechanical movements this brand has made its specialty.

▶▶ 3 *Maurice Lacroix, Pontos Décentrique GMT*
The Pontos Décentrique GMT by Maurice Lacroix displays two complete time zones on two totally off-centered subdials; a sun or a moon in a window serves as a day/night indication.

▶▶ 4 *Patek Philippe, Calatrava Travel Time Réf.4934*
The Calatrava Travel Time by Patek Philippe—introduced in 2007 in a feminine version decorated with mother-of-pearl and diamonds—has two superimposable hour hands.

▶▶ 5 *Jaeger-LeCoultre, Master Hometime*
The Master Hometime by Jaeger-LeCoultre has a double-hand system that is somewhat similar, but activated by the single crown at 3:00.

One hand can hide another

In most analog systems, the hour hand for the second zone is permanently visible, even when it's not needed. Patek Philippe got around this inconvenience in an elegant way. Its Calatrava Travel Time, which came out in a new women's mother-of-pearl with diamonds version last year, has two superimposed hands. Pressing one of the buttons in the caseband of the watch splits the hour hand of the second time zone so that the user can advance or turn it back according to whether she is traveling east or west. When the time-zone function is not required, the two hours hands run together as one. Jaeger-LeCoultre's Master Hometime works in a similar way, except that the single crown at 3:00 controls the split hand.

1. **Roger Dubuis, Globetimer**
On its triple-time-zone watch, Globetimer, Roger Dubuis has included two counters, each displaying twelve meridians.

2. **Jaquet Droz, Les Douze Villes**
In its Les Douze Villes model, Jaquet Droz combines a disk bearing the name of twelve cities with a jump-hour display.

3. **A.Lange&Söhne, Lange 1 Fuseaux horaires**
Featuring a "city bezel" instead of a window, the Lange 1 Fuseaux horaires, from A. Lange & Söhne, is notable for its two supplementary off-center dials.

4. **JeanRichard, GMT 2TimeZones**
JeanRichard's GMT 2TimeZones features 2 windows: one at 12:00 for the hour of the second time zone, with AM/PM indication, the other at 6:00 to display the name of one of the 24 reference cities.

1

2

3

In apertures

The times in different zones can also be shown on revolving disks. This popular system can also be rendered in different ways. JeanRichard's GMT 2TimeZones has two apertures on the dial, one at 12:00 for the second time zone with an AM/PM indication, the other at 6:00 to display one of the 24 reference cities. The two buttons on the left of the case are for turning the time-zone hands forwards or back, while an additional crown at 9:00 sets the time-zone city. In its Douze Villes model, Jaquet Droz combines a disk with 12 cities with jumping hours. Pressing the button sets the city and the corresponding time. In its triple-time-zone Globetimer, Roger Dubuis has configured two displays, each covering 12 meridians. Buttons enable the user to select the city, upon which its local hour is displayed by the big hand, while the small hand points to night or day. A. Lange & Söhne's Lange 1 Fuseaux Horaires features two off-center subdials. Home time is usually indicated on the larger dial, but thanks to an original setting system, the priorities can be changed to give the local time prominence when you're traveling, and to set Lange's patented large date accordingly.

The world on your wrist

In 1936, Louis Cottier a watchmaker from Carouge on the out-skirts of Geneva invented an ingenious device that enabled you to tell the time anywhere on the planet at a glance. His system was taken up and perfected in the celebrated World Time watches by Patek Philippe. The brand's Heure Universelle Ref. 5130 is a worthy successor to the originals. The central circle of the face carries the hands showing local time. It is surrounded by two mobile concentric disks: one with a 24-hour scale divided into day and night, the other marked with the names of 24 cities. The button at 10:00 changes the local time zone and at the same time synchronizes the 24-hour and cities disks accordingly. Girard-Perregaux also has a worldtime watch called ww.tc for worldwide time control. The women's version, ww.tc-Lady, dresses up the complication in diamonds, while the ww.tc-Financial not only shows the time in all 24 zones, but also the opening times of the major stock markets—Wall Street, London, Hong Kong and Tokyo. In its Master Geographic Worldtime, Jaeger-LeCoultre achieves the first combination between a second time-zone indication and world time. The crown at 2:00 turns the disk of cities to select the prominent time, which appears on the subdial at 7:00. The time in all the world's 24 time zones is also permanently displayed. The Vogard brand has come up with an exclusive patented system it calls Timezoner® to set the time by the bezel. The user turns the bezel to select the city and the local time and day/night indication are automatically displayed. The system also adjusts for summer time. In the latest race-inspired Vogard Black F1, the world's major automobile racetracks have replaced the city names. Antoine Preziuso's Transworld features a dial at the center of which rotates a map of the world in 24 hours. The outer part of the dial is graduated in 24 hours with zones for night and day. It's a fanciful way of telling world time, but the user must be familiar with geography and the intricacies of time zones.

▶▶ 1   *Antoine Preziuso, Transworld*
Antoine Preziuso's Transworld stands out for its dial, featuring
a central part decorated with a map of the globe making
a rotation every 24 hours and the exterior part divided into
24 sections, with day/night areas.

▶▶ 2   *Girard-Perregaux, ww.tc-lady*
Girard-Perregaux offers a world time display in its collection
called "ww.tc," which stands for World Wide Time Control.
The ww.tc-lady provides a feminine version of this complication
in a case that is highlighted by the sparkle of diamonds.

▶▶ 3   *Girard-Perregaux, ww.tc-financialT*
The ww.tc-financial, by Girard-Perregaux, shows—in addition
to the time in 24 times zones—the times when the world's four
major stock markets (Wall Street, London, Tokyo and Hong
Kong) are open.

▶▶ 4   *Patek Philippe, Heure Universelle Réf.5130*
In 1936, the Genevan watchmaker Louis Cottier invented an
ingenious system that allowed watch wearers to read at one
glance the time anywhere on the planet. Heure Universelle
Réf. 5130 by Patek Philippe pays tribute to this innovation.

▶▶ 5   *Vogard, Black F1*
On the new Vogard model "Black F1," with a look inspired by
auto racing, the city names have been replaced by those of the
world's major racing tracks.

▶▶ 6   *Jaeger-LeCoultre, Master Geographic Worldtime*
In its Master Geographic Worldtime, Jaeger-LeCoultre unites
for the first time the indication of a second time zone and the
universal time display.

A. LANGE & SÖHNE

LANGE 1 TIME ZONE

The Lange 1 Time Zone watch houses the Caliber L031.1 manually wound movement. Comprised of 417 parts and 54 jewels, this movement features twin mainspring barrels, a lever escapement and a balance spring with a frequency of 21,600 semi-oscillations per hour. The watch offers home time (hours, minutes, small seconds with stop seconds) with a day/night indicator, second time-zone indicator with day/night, and an outer city ring. Additionally there is a 72-hour power-reserve indicator, and a big-date indicator at 1:00. The easy-to-use watch features two off-center subdials. The larger subdial takes priority and displays home time. The smaller dial indicates time in another zone, which is set via a pushpiece. An ingenious adjustment mechanism makes it possible for the local time to become the home time when traveling, thereby reversing the priorities of the two subdials.

AUDEMARS PIGUET

JULES AUDEMARS DUAL TIME "ALL STARS" LIMITED EDITION
REF. 26090PT.00.D028CR.01

Crafted in 950 platinum, this limited-edition timepiece features a second time zone displaying hours and minutes with AM/PM indication, power reserve and date. The dial is silvered and decorated with a star pattern and twelve Roman numerals. This 99-piece limited edition commemorates Arnold Schwarzenegger's After-School All Stars Foundation providing academic, recreational, cultural, and life skills for children in underprivileged environments.

AUDEMARS PIGUET

ROYAL OAK DUAL TIME - REF.26120OR.OO.D002CR.01

Crafted in 18K pink gold, this Royal Oak Dual Time houses the self-winding Caliber 2846. This timepiece features a second time zone displaying hours and minutes with AM/PM indication, power reserve and date. The dial is engine-turned with a Grande Tapisserie pattern and offers riveted gold indexes with facets. Also available in rose or yellow gold with silvered white dial.

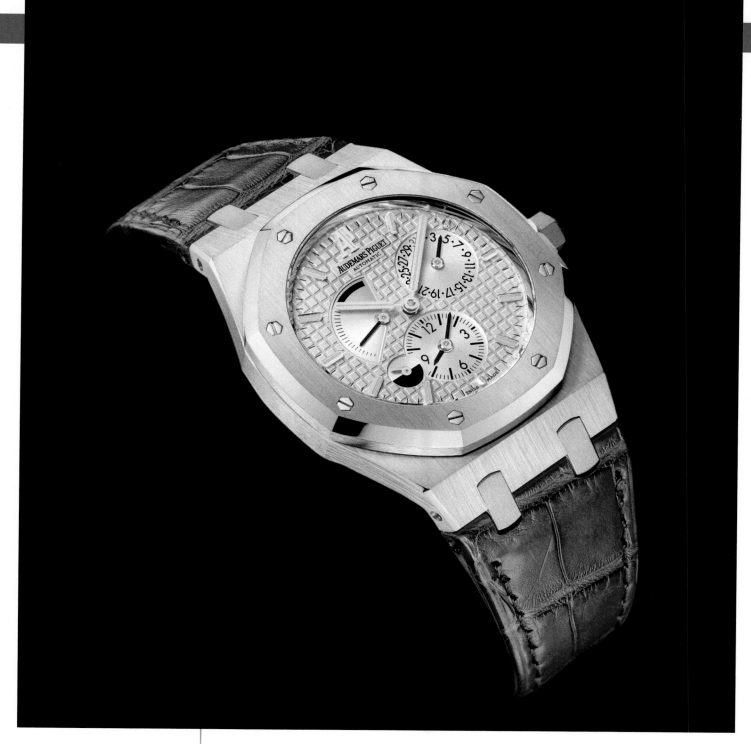

AUDEMARS PIGUET

ROYAL OAK DUAL TIME - REF. 26120BA.OO.D088CR.01

This 18K yellow-gold Royal Oak Dual Time houses the self-winding Caliber 2846 and features a second time zone displaying hours and minutes with AM/PM indication, power reserve and date. The dial is engine-turned with a Grande Tapisserie pattern and offers riveted gold indexes with facets.

AUDEMARS PIGUET

ROYAL OAK DUAL TIME - REF. 26120ST.OO.1220ST.01

Crafted in stainless steel, this Royal Oak Dual Time houses the self-winding Caliber 2846 and features a second time zone displaying hours and minutes with AM/PM indication, power reserve and date. The dial is engine-turned with Grande Tapisserie pattern and offers riveted gold indexes with facets. Also available with black or navy dial.

BOZEMAN WATCH CO.

CUTTHROAT - REF. 008

The hand-tooled Cutthroat features a mechanical automatic-winding ETA caliber 2893-2 GMT with a 24-hour second time zone, 21 jewels, 46-hour power reserve, and 28,800 vibrations per hour. Encased in Ø 42mm of mirror-finished solid stainless steel, the watch is accented with a red 24-hour GMT indicator resembling the throat coloration its namesake, the endangered native Montana Cutthroat trout. Is limited to 100 pieces in its first edition.

DE GRISOGONO

INSTRUMENTO DOPPIO TRE

This first double-faced watch with three time zones, the Instrumento Doppio Tre, combines a sophisticated movement with impeccable technical design. The watch offers two time-zone displays on one dial and one time on the other dial. All three displays work via a single-barrel movement comprised of more than 300 components. The case consists of two main parts, including a base cradle from which the case is lifted and rotated to reveal the second dial on the back. The front dial offers the double time-zone readout via superimposed counters and full date indication. The third time zone with analog hour and minute display is on the second dial, which is located uniquely under the rotor. The watch houses the mechanical ETA-based caliber with automatic-winding mechanism enhanced by de GRISOGONO.

DeWITT

TRIPLE COMPLICATION GMT3 - REF. AC.2041.40A.M121/120

Encased in palladium, the face of the Triple Complication GMT 3 imposes its strong personality through perfectly balanced architecture, blending the most sophisticated functions and original metal combinations. It is powered by the exclusive DeWitt caliber DW2041 with a 42-hour power reserve, GMT function, day and night indicator and a dissociated date. The dazzling black guilloché Côtes de Genève dial is set with brilliant-cut diamonds, the day and night disk is also set with white and black diamonds, as well as yellow sapphires. Limited edition of 99 pieces.

GUY ELLIA

TIME SQUARE Z1 - DUAL TIME GMT

Guy Ellia's new Time square Z1 Dual Time GMT—still as virile and technical as the last complications. Simple, curved, and lying as flat as possible, it sits perfectly on the wrist. An automatic Frédéric Piguet movement, Caliber PGE 5C50, operates this GMT with a second time zone and 3-day power reserve.

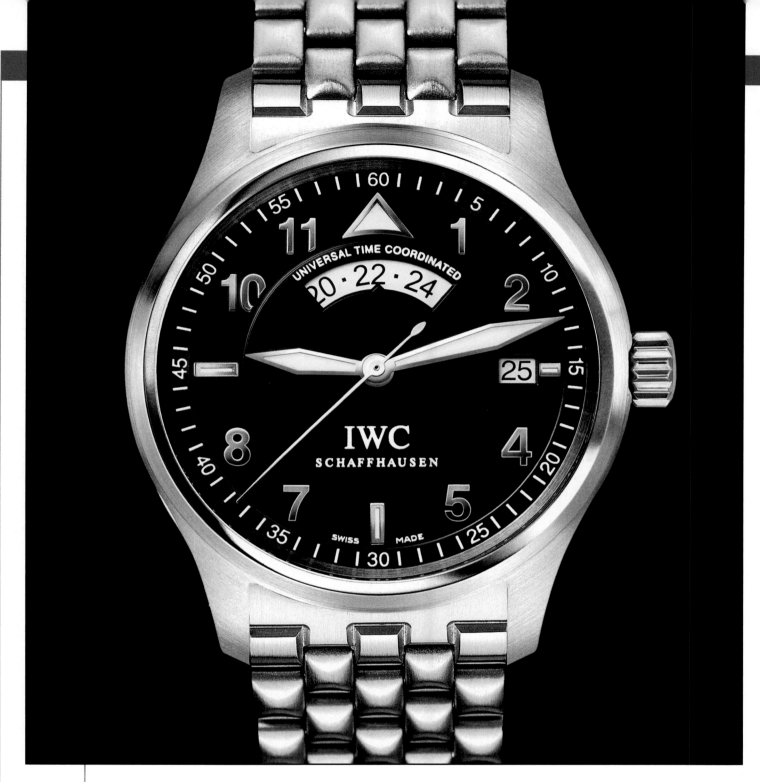

IWC

SPITFIRE UTC - REF. 3251

IWC's Spitfire UTC is crafted in steel and houses the caliber 37526 automatic movement, which oscillates at 28,800 vibrations per hour and features 21 rubies. It offers date indicator and 24-hour display. The time is adjusted in one-hour intervals and features a center second hand with stop device. The watch houses a soft iron inner case for protection against magnetic fields. It is water resistant to 6atm.

JAEGER-LECOULTRE

MASTER WORLD GEOGRAPHIC

This steel Master World Geographic is the latest in Jaeger-LeCoultre's line of multiple time-zone timepieces. On a single watch face is displayed the local time and all 24 time zones together with the precise time in one other selected time zone. This limited-series model is fitted with a new self-winding Jaeger-LeCoultre movement of remarkable toughness and reliability. The hours, minutes and seconds hands on the main dial track local time only, while a rotating dial ring and system of dial colors and shadings with colored arrows and sub-disks enable the easy legibility of universal and local timescales. An ingenious crown-operated mechanism makes it possible to highlight a major town in each time zone and it is even possible to distinguish between summer- and winter-time in both hemispheres. The date is displayed at 3:00 and there are indicators of the power reserve and months containing fewer than 31 days.

JAEGER-LECOULTRE

REVERSO SQUADRA HOMETIME BLACK

The Squadra Hometime Black is powered by the automatic Jaeger-LeCoultre Caliber 977, which is crafted, assembled and decorated by hand, beats at a frequency of 28,800 vibrations per hour and boasts a 48-hour power reserve. A number of technical innovations reinforce this watch's ruggedness and reliability: a balance-bridge screwed on either side to the mainplate to ensure enhanced stability, as well as two catches to avoid any distortion of the mainspring even in the case of violent impacts. The black guilloché dial displays the hours, minutes, seconds and date (at 3:00, linked to Travel time), as well as AM/PM indication linked to the second time zone, indicated by a red open-worked hand serving as an immediate reminder of one's Home time. Water resistant to 50 meters and equipped with a sapphire crystal caseback, the Reverso Squadra Hometime Black is presented on a new articulated molded rubber strap with folding clasp. Also available in steel, this 18K pink-gold version is produced in a limited series of 500.

JAEGER-LECOULTRE

MASTER HOMETIME

This Master Hometime watch houses Jaeger-LeCoultre's mechanical automatic movement 975 that beats at 28,000 vibrations an hour. It offers 50 hours of power reserve and features 230 parts and 29 jewels. The local hour hand (for travel time) can be moved forward or backward, date function is synchronized with the local hour hand, the home- or reference-time hour hand, minutes and small seconds hands, and day/night indicator. It is crafted in stainless steel or 18-karat pink gold and is water resistant to 5atm.

JAEGER-LECOULTRE

REVERSO GRANDE AUTOMATIQUE

For the first time, the Reverso Grande Automatique appears in a version fitted with an automatic movement, Jaeger-LeCoultre Caliber 970, a mechanical automatic movement with a barrel whose dimensions have been optimized to offer a 50-hour power reserve. The watch offers large date of travel time and second time zone with day and night indications. The 233-part movement vibrates at 28,800 beats per hour and is equipped with a unidirectional winding rotor mounted on ceramic balls requiring neither lubrication nor maintenance, a variable inertia balance to improve precision, and crown setting for all the indicators (local time, reference time, minutes, date, day/night display). It is offered in stainless steel or 18-karat pink gold.

JAEGER-LECOULTRE

REVERSO GRANDE GMT

The principle of two watches in one—such as the Reverso—has long delighted watch connoisseurs. The Reverso Grande GMT features a single movement driving back-to-back dials displaying different time zones. Crafted in stainless steel or 18-karat pink gold, the front dial displays hours, minutes, large date, small seconds, and day/night indicator. The dial has a silvered guilloché wave design. The contrasting black back dial features the 8-day power-reserve indicator and the symmetrically arranged day/night indicator, as well as the extraordinary GMT device. Reverso Grande GMT is powered by the manually wound Caliber 878 beating at 28,800 vibrations per hour and consisting of 276 parts and 35 jewels.

JEAN-MAIRET & GILLMAN

CONTINENTES

This square Continentes offers three retrograde hands and depicts time in three sections of the world: the Americas, Asia/Pacific and Europe/Africa. The mother-of-pearl dial of the watch has a world map decoration to indicate the three zones. Crafted in 18-karat rose gold, the watch houses the automatic JMG 3101TR/1153 caliber with 40 jewels, and is equipped with a 24-karat gold hand-decorated rotor.

PARMIGIANI FLEURIER

KALPA HEMISPHERES

This watch houses the manual-winding PF337 movement with a 50-hour power reserve and beats at 28,800 vibrations per hour. The 38-jeweled movement features the Côtes de Genève decoration and hand-chamfered bridges. The watch's functions include hours, minutes, small seconds at 6:00, day/night indicator linked to local time at 6:00, 2nd time-zone hour and minute display at 12:00, 2nd time zone day/night indicator at 1:00, large calendar window. It is crafted in 18K rose gold or steel. The watch is water resistant to 30 meters and features sapphire crystals with antireflection treatment.

ULYSSE NARDIN

DUAL TIME - REF. 243-55-7/91

The 42mm Dual Time features a second time zone with patented quickset on the main dial, permanent home time displayed in window at 9:00, and big date in double window. Caliber UN-24 is visible through Dual Time's exhibition caseback. Offered with various dial combination and with a bracelet, the 42 mm Dual Time is also available in 18K rose gold.

ULYSSE NARDIN

QUADRATO DUAL TIME - REF. 243-92-7/601

The Quadrato Dual Time measures 42x42mm and features a second time zone with patented quickset on the main dial, permanent home time displayed in window at 9:00, and big date in double window. Caliber UN-24 is visible through Quadrato Dual Time's exhibition caseback. This timepiece is also available in 18K rose gold; strap or gold bracelet.

ULYSSE NARDIN

QUADRATO DUAL TIME - REF. 246-92/600

The Quadrato Dual Time measures 42x42mm and features a second time zone with patented quickset on the main dial, permanent home time displayed in window at 9:00, and big date in double window. Caliber UN-24 is visible through the exhibition caseback. This watch is also available in stainless steel and on a stainless steel or rose gold bracelet.

ULYSSE NARDIN

QUADRATO DUAL TIME - REF. 246-92/692

The Quadrato Dual Time measures 42x42mm and features a second time zone with patented quickset on the main dial, permanent home time displayed in window at 9:00, and big date in double window. Caliber UN-24 is visible through the exhibition caseback. This watch is also available in stainless steel and on a steel or gold bracelet.

ULYSSE NARDIN

LADY DUAL TIME - REF. 246-22B/391

The 37mm Lady Dual Time in 19K rose gold features a second time zone with patented quickset on the main dial, permanent home time in window at 9:00, big date in double window and small seconds. Caliber UN-24 is visible through the exhibition caseback. The Lady Dual Time is also available in stainless steel, on a bracelet, with various dial combinations, and with or without diamonds.

VACHERON CONSTANTIN

OVERSEAS DUAL TIME - REF. 47450/B01A

Encased in 316L surgical-grade steel on a steel bracelet, this Overseas Dual Time watch is powered by the mechanical automatic-winding Vacheron Constantin Caliber 1122 with 40 hours of power reserve. The 34-jeweled movement beats at 28,800 vibrations per hour, and is protected against magnetic fields by a soft inner iron case. The watch offers hours, minutes, seconds, date, and dual-time readout with day/night indication. Eight screws fasten the bezel and the sapphire crystal is antireflective. Water resistant to 15atm, Overseas Dual Time features a silvered dial with applied, luminescent gold trapezoid markers and luminescent hands.

VACHERON CONSTANTIN

MALTE DUAL TIME REGULATOR - REF. 42005

This Malte Dual Time Regulator is crafted in 18K pink gold in a half-hunter case with back lid, and houses the COSC-certified chronometer Vacheron Constantin Caliber 1206 RDT. The manually wound movement offers hours, minutes, date calendar at 6:00 and second time-zone indicator at 9:00 via a 24-hour subdial.

VACHERON CONSTANTIN

MALTE DUAL TIME - REF. 47400

This self-winding Malte Dual Time houses the Caliber 1222 and is available in 18K white or rose gold. It offers hours, minutes, date, power reserve, and second time-zone indication with day/night readout. The movement beats at 28,800 vibrations per hour; the watch is water resistant to 3atm.

ZENITH

GRANDE CLASS RESERVE DE MARCHE DUAL TIME ELITE

Housing the Elite 683 automatic extra-flat movement, this 44mm Grande Class Reserve de Marche Dual Time Elite consists of 192 parts and 36 jewels. Beating at 28,800 vibrations per hour, the watch offers 50 hours of power reserve (at 2:00) and features a 22K gold oscillating weight. In addition to hours and minutes, the watch gives small seconds, date and a 24-hour second-time-zone indication. Shown in 18K rose gold, it is also available in white and yellow gold, as well as steel.

Alarm watches

As the ultimate useful complication, alarms were often part of standard equipment for many mechanical wristwatches before being replaced by electronic alarm clocks...or by the classic hotel wake-up call. With the boom in business and tourist travel that dictated the strong comeback of multiple time-zone watches, the alarm function is enjoying renewed success. It has been popping up on extremely valuable timepieces and several renowned watch manufacturers have developed some innovative solutions to enhance its aesthetic appeal, its user-friendliness and/or its sound quality.

Frère Jacques

The alarm is undoubtedly the most ancient of all horological complications. It seems that as early as the 12th century there were monastery clocks that chimed as an audible reminder of church service times, even before the appearance of hands. By the 15th century, table clocks were often fitted with alarm mechanisms chiming on tiny bells, the 16th century saw the appearance of alarm pocket-watches with openworked covers facilitating the passage of the sound. In 1601, the Geneva Watchmakers Corporation even required anyone wanting to become a "master" to make a small alarm clock. In the 17th century, horologers also made large-sized "carriage watches" with mechanisms designed to awaken travelers so they would not miss the next connection.

Recently revived, Vulcain is tapping into its rich heritage. It has re-issued its famous Nautical model, which houses the brand's alarm movement called Cricket because of its shrill chirping sound.

A wristworn alarm

The first alarm wristwatch was presented by Eterna in 1914. Its unique barrel wound both the movement and the alarm mechanism. Around 1920, Zenith also created an alarm movement equipped with two barrels, but these mechanisms were not yet up to par. The vibrations tended to upset the running of the watch and the sound was not loud enough to actually wake someone sleeping. In 1947, Vulcain launched the first genuinely operational alarm wristwatch. The famous hand-wound Cricket movement featured two barrels, one for the movement and the other for the alarm, equipped with an alarm that lasted around 25 seconds. Thanks to a stud system fixed to a membrane and a double caseback with holes drilled into it, the mechanism emitted a strident sound capable of awakening even a sound sleeper. The Vulcain Cricket became extremely popular among such eminent figures as Truman, Eisenhower, Johnson and Nixon—earning it the nickname Presidents Watch. The mechanical alarm watch enjoyed its heyday during the 1950s. Many manufacturers took an interest in this booming area. In 1950, Jaeger-LeCoultre introduced its famous Memovox with a "bell-shaped back" enabling two types of sound: a loud one for the morning alarm, and a more discreet one for daily appointments. The trick was that the hammer directly struck the back that was protected by a perforated cover. When the watch was worn, this cover was in contact with the skin, thereby muffling the sound. In 1958, Jaeger-LeCoultre even presented the Memovox Parking, which coincided with the emergence of the first parking meters and short-term parking zones. In 1961, Vulcain launched the Cricket Nautical, water resistant to 300 meters and the first alarm watch with an alarm that was audible under water. By the 1970s however, the eruption of quartz and of electric alarm clocks seemed to spell the death of mechanical alarm watches.

1

3

2

A glorious awakening

The rebirth of mechanical watchmaking in the late 1980s also heralded the comeback of the mechanical alarm watch. In 1989, Jaeger-LeCoultre launched the first alarm wristwatch with perpetual calendar: the famous Grand Réveil. In 1994, the Manufacture in Le Sentier launched the Master Réveil, heir to the Memovox. The Cricket caliber also returned to the forefront. Engaged in a sweeping process of renewal, the Vulcain brand is determined to make the most of its rich heritage, while evolving the movement and enriching it with other useful complications, such as a dual time-zone and world-time displays. In particular, Vulcain re-issued the famous Nautical, with its rotating central dial displaying the diving decompression stages and a triple case-back serving as a resonance chamber. In 2005, the firm created a sensation with the Imperial Gong, the first wristwatch with alarm and tourbillon. This highly exclusive timepiece was equipped with a cathedral gong worthy of the finest minute repeater models. In 2006, Vulcain also distinguished itself by presenting a new collection called Golden Voice, with a gentle and discreet sound more like a "vibrate" mode than an alarm as such. The alarm time is indicated by the stylized V adorning the rotating dial.

Travel times

Vulcain is not the only brand to occupy the alarm-watch niche. In its Leman Réveil GMT "Anniversary 1735-2005" model, Blancpain combined this complication with a dual time-zone indication in an unusual way: the alarm hand is connected to the dual time-zone display, that of the temporary location, indicated by the large hour and minute hands. The date is also indexed to the travel time. Another practical innovation lies in the movement's automatic-winding mechanism enabling simultaneous winding of the winding mechanism. The Réveil

▶▶ 1 *Blancpain, Léman Réveil GMT*
   "Anniversaire 1735–2005"
   In its Léman Réveil GMT "Anniversaire 1735–2005,"
   Blancpain marries the alarm complication with
   the second time zone indication in an unusual way:
   the alarm hand is displayed with the second time
   zone display.

▶▶ 2 *Vulcain, Golden Voice*
   In 2006, Vulcain launched a new collection called
   Golden Voice, with a softer, more discreet sound,
   strictly speaking closer to a "vibrate setting" than
   an alarm.

▶▶ 3 *Vulcain, Impérial Gong*
   In 2005, Vulcain caused a sensation with its
   introduction of the Imperial Gong, the first watch
   with an alarm movement and tourbillon.

▶▶ 4 *Breguet, Réveil du Tsar)*
   The Réveil du Tsar, by Breguet, has an alarm indicator
   in a small aperture at 12:00.

▶▶ 5 *Jaeger-LeCoultre, Master Grand Réveil*
   In 2005, Jaeger-LeCoultre launched the Master
   Grand Réveil, with perpetual calendar.

1

▸▸ 1 *Zenith, Grande Class, Traveller Répétition minutes El Primero*
*The Grande Class Traveller Répétition Minutes El Primero
by Zenith (see* Multi-Complications *chapter) features,
among other functions, an alarm with two sound settings
or a vibrate setting, as well as two power-reserve
indicators: one for the movement, one for the alarm.*

du Tsar, by Breguet, features similar functions, along with a striking-mode indicator in a small window at 12:00. The Grande Class Traveller Minute Repeater El Primero by Zenith (see the chapter on Multi-Complications) includes an alarm function with a two-tone strike or vibrate mode, as well as two power-reserve indicators: one for the movement and the other for the striking mechanism. In 2005, Jaeger-LeCoultre launched the Master Grand Réveil, with perpetual calendar. The alarm mechanism features a barrel and lever independent from the main movement, as well as a hammer causing a gong suspended in the back of the watch to vibrate. The alarm may be set to strike or vibrate mode—a choice appearing in an aperture between 10:00 and 11:00. In a more sporty style, Jaeger-LeCoultre has saluted its partnership with Aston Martin by creating the AMVOX1 R-Alarm, distinguished by its distinctive appearance reminiscent of dashboard counters. More recently, the Manufacture from Le Sentier introduced the Master Compressor Extreme W-Alarm. In addition to its shock-absorbing case, this ultra-sturdy and ultra-resistant watch features several patented innovations relating to the alarm mechanism. Instead of being fixed to the back of the case (which makes the alarm less audible when the watch is strapped to the wrist), the gong is wrapped around the movement and secured to the case middle by two pins. Moreover, the hammer strikes the gong in a specific place close to its fastening point. The result is a more powerful sound and optimal resonance, whether the watch is worn or placed on a night-stand. The alarm is also indicated with a stop/start function controlled by two pushbuttons. The alarm time is selected in an original and accurate manner thanks to a double hour/minute disc in an aperture at 9:00. This timepiece also features a world-time display with rotating 24-hour ring and city disk. It has in particular been issued in two Master

▸▸ 2 *Villemont, Solar Navigator Limited
Edition Mario Julen*
*The Swiss brand Villemont and the
Norwegian watchmaker Amundsen Oslo
AS, recently united in the same group,
presented the Solar Navigator Limited
Edition Mario Julen in 2007.*

▸▸ 3 *Jaeger-LeCoultre, Master Compressor
Extreme W-Alarm*
*Jaeger-LeCoultre recently introduced
the Master Compressor Extreme
W-Alarm, which bears several patents
relating to its alarm mechanism.*

▸▸ 4 *Jaeger-LeCoultre, AMVOX1 R-Alarm*
*In a decidedly sporting mode, Jaeger-
LeCoultre celebrated its partnership
with Aston Martin by creating the
AMVOX1 R-Alarm, with an aesthetic
reminiscent of automobile dials.*

Compressor Extreme W-Alarm 46 limited editions dedicated to seven-time world motorcycling champion Valentine Rossi and his lucky starting number. And while on the topic of high adrenalin and adventurous feats, the Swiss Villemont brand and the Norwegian watchmaker Amundsen Oslo AS, which recently merged within the same group, presented the Solar Navigator Edition Mario Julen Limited Edition in 2007. This timepiece pays tribute to the Mount Everest expedition headed by Mario Julen in the spring of 2006 to commemorate the 50th anniversary of the first Swiss team to reach the roof of the world. It is particularly distinguished by its central alarm hand and its solar navigating system, a manual alternative to GPS.

JAEGER-LECOULTRE

AMVOX1 ALARM - REF. 190 T4 40

AMVOX1's alarm operates with a suspended gong, which creates an unusually strong sound. Encased in Ø 42mm of polished titanium that is water resistant to 5atm, the Jaeger-LeCoultre Memovox 918 caliber with a 45-hour power reserve is constructed, assembled and decorated by hand, and tested for 1,000 hours. AMVOX1's ruthenium dial is topped with a bidirectional turning center disk, a grained rhodium-plated ring, and luminescent numerals, markers, hands, and center sonnerie pointer. This model is shown on a brown Bridge of Weir calf leather strap, and the watch is also available in a stainless steel version with a black dial, on a black Bridge of Weir calf leather strap or on a stainless steel bracelet. Limited edition of 1,000 pieces.

JEAN-MAIRET & GILLMAN

CONTINENTES

This square Continentes offers three retrograde hands and depicts time in three sections of the world: the Americas, Asia/Pacific and Europe/Africa. The mother-of-pearl dial of the watch has a world map decoration to indicate the three zones. Crafted in 18-karat rose gold, the watch houses the automatic JMG 3101TR/1153 caliber with 40 jewels, and is equipped with a 24-karat gold hand-decorated rotor.

JEAN-MAIRET & GILLMAN

HORA MUNDI

From the Around the World Collection, this Hora Mundi watch is crafted in stainless steel and houses the mechanical JMG 1999 self-winding movement. The watch offers 44 hours of power reserve, hours, minutes, seconds, date, alarm function and a world-time function via a disk. The Ø 41mm case is water resistant to 3atm. The black dial is accented with a silver cities zone and the watch is fitted with a sapphire caseback.

IMPERIAL GONG

Imperial Gong combines a flying tourbillon with a mechanical alarm mechanism.

Glossary

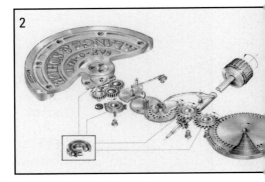

1

ACCURACY s. Precision

ALARM WATCH (image 1)
A watch provided with a movement capable of releasing an acoustic sound at the time set. A second crown is dedicated to the winding, setting and release of the striking-work; an additional center hand indicates the time set. The section of the movement dedicated to the alarm device is made up by a series of wheels linked with the barrel, an escapement and a hammer (s.) striking a gong (s.) or bell (s.). Works much like a normal alarm clock.

AMPLITUDE
Maximum angle by which a balance or pendulum wings from its rest position.

ANALOG or ANALOGUE
A watch displaying time indications by means of hands.

ANTIMAGNETIC
Said of a watch whose movement is not influenced by electromagnetic fields that could cause two or more windings of the balance-spring to stick to each other, consequently accelerating the rate of the watch. This effect is obtained by adopting metal alloys (e.g. Nivarox) resisting magnetization.

ANTIREFLECTION, ANTIREFLECTIVE
Superficial glass treatment assuring the dispersion of reflected light. Better results are obtained if both sides are treated, but in order to avoid scratches on the upper layer, the treatment of the inner surface is preferred.

ARBOR
Bearing element of a gear (s.) or balance, whose ends—called pivots (s.)—run in jewel (s.) holes or brass bushings.

AUTOMATIC (image 2)
A watch whose mechanical movement (s.) is wound automatically. A rotor makes short oscillations due to the movements of the wrist. Through a series of gears, oscillations transmit motion to the barrel (s.), thus winding the mainspring progressively.

AUTOMATON
Figures, placed on the dial or case of watches, provided with parts of the body or other elements moving at the same time as the sonnerie (s.) strikes. The moving parts are linked, through an aperture on the dial or caseback, with the sonnerie hammers (s.) striking a gong.

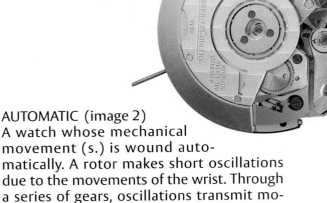

2

BALANCE (image 3)
Oscillating device that, together with the balance spring (s.), makes up the movement's heart inasmuch as its oscillations determine the frequency of its functioning and precision.

BALANCE SPRING (image 3)
Component of the regulating organ (s.) that, together with the balance (s.), determines the movement's precision. The material used is mostly a steel alloy (e.g. Nivarox, s.), an extremely stable metal compound. In order to prevent the

3

system's center of gravity from continuous shifts, hence differences in rate due to the watch's position, some modifications were adopted. These modifications included Breguet's overcoil (closing the terminal part of the spring partly on itself, so as to assure an almost perfect centering) and Philips curve (helping to eliminate the lateral pres-

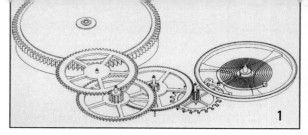

1

2

sure of the balance-staff pivots against their bearings). Today, thanks to the quality of materials, it is possible to assure an excellent precision of movement working even with a flat spring.

BARREL (image 1-2)
Component of the movement containing the mainspring (s.), whose toothed rim meshes with the pinion of the first gear of the train (s.). Due to the fact that the whole—made up of barrel and mainspring—transmits the motive force, it is also considered to be the very motor. Inside the barrel, the mainspring is wound around an arbor (s.) turned by the winding crown or, in the case of automatic movements, also by the gear powered by the rotor (s.).

BEARING
Part on which a pivot turns, in watches mostly a jewels (s.).

BEVELING (image 3)
Chamfering of edges of levers, bridges and other elements of a movement by 45∞, a treatment typically found in high-grade movements.

3

BEZEL
Top part of case (s.), sometimes holds the crystal. It may be integrated with the case middle (s.) or a separate element. It is snapped or screwed on to the middle.

BOTTOM PLATE s. Pillar-plate

BRACELET
A metal band attached to the case. It is called integral if there is no apparent discontinuity between case and bracelet and the profile of attachments is similar to the first link.

4

BRIDGE (image 4)
Structural metal element of a movement (s.)—sometimes called cock or bar—supporting the wheel train (s.), balance (s.), escapement (s.) and barrel (s.). Each bridge is fastened to the plate (s.) by means of screws and locked in a specific position by pins. In high-quality move-

5

ments the sight surface is finished with various types of decoration.

BREGUET HANDS (image 5)
A particular type of hands in a traditional elegant shape.

BRUSHED, BRUSHING
Topical finishing giving metals a line finish, a clean and uniform look.

CABOCHON (image 6)
Any kind of precious stone, such as sapphire, ruby or emerald, uncut and only polished, generally of a half-spherical shape, mainly used as an ornament of the winding crown (s.) or certain elements of the case.

6

CALENDAR, ANNUAL
An intermediate complication between a simple calendar and a perpetual calendar. This feature displays all the months with 30 or 31 days correctly, but needs a manual correction at the end of February. Generally, date, day of the week and month, or only day and month are displayed on the dial.

CALENDAR, GREGORIAN

With respect to the Julian Calendar (s. Calendar, Julian), the calendar reform introduced by Pope Gregory XIII in 1582 corrected the slight error of the former calendar by suppressing a leap year every hundred years, except for years whose numbers are divisible by 400 (this entailed the elimination of the leap years in 1700, 1800 and 1900, but not in 2000 and 2400). In non-Catholic countries this reform was introduced after 1700.

CALENDAR, FULL

Displaying date, day of the week and month on the dial, but needing a manual correction at the end of a month with less than 31 days. It is often combined with the moonphase (s.).

CALENDAR, JULIAN

The calendar established by Julius Caesar was based on the year duration of 365.25 days with a leap year with 366 days every 4 years. In 325 AD, this calendar was adopted by the Church. Due to the slight error (0.0078 day) implied in this time count, the Julian Calendar was later replaced by the Gregorian Calendar (s. Calendar, Gregorian).

CALENDAR, PERPETUAL (image 1)

This is the most complex horology complication related to the calendar feature, as it indicates the date, day, month and leap year and does not need manual corrections until the year 2100 (when the leap year will be ignored).

CALIBER (image 2)

Originally it indicated only the size (in lines, "") of a movement (s.), but now this indication defines a specific movement type and combines it with the constructor's name and identification number. Therefore the caliber identifies the movement.

CANNON

An element in the shape of a hollow cylinder, sometimes also called pipe or bush, for instance the pipe of the hour wheel bearing the hour hand.

CHAPTER-RING

Hour-circle, i.e. the hour numerals arranged on a dial.

Carousel

Device similar to the tourbillon (s.), but with the carriage not driven by the fourth wheel, but by the third wheel.

CARRIAGE or TOURBILLON CARRIAGE (image 3)

Rotating frame of a tourbillon (s.) device, carrying the balance and escapement (s.). This structural element is essential for a perfect balance of the whole system and its stability, in spite of its reduced weight. As today's tourbillon carriages make a rotation per minute, errors of rate in the vertical position are eliminated. Because of the widespread use of transparent dials, carriages became elements of aesthetic attractiveness.

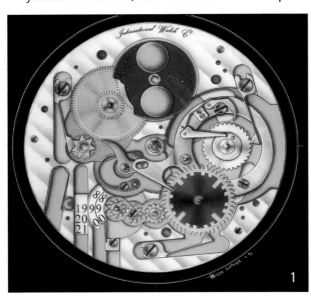

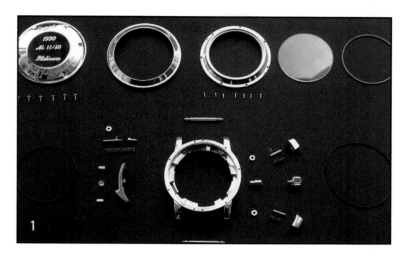

1

According to the Swiss law, a manufacture may put the word "chronometer" on a model only after each individual piece has passed a series of tests and obtained a running bulletin and a chronometer certificate by an acknowledged Swiss control authority, such as the COSC (s.).

CIRCULAR GRAINING (image 4)
Superficial decoration applied to bridges, rotors and pillar-plates in the shape of numerous slightly superposed small grains, obtained by using a plain cutter and abrasives. Also called Pearlage or Pearling.

2

4

CASE (image 1, next page)
Container housing and protecting the movement (s.), usually made up of three parts: middle, bezel, and back.

CENTER SECOND HAND, s. Sweep second hand.

CENTER-WHEEL
The minute wheel in a going-train.

CHAMPLEVÉ (image 2)
Hand-made treatment of the dial or case surface. The pattern is obtained by hollowing a metal sheet with a graver and subsequently filling the hollows with enamel.

CHIME
Striking-work equipped with a set of bells that may be capable of playing a complete melody. A watch provided with such a feature is called chiming watch.

CHRONOGRAPH (image 3)
A watch that includes a built-in stopwatch function, i.e. a timer that can be started and stopped to time an event. There are many variations of the chronograph.

CHRONOMETER
A high-precision watch.

CLICK s. Pawl

CLOISONNÉ (image 5)
A kind of enamel work— mainly used for the decoration of dials—in which the outlines of the drawing are formed by thin metal wires. The colored enamel fills the hollows formed in this way. After oven firing, the surface is  smoothed until the gold threads appear again.

CLOUS DE PARIS (image 6)
Decoration of metal parts characterized by numerous small pyramids.

3

5

COCK, s. Bridge.

COLIMAÇONNAGE (image 1 next page), s. Snailing.

COLUMN-WHEEL (image 2)
Part of chronograph movements, governing

the functions of various levers and parts of the chronograph operation, in the shape of a small-toothed steel cylinder. It is controlled by pushers through levers that hold and release it. It is a very precise and usually preferred type of chronograph operation.

COMPLICATION
Additional function with respect to the manual-winding basic movement for the display of hours, minutes and seconds. Today, certain features, such as automatic winding or date, are taken for granted, although they should be defined as complications. The main complications are moonphase (s.), power reserve (s.), GMT (s.), and full calendar (s.). Further functions are performed by the so-called great complications, such as split-second (s.) chronograph, perpetual calendar (s.), tourbilon (s.) device, and minute repeater (s.).

CORRECTOR
Pusher (s.) positioned on the case side that is normally actuated by a special tool for the quick setting of different indications, such as date, GMT (s.), full or perpetual calendar (s.).

COSC
Abbreviation of "Contrôle Officiel Suisse des Chronomètres," the most important Swiss institution responsible for the functioning and precision tests of movements of chronometers (s.). Tests are performed on each individual watch at different temperatures and in different positions before a functioning bulletin and a chronometer certificate are issued, for which a maximum gap of -4/+4 seconds per day is tolerated.

CÔTES CIRCULAIRES (image 3)
Decoration of rotors and bridges of movements, whose pattern consists of a series of concentric ribs.

CÔTES DE GENÈVE (image 4)
Decoration applied mainly to high-quality movements, appearing as a series of parallel ribs, realized by repeated cuts of a cutter leaving thin stripes.

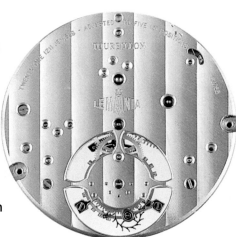

COUNTER (image 5)
Additional hand on a chronograph (s.), indicating the time elapsed since the beginning of the measuring. On modern watches the second counter is placed at the center, while minute and hour counters have off-center hands in special zones (s.), also called subdials.

CROWN
Usually positioned on the case middle (s.) and allows winding, hand setting and often date or GMT hand setting. As it is linked to the movement through the winding stem (s.) passing through a hole in the case. For waterproofing purposes, simple gaskets are used in water-resistant watches, while diving watches adopt screwing systems (screw-down crowns).

CROWN-WHEEL
Wheel meshing with the winding pinion and with the ratchet wheel on the barrel-arbor.

DECK WATCH
A large-sized ship's chronometer.

DEVIATION
A progressive natural change of a watch's rate with respect to objective time. In case of a watch's faster rate, the deviation is defined positive, in the opposite case negative.

DIAL (image 1)
Face of a watch, on which time and further functions are displayed by markers (s.), hands (s.), discs or through windows (s.). Normally it is made of a brass—sometimes silver or gold.

DIGITAL
Said of watches whose indications are displayed mostly inside an aperture or window (s.) on the dial.

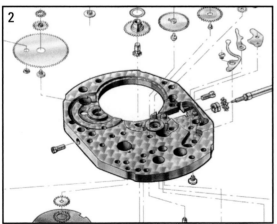

EBAUCHE (image 2)
Incomplete (jeweled or non-jew-

eled) watch movement without regulating organs, mainspring, dial and hands.

ENDSTONE (image 3)
Undrilled jewel, placed on the balance jewel with the tip of the balance-staff pivot resting against its flat surface, to reduce pivot friction. Sometimes used also for pallet staffs and escape wheels.

ENGINE-TURNED, s. Guilloché.

EQUINOX (image 4)
The time when day and night are of equal length, when the sun is on the plane of the equator. Such times occur twice in a year: the vernal equinox on March 21st-22nd and the autumnal equinox on September 22nd-23rd.

EQUATION OF TIME (image 4)
Indication of the difference, expressed in minutes, between conventional mean time and real solar time. This difference varies from -16 to +16 seconds between one day and the other.

ESCAPE WHEEL (image 5)
A wheel belonging to the mechanism called escapement (s.).

ESCAPEMENT (image 5)
Positioned between the train (s.) and the balance wheel and governing the rotation speed of the wheel-train wheels. In today's horology the most widespread escapement type is the lever escapement. In the past, numerous types of escapements were realized, such as: verge, cylinder, pin-pallet, detent and duplex escapements.

Recently, George Daniels developed a so-called "coaxial" escapement.

FLINQUÉ (image 6)
Engraving on the dial or case of a watch, covered with an enamel layer.

FLUTED (image 1)
Said of surfaces worked with thin parallel grooves, mostly on dials or case bezels.

FLY-BACK (image 2)
Feature combined with chronograph (s.) functions, that allows a new measurement starting from zero (and interrupting a measuring already under way) by pressing down a single pusher, i.e. without stopping, zeroing and restarting the whole mechanism. Originally, this function was developed to meet the needs of air forces.

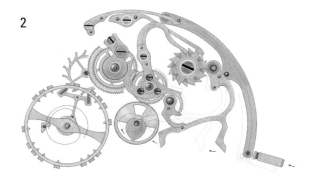

FOLD-OVER CLASP (image 3)
Hinged and jointed element, normally of the same material as the one used for the case. It allows easy fastening of the bracelet on the wrist. Often provided with a snap-in locking device, sometimes with an additional clip or push-piece.

FOURTH-WHEEL
The seconds wheel in a going-train.

FREQUENCY, s. Vibration
Generally defined as the number of cycles per time unit; in horology it is the number of oscillations of a balance every two seconds or of its vibrations per second. For practical purposes, frequency is expressed in vibrations per hour (vph).

FUSEE
A conical part with a spiral groove on which a chain or cord attached to the barrel (s.) is wound. Its purpose is to equalize the driving power transmitted to the train.

GENEVA SEAL, s. Poinçon de Genève.

GLUCYDUR
Bronze and beryllium alloy used for high-quality balances (s.). This alloy assures high elasticity and hardness values; it is non-magnetic, rustproof and has a very reduced dilatation coefficient, which makes the balance very stable and assures high accuracy of the movement.

GMT (image 4)
Abbreviation for Greenwich Mean Time. As a feature of watches, it means that two or more time zones are displayed. In this case, the second time may be read from a hand making a full rotation in a 24-hour ring (thereby also indicating whether it is a.m. or p.m. in that zone).

GOING TRAIN s. Train.
GONG (image 1, next page)
Harmonic flattened bell in a steel alloy, generally positioned along the circumference of the move-

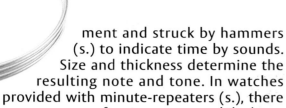

1

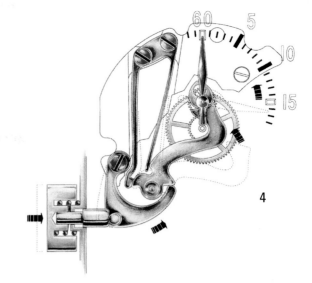

4

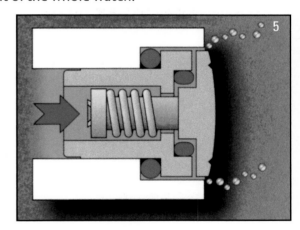

ment and struck by hammers (s.) to indicate time by sounds. Size and thickness determine the resulting note and tone. In watches provided with minute-repeaters (s.), there are often two gongs and the hammers strike one note to indicate hours, both notes together to indicate quarters and the other note for the remaining minutes. In more complex models, equipped also with en-passant sonnerie (s.) devices, there may be up to four gongs producing different notes and playing even simple melodies (such as the chime of London's Big Ben).

GRAND (or GREAT) COMPLICATIONS s. Complication

GUILLOCHé (image 2)
Decoration of dials, rotors or case parts consisting of patterns made by hand or engine-turned. By the thin pattern of the resulting engravings—consisting of crossing or interlaced lines—it is possible to realize even complex drawings. Dials and rotors decorated in this way are generally in gold or in solid silver.

HAMMER
Steel or brass element used in movements

provided with a repeater or alarm sonnerie (s.). It strikes a gong (s.) or bell (s).

HAND (image 3)
Indicator for the analogue visualization of hours, minutes and seconds as well as other functions. Normally made of brass (rhodium-plated, gilded or treated otherwise), but also steel or gold. Hands are available in different shapes and take part in the aesthetic result of the whole watch.

5

HEART-PIECE (image 4)
Heart-shaped cam generally used to realign the hands of chronograph counters.

HELIUM VALVE (image 5)
Valve inserted in the case of some professional diving watches to discharge the helium contained in the air mixture inhaled by divers.

HEXALITE
An artificial glass made of a plastic resin.

3

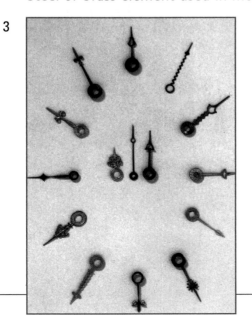

1

HUNTER CALIBER
A caliber (s.) characterized by the seconds hand fitted on an axis perpendicular to the one of the winding-stem (s.).

IMPULSE
In a lever escapement (s.) the action of the escape-wheel tooth on the impulse face of the pallet; in the Swiss lever escapement it is produced by the impulse face of the wheel tooth and that of the pallet.

INCABLOC, s. Shockproof.

INDEX s. Regulator

JEWEL (image 1)
Precious stone used in movements as a bearing surface. Generally speaking, the steel pivots (s.) of wheels in movements turn inside synthetic jewels (mostly rubies) lubricated with a drop of oil. The jewel's hardness reduces wear to a minimum even over long periods of time (50 to 100 years). The quality of watches is determined mainly by the shape and finishing of jewels rather than by their number (the most refined jewels have rounded holes and walls to greatly reduce the contact between pivot and stone).

2

JUMPING HOUR (image 2)
Feature concerning the digital display of time in a window. The indication changes almost instantaneously at every hour.

LEAP-YEAR CYCLE
Leap or bissextile years have 366 days and occur every 4 years (with some exceptions, s. Calendar, Gregorian). Some watches display this datum.

LÉPINE CALIBER
A caliber (s.) typical for pocket-watches, characterized by the seconds hand fitted in the axis of the winding-stem (s.)

LIGNE s. Line.

LINE
Ancient French measuring unit maintained in horology to indicate the diameter of a movement (s.). A line (expressed by the symbol ''') equals 2.255mm. Lines are not divided into decimals; therefore, to indicate measures inferior to the unit, fractions are used (e.g. movements of 13'''3/4 or 10'''1/2).

LUBRICATION
To reduce friction caused by the running of wheels and other parts. There are points to be lubricated with specific low-density oils such as the pivots (s.) turning inside jewels (s.), the sliding areas between levers, and the spring inside the barrel (requiring a special grease), as well as numerous other parts of a movement.

LUG
Double extension of the case middle (s.) by which a strap or bracelet is attached. Normally, straps and bracelets are attached with removable spring bars.

LUMINESCENT
Said of materials applied on markers (s.) and/or hands (s.), emitting the luminous energy previously absorbed as electromagnetic light rays. Tritium is no longer used and was replaced by other substances having the same emitting powers, but with virtually zero radioactivity, such as Super-LumiNova and Lumibrite.

3

MAINSPRING
This and the barrel (s.) make up the driving element of a movement (s.). It stores and transmits the power force needed for its functioning.

MANUAL
A mechanical movement (v.) in which winding is performed by hand. The motion transmitted from the user's fingers to the crown is forwarded to the movement through the winding stem (s.), from this to the barrel (s.) through a series of gears (s.) and finally to the mainspring (s.).

MARINE CHRONOMETER
A large-sized watch enclosed in a box (therefore also called box chronometer) mounted on gimbals and used, on board of ships, to determine the respective longitude.

MARKERS
Elements printed or applied on the dial, sometimes they are luminescent (s.), used as reference points for the hands to indicate hours and fifteen- or five-minute intervals.

MEAN TIME
The mean time of the meridian of the Greenwich Observatory, considered the universal meridian, is used as a standard of the civil time system, counted from midnight to midnight.

MICROMETER SCREW (image 1)
Element positioned on the regulator, allowing to shift it by minimal and perfectly gauged ranges so as to obtain accurate regulations of the movement.

MICRO-ROTOR, s. Rotor. (image 2)

MINUTE REPEATER, s. Repeater.

MODULE (image 3)
Self-contained mechanism, independent of the basic caliber (s.), added to the movement (s.) to make an additional function available: chronograph (s.), power reserve (s.), GMT (s.), perpetual or full calendar (s).

MOONPHASE (image 3)
A function available in many watches, usually combined with calendar-related features. The moonphase disc advances one tooth every 24 hours. Normally, this wheel has 59 teeth and assures an almost perfect synchronization with the lunation period, i.e. 29.53 days (in fact, the disc shows the moonphases twice during a single revolution). However, the difference of 0.03 days, i.e. 44 minutes each month, implies the need for a manual adjustment every two and a half years to recover one day lost with respect to the real state of moonphase. In some rare case, the transmission ratio between the gears controlling the moonphase are calculated with extreme accuracy so as to require manual correction only once in 100 years.

MOVEMENT (s. page 602)
The entire mechanism of a watch. Movements are divided into two great families: quartz and mechanical; the latter are available with manual (s.) or automatic (s.) winding devices.

MOVEMENT-BLANK s. Ebauche

NIVAROX
Trade name (from the producer's name) of a steel alloy, resisting magnetization, used for modern self-compensating balance springs (s.). The quality level of this material is indi-

cated by the numeral following the name in decreasing
value from 1 to 5.

OBSERVATORY CHRONOMETER
An observatory-tested precision watch that obtained the
relevant rating certificate.

OPEN-FACE CALIBER
s. Lépine Caliber.

OSCILLATION
Complete oscillation or rotation movement of the bal-
ance (s.), formed by two vibrations (s.).

OVERCOIL s. Balance spring.

PALLETS
Device of the escapement
(s.) transmitting part of the
motive force to the balance
(s.), in order to maintain the
amplitude of oscillations un-
changed by freeing a tooth
of the escape wheel at one time.
PAWL
Lever with a beak that engages in the teeth
of a wheel under the action of a spring.

PILLAR-PLATE OR MAIN PLATE
Supporting element of bridges (s.) and other
parts of a movement (s).
PINION
Combines with a wheel and an arbor (s.) to
form a gear (s.). A pinion has less teeth than
a wheel and transmits motive force to a
wheel. Pinion teeth (normally 6 to 14) are
highly polished to reduce friction to a minimum.

PIVOT
End of an arbor (s.) turning on a jewel (s.)
support. As their shape and size can influence friction, the pivots of the balance-staff
are particularly thin and, hence, fragile, so

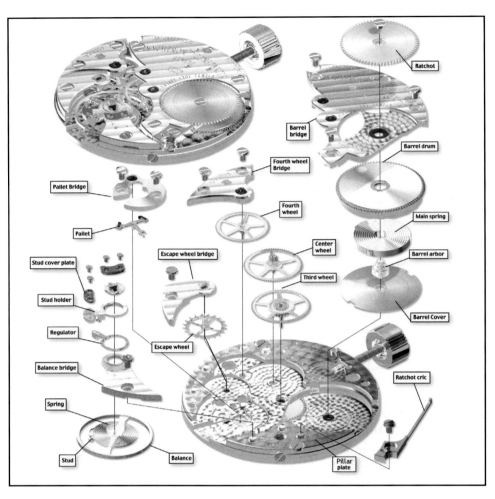

they are protected by a shockproof (s.) system.

PLATE s. Pillar-plate.

PLATED
Said of a metal treated by a galvanizing pro-
cedure in order to apply a slight layer of gold
or another precious metal (silver, chromium,
rhodium or palladium) on a brass or steel
base.

PLEXIGLAS
A synthetic resin used for watch crystal.

POINÇON DE GENÈVE (image 1)
Distinction assigned by the Canton of Geneva to movements produced by watchmaker
firms of the Region and complying with all
the standards of high horology with respect
to craftsmanship, small-scale production,

working quality, accurate assembly and setting. The Geneva Seal is engraved on at least one bridge and shows the Canton's symbol, i.e. a two-field shield with an eagle and a key respectively in each field.

POWER RESERVE (image 2)
Duration (in hours) of the residual functioning autonomy of a movement after it has reached the winding peak. The duration value is displayed by an instantaneous indicator: analog (hand on a sector) or digital (through a window). The related mechanism is made up of a series of gears linking the winding barrel and hand. Recently, specific modules were introduced which may be combined with the most popular movements.

PRECISION
Accuracy rate of a watch, a term difficult to define exactly. Usually, a precision watch is a chronometer whose accuracy-standard is certified by an official watch-rating bureau, and a high-precision watch is a chronometer certified by an observatory.

PULSIMETER CHRONOGRAPH
The pulsimeter scale shows, at a glance, the number of pulse beats per minute. The observer releases the chronograph hand when starting to count the beats and stops at the 30th, the 20th or the 15th beat according to the basis of calibration indicated on the dial.

PUSHER, PUSH-PIECE or PUSH-BUTTON
Mechanical element mounted on a case (s.) for the control of specific functions. Generally, pushers are used in chronographs (s.), but also with other functions.

PVD
Abbreviation of Physical Vapor Deposition, a plating process consisting of the physical transfer of substance by bombardment of electrons.
RATCHET (WHEEL)
Toothed wheel prevented from moving by a click pressed down by a spring.

RATING CERTIFICATES s. Chronometer and COSC.

REGULATING UNIT (image 3)
Made up by balance (s.) and balance spring (s.), governing the division of time within the mechanical movement, assuring its regular running and accuracy. As the balance works like a pendulum, the balance spring's function consists of its elastic return and starting of a new oscillation. This combined action determines the frequency, i.e. the number of vibrations per hour, and affects the rotation speed of the different wheels. In fact the balance, by its oscillations, at every vibration (through the action of the pallets), frees a tooth of the escape wheel (s. Escapement). From this, motion is transmitted to the fourth wheel, which makes a revolution in one minute, to the third and then the center wheel, the latter making a full rotation in one hour. However, everything is determined by the correct time interval of the oscillations of the balance.

REGULATOR (image 3)
Regulating the functioning of a movement by lengthening and shortening the active section of the balance spring (s.). It is positioned on the balance-bridge and encompasses the balance spring with its two pins near its fixing point on the bridge itself. By shifting the index, the pins also are moved and, by consequence, the portion of the balance spring capable of bringing the balance back is lengthened or shortened by its elastic force. The shorter it is, the more reactive

it tends to be and the more rapidly it brings the balance back and makes the movement run faster. The contrary happens when the active portion of the balance spring is lengthened. Given today's high frequencies of functioning, even slight index shifts entail daily variations of minutes. Recently, even more refined index-regulation systems were adopted (from eccentric (s.) to micrometer screws (s.)) to limit error margins to very few seconds per day.

REMONTOIR, CONSTANT-FORCE
Old term used to denote any mechanism assuring a constant transmission of the driving power to the escape wheel.

REPEATER (image 1)
Mechanism indicating time by acoustic sounds. Contrary to the watches provided with en-passant sonnerie (s.) devices, that strike the number of hours automatically, repeaters work on demand by actuating a slide (s.) or pusher (s.) positioned on the case side. Repeaters are normally provided with two hammers and two gongs: one gong for the minutes and one for the hours. The quarters are obtained by the almost simultaneous strike of both hammers. The mechanism of the striking work is among the most complex complications.

1

RETROGRADE (image 2)
Said of a hand (s.) that, instead of making a revolution of 360 before starting a new measurement, moves on an arc scale (generally of 90 to 180) and at the end of its trip comes back instantaneously.

Normally, retrograde hands are used to indicate date, day or month in perpetual calendars, but there are also cases of retrograde hours, minutes or seconds. Unlike the case of the classical indication over 360, the retrograde system requires a special mechanism to be inserted into the basic movement.

ROLLER TABLE or ROLLER
Part of the escapement in the shape of a disc fitted to the balance staff and carrying the impulse pin that transmits the impulses given by the pallets to the balance.

ROTOR (image 3)
In automatic-winding mechanical movements the rotor is the part that, by its complete or partial revolutions and the movements of human arm, allows winding of the mainspring (s.).

3

SCALE (image 4)
Graduation on a measuring instrument, showing the divisions of a whole of values, especially on a dial, bezel. The scales mostly used in horology are related to the following measuring devices: tachometer (s.) (indicating the average speed), telemeter (s.) (indicating the distance of a simultaneously luminous and acoustic source, e.g. a cannon-shot or a thunder and related lightning), pulsometer (to calculate the total number of heartbeats per minute by counting only a certain quantity of them). For all of these scales, measuring starts at the beginning of the event concerned and stops at its end; the reading refers directly to the chronograph second hand, without requiring further calculations.

2

4

SECOND TIME-ZONE INDICATOR, s. GMT and World Time.

SECTOR, s. Rotor.

SELF-WINDING, s. Automatic.

SHOCKPROOF or SHOCK-RESISTANT (image 1)
Watches provided with shock-absorber systems (e.g. Incabloc) help prevent damage from shocks to the balance pivots. Thanks to a retaining spring system, it assures an elastic play of both jewels, thus absorbing the movements of the balance-staff pivots when the watch receives strong shocks. The return to the previous position is due to the return effect of the spring. If such a system is lacking, the shock forces exert an impact on the balance-staff pivots, often causing bending or even breakage.

SIDEREAL TIME
The conventional time standard refers to the sidereal year (defined in terms of an average of 365.25636 days) considered to be perfectly regular until very recently, but – even though this is not true – the difference is so slight that it is virtually neglected. As a unit of time, the sidereal day is used mainly by astronomers to define the interval between two upper transits of the vernal point in the plane of the meridian.

SKELETON, SKELETONIZED (image 2)
Watches whose bridges and pillar-plates are cut out in a decorative manner, thus revealing all the parts of the movement.

SLIDE
Part of a mechanism moving with friction on a slide-bar or guide.
SMALL SECOND
Time display in which the second hand is placed in a small subdial.

SNAILING (image 3)
Decoration with a spiral pattern, mainly

used on the barrel wheel or on big-sized full wheels.

SOLAR TIME
Generally speaking, the time standard referred to the relative motion of the Earth and the Sun governing the length of day and night. The true solar day is the period measured after the Sun appears again in the same position from our point of observation. Due to the non-uniform rotation of the Earth around the Sun, this measure is not regular. As an invariable measure unit, the mean solar day corresponds to the average duration of all the days of the year.

SOLSTICE
The time when the sun is farthest from the equator, i.e. on June 21st (Summer solstice) and December 21st (Winter solstice).

SONNERIE (EN PASSANT)
Function consisting of an acoustic sound, obtained by a striking work made up of two hammers (s.) striking gongs (s.) at set hours, quarter- and half-hours. Some devices can emit a chime (with three or even four hammers and gongs). By a slide (s.) or an additional pusher (s.) it is possible to exclude the sonnerie device and to select a so-called grande sonnerie.

SPLIT-SECOND CHRONOGRAPH (image 4)
Chronographs with split-second mechanisms are particularly useful for timing simultaneous phenomena which begin at the same time, but end at different times, such as sporting events in which several competitors are taking part. In chronographs of this type, an additional hand is superimposed on the chronograph hand. Pressure on the pusher starts both hands, which remain superimposed as long as the split-second mechanism is not blocked. This is achieved when the split-second hand is stopped while the chronograph hand continues to move. After record-

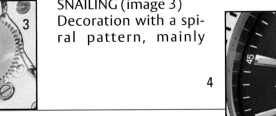

4

ing, the same pusher is pressed a second time, releasing the split-second hand, which instantly joins the still-moving chronograph hand, synchronizing with it, and is thus ready for another recording. Pressure on the return pusher brings the hands back to zero simultaneously, provided the split-second hand is not blocked. Pressure on the split pusher releases the split-second hand, which instantly joins the chronograph hand if the split-second hand happens to be blocked.

STAFF or STEM, s. Arbor.

STOPWORK
Traditional device (now obsolete) provided with a finger piece fixed to the barrel arbor and a small wheel in the shape of a Maltese cross mounted on the barrel cover, limiting the extent to which the barrel (s.) can be wound.

STRIKING WORK, s. Sonnerie and Repeater.

SUBDIAL, s. Zone.

SUPER-LUMINOVA, s. Luminescent.

SWEEP SECOND HAND
A center second hand, i.e. a second hand mounted on the center of the main dial.

TACHOMETER or TACHYMETER (image 1)
Function measuring the speed at which the wearer runs over a given distance. The tachometer scale is calibrated to show the speed of a moving object, such as a vehicle, over a known distance. The standard length on which the calibration is based is always shown on the dial, e.g. 1,000, 200 or 100 meters, or—in some cases—one mile. As the moving vehicle, for instance, passes the starting-point of the measured course whose length corresponds to that used as the basis of cali-

bration, the observer releases the chronograph hand and stops it as the vehicle passes the finishing point. The figure indicated by the hand on the tachometer scale represents the speed in kilometers or miles per hour.

TELEMETER (image 1)
By means of the telemeter scale, it is possible to measure the distance of a phenomenon that is both visible and audible. The chronograph hand is released at the instant the phenomenon is seen; it is stopped when the sound is heard, and its position on the scale shows, at a glance, the distance in kilometers or miles separating the phenomenon from the observer. Calibration is based upon the speed at which sound travels through the air, viz. approximately 340 meters or 1,115 feet per second. During a thunderstorm, the time that has elapsed between the flash of lightning and the sound of the thunder is registered on the chronograph scale.

THIRD WHEEL
Wheel positioned between the minutes and seconds wheels.

TIME ZONES
The 24 equal spherical lunes unto which the surface of the Earth is conventionally divided, each limited by two meridians. The distance between two adjacent zones is 15° or 1 hour. Each country adopts the time of its zone, except for countries with more than one zone. The universal standard time is that of the zero zone whose axis is the Greenwich meridian.

TONNEAU (image 2)
Particular shape of a watchcase, imitating the profile of a barrel, i.e. with straight, shorter, horizontal sides and curved, longer, vertical sides.

TOURBILLON (image 1, facing page)
Device invented in 1801 by A. L. Breguet. This function equalizes position errors due to changing positions of a watch and related effects of gravity. Balance, balance spring and escapement are housed inside a carriage (s.),

2

1

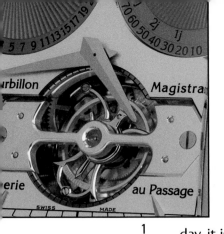

1

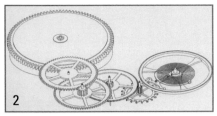

2

also called a cage, rotating by one revolution per minute, thus compensating for all the possible errors over 360. Although this device is not absolutely necessary for accuracy purposes today, it is still appreciated as a complication of high-quality watches.

TRAIN (image 2)
All the wheels between barrel (s.) and escapement (s.).

TRANSMISSION WHEEL s. Crown-wheel

UNIVERSAL TIME
The mean solar time (s.) of the Greenwich meridian, counted from noon to noon, Often confused with the mean time (s.) notion.

VARIATION
In horology the term is usually referred to the variation of the daily rate, i.e. the difference between two daily rates specified by a time interval.

WINDING, AUTOMATIC s. Automatic
VIBRATION
Movement of a pendulum or other oscillating bodies, limited by two consecutive extreme positions. In an alternate (pendulum or balance) movement, a vibration is a half of an oscillation (s.). The number of hourly vibrations corresponds to the frequency of a watch movement, determined by the mass and diameter of a balance (s.) and the elastic force of the balance spring. The number of vibrations per hour (vph) determines the breaking up of time (the "steps" of a second hand). For instance, 18,000 vph equals a vibration duration of 1/5 second; in the same way 21,600 vph = 1/6 second; 28,800 vph = 1/8 second; 36,000 vph = 1/10 second. Until the 1950s, wristwatches worked mostly at a frequency of 18,000 vph; later, higher frequencies were adopted to produce a lower percentage of irregularities to the rate. Today, the most common frequency adopted is 28,800 vph, which as-

3

sures a good precision standard and less lubrication problems than extremely high frequencies, such as 36,000 vph.

WATER RESISTANT or WATERPROOF (image 1)
A watch whose case (s.) is designed in such a way as to resist infiltration by water (3 atmospheres, corresponding to a conventional depth of 30 meters; 5 atmospheres, corresponding to a conventional depth of 50 meters.)

WHEEL
Circular element, mostly toothed, combines with an arbor (s.) and a pinion (s.) to make up a gear (s.). Wheels are normally made of brass, while arbors and pinions are made of steel. The wheels between barrel (s.) and escapement (s.) make up the so-called train (s.).

WINDING STEM
Element transmitting motion from the crown (s.) to the gears governing manual winding and setting.

WINDOW
Aperture in the dial, that allows reading the underlying indication, mainly the date, but also indications concerning a second zone's time or jumping hour (s.).

WORLD TIME (image 3)
Additional feature of watches provided with a GMT (s.) function, displaying the 24 time zones on the dial or bezel, each zone referenced by a city name, providing instantaneous reading of the time of any country.

ZODIAC
Circular belt with the ecliptic in the middle containing the twelve constellations through which the sun seems to pass in the course of a year.

ZONE
Small additional dial or indicator that may be positioned, or placed off-center on the main dial, used for the display of various functions (e.g. second counters).

BRAND DIRECTORY

AUDEMARS PIGUET
1348 Le Brassus
Switzerland
Tel: 41 21 845 14 00
USA: 212 758 8400

BELL & ROSS
350, rue Saint Honoré
75001 Paris, France
Tel: 33 1 55 35 36 00
USA: 888 307 7887

BOVET FLEURIER SA
9 rue Ami-Lévrier
1201 Geneva
Switzerland
Tel: 41 22 731 46 38
USA: 305 965 3277

BOZEMAN WATCH CO.
11 East Main Street
Bozeman
MT 59715 USA
Tel: 877 878 1780

BREGUET
1344 L'Abbaye
Switzerland
Tel: 41 21 841 90 90
USA: 866 458 7488

BVLGARI
34 rue de Monruz
2000 Neuchâtel
Switzerland
Tel: 41 32 722 78 78
USA: 212 315 9700

CHANEL
25 Place du Marché St Honoré
75001 Paris, France
Tel: 33 1 55 35 50 00
USA: 212 688 5055

CHOPARD
Rue de Veyrot 8
1217 Meyrin-Geneva 2
Switzerland
Tel: 41 22 719 31 31
USA: 212 821 0300

CONCORD
MGI Luxury Group S.A.
Rue de Nidau 35
2501 Bienne, Switzerland
Tel: 41 32 329 34 00
USA: 201 267 8000

DANIEL ROTH
4, rue de la Gare
1347 Le Sentier, Switzerland
Tel: 41 21 845 15 55
USA: 212 315 9700

de GRISOGONO
Route de St. Julien 176 bis
1228 Plan-les-Ouates
Switzerland
Tel: 41 22 817 81 00
USA: 212 439 4240

DeWITT
2, Rue du Pré-de-la-Fontaine
PO Box 58
Satigny - 1217 Meyrin 2
Switzerland
Tel: 41 22 750 97 97
USA: 305 572 9812

F. P. JOURNE
Rue de l'Arquebuse 17
1204 Geneva, Switzerland
Tel: 41 22 322 09 09
USA: 305 572 9802

GÉRALD GENTA
4, rue de la Gare
1347 Le Sentier, Switzerland
Tel: 41 22 977 17 17
USA: 212 315 9700

GREUBEL FORSEY
19-21 rue du Manège
2300 La Chaux-de-Fonds
Switzerland
Tel: 41 32 751 71 76
USA: 310 205 5555

GUY ELLIA
21 rue de la Paix
75002 Paris, France
Tel: 33 1 53 30 25 25
USA: 800 CELLINI

HUBLOT
44 Route de Divonne
1260 Nyon 2, Switzerland
Tel: 41 22 990 90 00
USA: 800 536 0636

IWC
Baumgarten Strasse 15
8201 Schaffhausen, Switzerland
Tel: 41 52 635 65 90
USA: 212 891 2460

JACOB & CO
14 rue du Rhone, 4th Floor
1204 Geneva, Switzerland
Tel: 44 22 819 18 42
USA: 212 719 5887

JAEGER-LECOULTRE
Rue de la Golisse 8
1347 Le Sentier, Switzerland
Tel: 41 21 845 02 02
USA: 212 308 2525

JEAN DUNAND Pièces Uniques
WPW SA
Pré-Fleuri 31
1228 Plan les Ouates
Switzerland
Tel: 41 22 706 19 60

JEAN-MAIRET & GILLMAN
11 Chemin du Petray
1222 Vesenaz
Switzerland
Tel: 41 22 703 40 20
USA: 561 651 7272

LEVIEV
31 Old Bond Street
LondonW1S4QH
Tel: 44 20 7493 3333
USA: 212 763 5333

MAURICE LACROIX
Brandschenkestrasse 2
8001 Zürich, Switzerland
Tel: 41 44 209 11 11
USA: 800 794 7736

PARMIGIANI FLEURIER
Rue du Temple 11
2114 Fleurier, Switzerland
Tel: 41 32 862 66 30
USA: 949 489 2885

PATEK PHILIPPE
Chemin du Pont du Centenaire 141
1228 Plan-les-Ouates
Switzerland
Tel: 41 22 884 20 20
USA: 212 218 1240

PIAGET
37, Chemin du Champ-des-Filles
1228 Plan-les-Ouates
Switzerland
Tel: 41 22 884 48 44
USA: 212 355 6444

RICHARD MILLE
11 rue du Jura
2345 Les Breuleux Jura
Switzerland
Tel: 41 32 959 43 53
USA: 310 205 5555

ROLEX
Rue François Dussaud 3-7
1211 Geneva 24, Switzerland
Tel: 41 22 302 22 00
USA: 212 758 7700

ROMAIN JEROME
Rue Robert Céard 8
1204 Geneva, Switzerland
Tel: 41 22 319 29 39
USA: 813 792 0402

TAG HEUER
Louis-Joseph Chevrolet 6A
2300 La Chaux-de-Fonds
Switzerland
Tel: 41 32 919 80 00
USA: 973 467 1890

ULYSSE NARDIN
3, Rue du Jardin
2400 Le Locle
Switzerland
Tel: 41 32 930 74 00
USA: 561 988 8600

VACHERON CONSTANTIN
Rue des Moulins 1
1204 Geneva, Switzerland
Tel: 41 22 316 17 40
USA: 212 713 0707

VULCAIN
PMH-Production &
Marketing Horloger SA
Chemin des Tourelles 4
Le Locle, Switzerland
Tel: 41 32 930 80 10

WYLER GENÈVE
58, rue de Moillebeau
1209 Geneva, Switzerland
Tel: 41 22 365 68 68
USA: 786 417 5478

ZENITH
2400 Le Locle
Switzerland
Tel: 41 32 930 62 62
USA: 973 467 1890

ZENITH

SWISS WATCH MANUFACTURE

SINCE 1865

"Time is the moving symbol of a motionless Eternity.

PLATO

ACADEMY
Tourbillon
El Primero
QUANTIÈME PERPÉTUEL

ACADEMY
Tourbillon
El Primero

Academy Tourbillon El Primero – Paris, France : An Academic range
Academy, a timepiece collection incorporating highly complex Grand Complications, combines the El Primero movement manufactured in-house with the world's fastest and most accurate Tourbillon mechanism. Housed in a rose gold case, the Academy Tourbillon El Primero "Perpetual Calendar" is an ode to eternity because once wound, it will show the time, date, day, month and year with great accuracy and will not need to be reset for a century. The hand-finished guilloché dial is adorned with asymmetrically facetted numerals that signal the triumph of a new classicism. The integral alligator strap has a gold triple folding clasp.

ZENITH INTERNATIONAL   TEL. +41 32 930 62 62   WWW.ZENITH-WATCHES.COM

de GRISOGONO
GENEVE

FG ONE

U.S. $25.00 CAN. $28.00
ISBN 978-0-8478-3126-5